The LITTLE, BROWN ESSENTIAL HANDBOOK for WRITERS

Third Edition

Jane E. Aaron

LONGMAN

An imprint of Addison Wesley Longman, Inc.

New York • Reading, Massachusetts • Menlo Park, California
Harlow, England • Don Mills, Ontario • Sydney • Mexico City
Madrid • Amsterdam

Sponsoring Development Manager: Arlene Bessenoff
Development Editor: Tom Maeglin
Supplements Editor: Donna Campion
Marketing Manager: Renée Ortbals
Project Manager: Bob Ginsberg
Design Manager: Wendy Ann Fredericks
Text Designer: Dorothy Bungert/EriBen Graphics
Cover Designer: Kay Petronio
Art Studio: EriBen Graphics
Electronic Production Specialist: Sarah Johnson
Senior Print Buyer: Hugh Crawford
Electronic Page Makeup: Dorothy Bungert/EriBen Graphics
Printer and Binder: Webcrafters, Inc.
Cover Printer: Webcrafters, Inc.

Library of Congress Cataloging-in-Publication Data

Aaron, Jane E.
    The Little, Brown essential handbook for writers / Jane E.
Aaron.—3rd ed.
        p.   cm.
    Includes index.
    ISBN 0-321-04970-5
    1. English language—Grammar—Handbooks, manuals,
etc.   2. English language—Rhetoric—Handbooks, manuals,
etc.   I. Title
PE1112.A24   1999   99-28869
808'.042--dc21   CIP

The Little, Brown Essential Handbook for Writers substantially abridges parts of *The Little, Brown Compact Handbook,* by Jane E. Aaron, and *The Little, Brown Handbook,* by H. Ramsey Fowler and Jane E. Aaron.

Please visit our Web site at
http://www.awlonline.com/littlebrown

ISBN 0-321-04970-5

    45678910—WC—020100

USING THIS BOOK

This small book contains essential information for writing. It covers the writing process, usage, grammar, punctuation, document design, research (including Internet research), and source citation—all in a convenient, accessible format.

You can use this book at any level of writing, in any discipline, and in or out of school. The explanations assume no special knowledge of the terminology of writing: needless terms are omitted, and essential terms, marked °, are defined in the Glossary of Terms. Material especially for writers using English as a second language is marked ESL. Examples come from a wide range of subjects, science to literature to business.

The guide on the next page shows how the book works, and the complete table of contents inside the back cover details the coverage. The book has three main components.

The big picture

An overview of the writing process begins the book. It can help you make choices about purpose, content, use of sources, format, and other writing options. The chapter also suggests ways to develop your subject and to revise and edit your drafts.

Considering the context for your writing is important because, contrary to much popular opinion, writing is not solely, or even primarily, a matter of correctness. True, any written message will find a more receptive audience if it is correct in grammar, punctuation, and similar matters that this book covers. But these should come late in the process, after you've allowed yourself to discover and shape what you have to say, freeing yourself to make mistakes along the way. As one writer put it, you need to get the clay on the potter's wheel before you can form it into a bowl, and you need to form the bowl before you can perfect it. So get your clay on the wheel and work with it until it looks like a bowl. Then edit.

Editing

Many of this book's chapters will help you write clearly and correctly. You'll never need or use every chapter because you already know much of what's here, whether consciously or not. The trick is to figure out what you *don't* know, focus on those areas, and back yourself up with this book.

Finding What You Need

Use the table of contents.

Inside the back cover, this detailed outline lists all the book's topics in one place.

Use the index.

At the end of the book (p. 227), this alphabetical list includes all topics, terms, and problem words and expressions.

Use the glossaries.

The alphabetical Glossary of Usage (p. 203) clarifies words and expressions that are often misused or confused, such as *hopefully* or *affect/effect.* The Glossary of Terms (p. 214) defines grammatical terms, such as *pronoun* or *agreement,* including all terms marked ° in the text.

Use the elements of the page.

❶Running head (header) showing the topic being discussed on this page.

❷Chapter number and title.

❸Section heading containing a main topic or convention. Heading code consists of chapter number (**21**) and heading letter (**a**).

❹Section subheading.

❺Explanation.

❻Page tab containing the code of the last heading on the page (**21b**).

❼Small raised circles indicating terms defined in the Glossary of Terms (p. 214).

❽Examples, always indented, often showing revision.

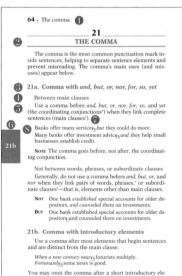

64 • The comma ❶

21
THE COMMA ❷

The comma is the most common punctuation mark inside sentences, helping to separate sentence elements and prevent misreading. The comma's main uses (and misuses) appear below.

❸ 21a. Comma with *and, but, or, nor, for, so, yet*

❹ Between main clauses

❺ Use a comma before *and, but, or, nor, for, so,* and *yet* (the coordinating conjunctions°) when they link complete sentences (main clauses°). ❼

❻ ❽ Banks offer many services, *but* they could do more.
Many banks offer investment advice, *and* they help small businesses establish credit.

NOTE The comma goes before, not after, the coordinating conjunction.

Not between words, phrases, or subordinate clauses

Generally, do not use a comma before *and, but, or,* and *nor* when they link pairs of words, phrases,° or subordinate clauses°—that is, elements other than main clauses.

NOT One bank *established* special accounts for older depositors, *and counseled* them on investments.
BUT One bank established special accounts for older depositors and counseled them on investments.

21b. Comma with introductory elements

Use a comma after most elements that begin sentences and are distinct from the main clause.

When a new century nears, futurists multiply.
Fortunately, some news is good.

You may omit the comma after a short introductory element if there's no risk that the reader will run the introductory element and main clause together: *By the year 2000 we may have reduced pollution.*

NOTE The subject° of a sentence is not an introductory element but a part of the main clause. Thus, do not use a comma to separate the subject and its verb.

NOT Some *pessimists, may* be disappointed.
BUT Some pessimists may be disappointed.

Checklists for editing appear on pages 8 (clarity and style), 28 (sentence parts and patterns), 62 (punctuation), 82 (form and appearance), and 116 (using and documenting sources). But you can develop a personal editing checklist as well, by keeping a list of mistakes and other writing problems that your readers point out to you.

When using any checklist, don't try to find every problem in a single reading: you may need to read once for repetition, say, and once for apostrophes. And read with your own eyes: don't depend too much on your computer's grammar or spelling checker because neither can catch every error (a spelling checker, for instance, can't distinguish between *no, not,* and *now*).

Research and documentation

When you need to consult sources for your writing, this book can help you find them, evaluate them, and acknowledge them. Chapters 33–38 guide you through the process of research writing, with special attention to locating and evaluating sources that you find online. Then Chapters 39–42 detail the four most widely used styles for citing sources: Modern Language Association, Chicago, American Psychological Association, and Council of Biology Editors. Because several of these styles do not yet provide extensive models for electronic sources, Chapter 43 details the Columbia style for documenting online sources in either the humanities or the sciences.

Acknowledgments

Representing biology, business, English composition, engineering, history, psychology, and other disciplines, many teachers offered expert advice for this revision:

Daniel R. Anderson, University of North Carolina, Chapel Hill
Linda S. Bergmann, University of Missouri, Rolla
Gary D. Calpas, University of Pittsburgh
Locke Carter, Texas Tech University
Adrienne Cassel, Wright State University
Charles Creutz, University of Toledo
Dorothy Dvorsky-Rohner, University of North Carolina, Asheville
Sylvia Gillett, Dundalk Community College
Michael J. Hricik, Westmoreland County Community College
Laura Hyatt, Barton College
David Leight, Reading Area Community College
Ruth S. MacDonald, University of Missouri, Columbia

David MacWilliams, University of North Carolina, Greensboro

Miles S. McCrimmon, J. Sargeant Reynolds Community College

Patricia A. Peroni, Davidson College

Mary Prescott, Bryant College

Ross Primm, Columbia College

Gerald Richman, Suffolk University

Michael D. Roberts, Fresno City College

Kristen L. Sanford, University of Missouri, Columbia

Benyamin Schwarz, University of Missouri, Columbia

Joseph A. Scimecca, George Mason University

Erica L. Scott, Slippery Rock University

Timothy J. Shannon, Gettysburg College

Karen R. Smith, Clarion University of Pennsylvania

Betsy Stevens, Cornell University

Kenneth Wilburn, East Carolina University

Many thanks to all of these teachers for their constructive suggestions.

Thanks also to my friends at and around Longman, especially Arlene Bessenoff, Thomas Maeglin, Renée Ortbals, Robert Ginsberg, and Dorothy Bungert.

1
THE PROCESS OF WRITING

When writing for others, you face a particular situation and work through a process that takes you from rough ideas to a finished piece. The next pages outline the elements of any writing situation and the stages you may cycle through as you develop and express your ideas. For any given writing project, some elements and some stages may be more important than others.

1a. The writing situation

The WRITING SITUATION consists of the requirements and the options that determine what and how you will write. Considering your situation at the start of a project will tell you a great deal about how to proceed.

Topic, audience, and purpose

Whenever you write to be read by others, you are communicating something about a topic to a particular audience of readers for a specific reason.

TOPIC

- What does your writing assignment tell you to do? If you don't have an assignment, what do you want to write about?
- What interests you about the topic? What do you already have ideas about or want to know more about? What is your attitude toward the topic: serious, angry, puzzled, amused?
- Is your topic limited enough so that you can cover it well in the space and time you have?

AUDIENCE

- Who will read your writing? What do your readers already know and think about your topic?
- Do your readers have any characteristics—such as educational background, experience in your field, or political views—that could influence their reception of your writing?
- What is your relationship to your readers? How formal or informal should your writing be?
- What do you want readers to do or think after they read your writing?

For Web sites on the process of writing, see page 197.

PURPOSE

- What aim does your assignment specify? For instance, does it ask you to explain something or argue a point?
- Why are you writing? What do you want your work to accomplish?
- How can you best achieve your purpose?

Research

- What kinds of evidence—such as facts, examples, and the opinions of experts—will best suit your topic, audience, and purpose?
- Does your assignment require you to consult sources of information or conduct other research, such as interviews, surveys, or experiments?
- Besides the requirements of the assignment, what additional information do you need to develop your topic? How will you obtain it?
- What style should you use to cite your sources? (See pp. 140–41 on source documentation in the academic disciplines.)

Deadline and length

- When is the assignment due? How will you apportion the work you have to do in the available time?
- How long should your writing be? If no length is assigned, what seems appropriate for your topic, audience, and purpose?

Document design

- What organization and format does the assignment require? (See pp. 89–101 on format in the academic disciplines and in business.)
- Even if a particular format is not required, how might you use margins, headings, illustrations, and other elements to achieve your purpose? (See pp. 83–88.)

1b. Development and focus

With a sense of your writing situation, you can begin to develop a draft of your paper. The guidelines below appear as stages to emphasize the kinds of thinking involved at various points in composing. But the stages are not fixed: you will inevitably circle back through them as your paper evolves, and you may find that some other sequence helps you touch the same bases.

Exploration

Most writers start a project by exploring ideas about their topic.

- Either in an actual draft or in some other form of writing, such as a list or diagram, try to discover and gather your own thoughts on your topic. Concentrate on opening up avenues: delay editing your ideas until you've seen how they come out in writing.
- Begin finding and evaluating appropriate sources of information and opinion to support and extend your own ideas. (See pp. 117–31 for tips on research.)

Thesis

The THESIS is the central idea of a piece of writing: the entire work develops and supports that idea. Though sometimes unstated, the thesis usually appears in a THESIS SENTENCE, or sentences, somewhere in the paper.

- Focus your thoughts and information on a single dominant question you seek to answer.
- Try to assert the answer to your question in one or two sentences, stating the idea that you want readers to carry away with them. This thesis sentence will probably change as your paper changes. Eventually, though, its final version will govern everything in the paper.

Plan

Even with a short piece of writing such as a letter or memo, your work will proceed more smoothly when you have a plan for it. You may need nothing more than a scratch outline that lists the major points you want to cover, perhaps with the most significant support for each point.

Most essays or papers divide into three parts:

- The INTRODUCTION—usually a paragraph or two—presents the topic, sometimes provides background, narrows the topic, and often includes the thesis sentence.
- The BODY, the longest part, contains the substance of the paper, developing parts of the thesis. See "Paragraphs" below.
- The CONCLUSION—usually a paragraph—ties together the parts of the body, sometimes restating the thesis, summarizing the major points, suggesting implications of the thesis, or calling for action.

Paragraphs

The body of your paper will consist of paragraphs that develop the major points contributing to the thesis. A point may require a single paragraph or two or three paragraphs. Generally, body paragraphs have their own structures:

- A TOPIC SENTENCE (often the first or second sentence) states the point that the paragraph develops.

1c

- The other sentences offer examples, facts, expert opinions, and other evidence to support the topic sentence.
- Occasionally, a concluding sentence ties the evidence together or prepares for the point of the next paragraph.
- To bind paragraphs and sentences so that they flow smoothly, you can use TRANSITIONAL EXPRESSIONS such as *first, however,* and *in addition.* (See p. 255 for a list.)

1c. Revision

When you have a draft of your paper, let it rest for a while to give you some distance from it. Then revise it against the checklist below, concentrating on the effectiveness of the whole. (Leave style, correctness, and other specific issues for editing.)

Revision Checklist

- **PURPOSE** What is the paper's purpose? Does it conform to the assignment? Will it be clear to readers?
- **THESIS** What is the thesis? Does the paper demonstrate it? What does each paragraph and each sentence contribute to the thesis? If there are digressions, should they be cut or reworked?
- **ORGANIZATION** What are the major points supporting the thesis? (List them.) How effective is their arj8rangement for the paper's purpose? Does the paper flow smoothly so that readers will follow easily?
- **DEVELOPMENT** How well do facts, examples, and other evidence support each major point and the thesis as a whole? Will readers find the paper convincing?
- **TONE** Is the paper appropriately formal or informal for its readers? Does it convey your attitude appropriately—for instance, is it neither too angry nor too flippant?
- **USE OF SOURCES** Have you used sources to support, not substitute for, your own ideas? Have you integrated borrowed material into your own sentences? (See pp. 127–40.)
- **TITLE, INTRODUCTION, AND CONCLUSION** Does the title convey the paper's content accurately and interestingly? Does the introduction engage and focus readers' attention? Does the conclusion provide a sense of completion?
- **FORMAT** Does the format of your paper suit your purpose and your audience's likely expectations for such papers?

1e

NOTE If you write on a computer, print your draft and revise it on paper. You'll be able to view whole sections at once, and the different medium can help you see flaws you may have missed on screen.

1d. Source documentation

If you draw on outside sources in writing your paper, you must clearly acknowledge those sources:

- See pages 133–36 for advice on when to acknowledge sources so that you avoid even the appearance of plagiarism.
- See pages 142–84 on documenting sources in the discipline you are writing in: MLA for English and many other humanities, Chicago for history and other humanities, APA for the social sciences, and CBE for the biological and other sciences. See also pages 184–95 for the Columbia style of documenting online sources in either the humanities or the sciences.

1e. Editing and proofreading

Much of this book concerns editing—tightening or clarifying sentences, polishing words, repairing mistakes in grammar and punctuation. Leave this work until after revision so that your content and organization are set before you tinker with your expression. For editing guidelines, see the checklists on pages 8 (clarity and style), 28 (sentence parts and patterns), 62 (punctuation), and 82 (form and appearance).

Most writers find that they spot errors better on paper than on a computer screen, so edit a printout if you can. And be sure to proofread your final draft before you submit it, even if you have used a spelling checker or similar aid. Spelling checkers are limited—for instance, they cannot distinguish between commonly confused words such as *their/there/they're* and *its/it's* or find common typos such as *not* for *now* and *you* for *your.* (See also p. 101.)

I

CLARITY AND STYLE

Checklist for
Clarity and Style

To improve the clarity and style of your drafts, use the following questions as a guide to editing.

✓ **EMPHASIS** Are your sentences emphatic? Do their subjects and verbs express their main actors and actions? Do their beginnings and endings stress main ideas and move from old information to new? Does coordination link ideas that are equally important? Does subordination de-emphasize less important ideas? (See Chapter 2.)

✓ **PARALLELISM** Have you used parallelism to show the equivalence of elements connected by *and, or, not only . . . but also,* and similar words? (See Chapter 3.)

✓ **VARIETY AND DETAILS** Have you varied sentence lengths and structures to stress your main ideas and hold readers' attention? Are your sentences well detailed so that readers will find them clear and interesting? (See Chapter 4.)

✓ **APPROPRIATE WORDS** Is your language appropriate for your writing situation? (Standard English suits most academic and business writing.) Have you avoided biased language? (See Chapter 5.)

✓ **EXACT WORDS** Are your words exact: suited to your meaning, concrete and specific, correct in idiom, and fresh, not clichéd? (See Chapter 6.)

✓ **CONCISENESS** Is your writing concise? Have you focused your subjects and verbs on key actors and actions? Have you cut empty words and unneeded repetition and recast unneeded *there is* and *it is* constructions? Have you reduced word groups to their essence and combined sentences where appropriate? (See Chapter 7.)

2
EMPHASIS

Emphatic writing leads readers to see your main ideas both within and among sentences.

2a. Subjects and verbs

The heart of every sentence is its subject,° which usually names the actor, and its verb,° which usually specifies the subject's action: *Children* [subject] *grow* [verb]. When these elements do not identify the key actor and action in the sentence, readers must find that information elsewhere and the sentence may be wordy and unemphatic. In the following sentences, the subjects and verbs are italicized:

UNEMPHATIC The *intention* of the company *was* to expand its workforce. A *proposal was* also *made* to diversify the backgrounds and abilities of employees.

These sentences are unemphatic because their key ideas (the company's intending and deciding) do not appear in their subjects and verbs. Revised, the sentences are not only clearer but more concise:

REVISED The *company intended* to expand its workforce. *It* also *proposed* to diversify the backgrounds and abilities of employees.

Several constructions can drain meaning from a sentence's subject and verb:

- Nouns made from verbs can obscure the key actions of sentences and add words. These nouns include *intention* (from *intend*), *proposal* (from *propose*), *decision* (from *decide*), *expectation* (from *expect*), *persistence* (from *persist*), *argument* (from *argue*), and *inclusion* (from *include*).

UNEMPHATIC After the company made a *decision* to hire more disabled workers, its next step was the *construction* of wheelchair ramps and other facilities.

°The degree sign (°) marks every term defined in the Glossary of Terms, beginning on page 214.

For Web sites on clarity and style, see page 197.

REVISED	After the company *decided* to hire more disabled workers, it next *constructed* wheelchair ramps and other facilities.

- Weak verbs, such as *made* and *was* in the unemphatic sentence above, tend to stall sentences just where they should be moving and often bury key actions:

UNEMPHATIC	The company *is* now the leader among businesses in complying with the 1990 Americans with Disabilities Act. Its officers *make* frequent speeches on the act to business groups.
REVISED	The company now *leads* other businesses in complying with the 1990 Americans with Disabilities Act. Its officers frequently *speak* on the act to business groups.

- Verbs in the passive voice° state actions received by, not performed by, their subjects. Thus the passive de-emphasizes the true actor of the sentence, sometimes omitting it entirely. Generally, prefer the active voice,° in which the subject performs the verb's action. (See also p. 39.)

UNEMPHATIC	The 1990 *law is seen* by most businesses as fair, but the *costs* of complying *have* sometimes *been exaggerated.*
REVISED	Most *businesses see* the 1990 law as fair, but some *opponents have exaggerated* the costs of complying.

2b. Concise writing

Unneeded words sap the energy from sentences and interfere with readers' ability to pick out main ideas. You can tighten wordy sentences by focusing on subjects and verbs, as suggested in the previous section. You can also use the techniques listed below, all discussed in more detail in Chapter 7, "Conciseness":

- Cut empty words (p. 24).
- Cut unneeded repetition (p. 25).
- Reduce clauses and phrases (p. 26).
- Cut *there is* and *it is* (p. 26).
- Combine sentences (p. 26).

2c. Sentence beginnings and endings

The beginning and ending of a sentence are the most emphatic positions, and the ending is usually more emphatic than the beginning. To emphasize information, place it first or last, reserving the middle for incidentals.

> UNEMPHATIC   Education remains the single best means of economic advancement, despite its shortcomings.
>
> **REVISED**   Education remains, despite its shortcomings, the single best means of economic advancement.

2d

Generally, readers expect the beginning of a sentence to contain information that they already know or that you have already introduced. They then look to the ending for new information. In the unemphatic passage below, the second and third sentences both begin with new topics (in italics), while the old topics (the controversy and education) appear at the end:

> UNEMPHATIC   Education almost means controversy these days, with rising costs and constant complaints about its inadequacies. But the *value of schooling* should not be obscured by the controversy. The *single best means of economic advancement*, despite its shortcomings, remains education.

In the more emphatic revision, the italicized old information begins each sentence and new information ends the sentence. The passage follows the pattern A→B. B→C. C→D.

> **REVISED**   Education almost means controversy these days, with rising costs and constant complaints about its inadequacies. But *the controversy* should not obscure the value of schooling. *Education* remains, despite its shortcomings, the single best means of economic advancement.

2d. Coordination

Use COORDINATION to show that two or more elements in a sentence are equally important in meaning:

- Link two complete sentences (main clauses°) with a comma and a coordinating conjunction° (*and, but, or, nor, for, so, yet*).

  Independence Hall in Philadelphia is now restored, <u>but</u> *fifty years ago it was in bad shape.*

- Link two main clauses with a semicolon alone or a semicolon and a conjunctive adverb,° such as *however, indeed,* or *therefore.*

The building was standing; <u>however</u>, it suffered from decay and vandalism.

- Within clauses, link words and word groups with a coordinating conjunction (*and, but, or, nor*) but no comma.

The people <u>and</u> officials of the nation were indifferent to Independence Hall <u>or</u> took it for granted.

Coordination clarifies meaning and smooths choppy sentences.

CHOPPY SENTENCES	We should not rely so heavily on oil. Coal and uranium are also overused. We have a substantial energy resource in the moving waters of our rivers. Smaller streams add to the total volume of water. The resource renews itself. Coal and oil are irreplaceable. Uranium is also irreplaceable. The cost of water does not increase much over time. The costs of coal, oil, and uranium rise dramatically.
IDEAS COORDINATED	We should not rely so heavily on coal, oil, <u>and</u> uranium, <u>for</u> we have a substantial energy resource in the moving waters of our rivers <u>and</u> streams. Coal, oil, <u>and</u> uranium are irreplaceable <u>and</u> thus subject to dramatic cost increases; water, <u>however</u>, is self-renewing <u>and</u> more stable in cost.

NOTES A string of main clauses connected by *and* implies that all ideas are equally important and creates a dull, plodding rhythm. Use subordination (see below) to revise such excessive coordination.

Two punctuation errors, the comma splice and the fused sentence, can occur when you link main clauses. See pages 59–60.

2e. Subordination

Use SUBORDINATION to indicate that some elements in a sentence are less important than others for your meaning. Usually, the main idea appears in the main clause,° and supporting information appears in subordinate structures such as the following:

- Subordinate clauses° containing a subject and a verb (like a complete sentence) but beginning with a subordinating word such as *although, because, before, if, since, that, when, where, which,* or *who* (*whom*).

<u>Although</u> production costs have declined, they are still high. [Stresses that costs are still high.]

Costs, _which include labor and facilities,_ are difficult to control. [Stresses that costs are difficult to control.]

- Phrases.°

Despite some decline, production costs are still high.
Costs, _including labor and facilities,_ are difficult to control.

- Single words.

Declining costs have not matched prices.
Labor costs are difficult to control.

Subordination can transform a monotonous string of main clauses into a more emphatic and interesting passage.

STRING OF MAIN CLAUSES	In recent years computer prices have fallen, and production costs have fallen more slowly, and computer manufacturers have had to struggle, for their profits have been shrinking.
REVISED	_Because_ production costs have fallen more slowly _than computer prices_ in recent years, computer manufacturers have had to struggle _with shrinking profits._

Generally, subordinate clauses give the most emphasis to secondary information, phrases give less, and single words give the least.

NOTE A subordinate clause or a phrase is not a complete sentence and should not be set off and punctuated as one. See pages 57–58 on sentence fragments.

3
PARALLELISM

PARALLELISM matches the form of your sentence to its meaning: when your ideas are equally important, or parallel, you express them in similar, or parallel, grammatical form.

The air is dirtied by _factories belching smoke_
and
vehicles spewing exhaust.

The parallelism clarifies and emphasizes the likeness between the two italicized word groups in a way that nonparallel phrases would not, as in _The air is dirtied by factories that belch smoke and exhaust from vehicles._

To spot elements that should be parallel, look for two or more words or phrases connected by coordinating conjunctions or correlative conjunctions, as shown in the sections following.

NOTE Parallelism can work like glue to link the sentences of a paragraph as well as the parts of a sentence: *Pulleys are ancient machines for transferring power. Unfortunately, they are also inefficient machines.*

3a. Parallelism with *and, but, or, nor, yet*

The coordinating conjunctions° *and, but, or, nor,* and *yet* signal a need for parallelism.

The industrial base was *shifting* <u>and</u> *shrinking.*

Politicians seldom *acknowledged the problem* <u>or</u> *proposed alternatives.*

Industrial workers were understandably disturbed *that they were losing their jobs* <u>and</u> *that no one seemed to care.*

> **NONPARALLEL** Three reasons why steel companies kept losing money were that their plants were inefficient, high labor costs, <u>and</u> foreign competition was increasing.
>
> **REVISED** Three reasons why steel companies kept losing money were *inefficient plants,* high labor costs, <u>and</u> *increasing foreign competition.*

NOTES As the preceding example shows, parallel elements match in structure, but they need not match word for word.

Be careful not to omit needed words in parallel structures.

> **NONPARALLEL** Many workers found it difficult to have faith <u>and</u> work for the future. [*Faith* and *work* require different prepositions,° so both must be stated.]
>
> **REVISED** Many workers found it difficult to have faith *in* <u>and</u> work for the future.

3b. Parallelism with *both . . . and, either . . . or,* and so on

Correlative conjunctions° stress equality and balance between elements. Parallelism confirms the equality. The correlative conjunctions include *both . . . and, either . . . or, neither . . . nor, not only . . . but also,* and *whether . . . or.*

At the end of the novel, Huck Finn <u>both</u> *rejects society's values by turning down money and a* <u>home</u> <u>and</u> *affirms his own values by setting out for "the territory."*

With correlative conjunctions, the element after the second connector must match the element after the first connector.

NONPARALLEL Huck Finn learns <u>not only</u> that human beings have an enormous capacity for folly <u>but also</u> enormous dignity. [The first element includes *that human beings have;* the second element does not.]

REVISED Huck Finn learns *that human beings have* <u>not only</u> an enormous capacity for folly <u>but also</u> enormous dignity. [Repositioning *not only* makes the two elements parallel.]

4
VARIETY AND DETAILS

To make your writing interesting as well as clear, use varied sentences that are well textured with details.

4a. Varied sentence lengths and structures

In most contemporary writing, sentences tend to vary from about ten to about forty words, with an average of fifteen to twenty-five words. If your sentences are all at one extreme or the other, your readers may have difficulty locating main ideas and seeing the relations among them.

- If most of your sentences contain thirty-five words or more, your main ideas may not stand out from the details that support them. Break some of the long sentences into shorter, simpler ones that stress key ideas.
- If most of your sentences contain fewer than ten or fifteen words, all your ideas may seem equally important and the links between them may not be clear. Try combining sentences with coordination (p. 11) and subordination (p. 12) to show relationships and stress main ideas over supporting information.

A good way to focus and hold readers' attention is to vary the structure of sentences so that they do not all follow the same pattern, like soldiers in a parade. Some suggestions:

- Avoid strings of main clauses,° which can make all ideas seem equally important and create a plodding rhythm. You want to emphasize your key subjects and verbs, moving in each sentence from old information to new (see p. 11). Subordinating less important information (italics in the revision below) can help you achieve this emphasis.

UNVARIED The moon is now drifting away from the earth. It moves away about one inch a year. This movement is lengthening our days, and they grow about a thousandth of a second every century. Forty-seven of our present days will someday make up a month. We might eventually lose the moon altogether. Such great planetary movement rightly concerns astronomers, but it need not worry us. It will take 50 million years.

REVISED The moon is now drifting away from the earth *about one inch a year. At a thousandth of a second or so every century,* this movement is lengthening our days. Forty-seven of our present days will someday make up a month, *if we don't eventually lose the moon altogether.* Such great planetary movement rightly concerns astronomers, but it need not worry us. It will take 50 million years.

• Vary the beginnings of sentences. Although you want to link sentences by moving from old to new information in each one (see p. 11), you need not begin every sentence with its subject.° A word or word group opening a sentence can provide descriptive information about timing, purpose, manner, and other aspects of the subject or action. And transitional expressions° can link sentences by indicating addition (for instance, *finally*), comparison (*similarly*), intensification (*indeed*), and other relationships. (See p. 225 for a list of such expressions.)

UNVARIED The lawyer cross-examined the witness for two days. The witness had expected to be dismissed within an hour. He was visibly irritated. He did not cooperate. He was reprimanded by the judge.

REVISED *For two days,* the lawyer cross-examined the witness. *Expecting to be dismissed within an hour,* the witness was visibly irritated. He did not cooperate. *Indeed,* he was reprimanded by the judge.

• Occasionally, to achieve special emphasis, reverse the usual word order of a sentence.

A dozen witnesses testified, and the defense attorney barely questioned eleven of them. *The twelfth, however, he grilled.* [Compare normal word order: *He grilled the twelfth, however.*]

4b. Details

Relevant details such as facts and examples create the texture and life that keep readers alert and help them grasp your meaning. For instance:

FLAT   Constructed after World War II, Levittown, New York, comprised thousands of houses in two basic styles. Over the decades, residents have altered the houses so dramatically that the original styles are often unrecognizable.

DETAILED   Constructed *on potato fields* after World War II, Levittown, New York, comprised *more than 17,000* houses in *Cape Cod and ranch* styles. Over the decades, residents have *added expansive columned porches, punched dormer windows through roofs, converted garages to sun porches, and otherwise* altered the houses so dramatically that the original styles are often unrecognizable.

5
APPROPRIATE WORDS

A country as diverse as the United States naturally encompasses varied subcultures with their own rich and vital vocabularies, such as the dialects of many African Americans and Hawaiians or the technical slang of computer hackers. The common language that brings all speakers together is STANDARD ENGLISH, usually defined as the English expected and used by educated readers and writers. Standard English is "standard" not because it is better than other forms of English but because it is accepted as the common language, much as dimes and quarters are accepted as the common currency. Standard English allows diverse people to communicate.

In situations calling for standard English, including most academic and business writing, you should use some specialized vocabularies only cautiously, as when aiming for a particular effect with an audience you know will appreciate it. You should entirely avoid some other vocabularies, especially those expressing prejudice.

5a. Dialect

Like many countries, the United States includes scores of regional, social, or ethnic groups with their own distinct DIALECTS, or versions of English: standard English, Black English, Appalachian English, and Creole are examples. All the dialects of English share many features, but each also has its own vocabulary, pronunciation, and grammar.

If you speak a dialect of English besides standard English, you need to be careful about using your dialect in situations where standard English is the norm, such as in academic or business writing. Otherwise, your readers may not understand your meaning, or they may perceive your usage as incorrect. (Dialects are not wrong in themselves, but forms imported from one dialect into another may still be perceived as wrong.)

Edit your drafts carefully to eliminate dialect expressions, especially those which dictionaries label "nonstandard," such as *hisn, hern, hisself, theirselves, them books, them courses, this here school, that there building, knowed, throwed, hadn't ought, could of, didn't never, might could do,* and *haven't no.*

5b. Slang

SLANG is the insider language used by a group, such as musicians or football players, to reflect common experiences and to make technical references efficient. The following example is from an essay on the slang of "skaters" (skateboarders):

> Curtis slashed ultra-punk crunchers on his longboard, while the Rube-man flailed his usual Gumbyness on tweaked frontsides and lofty fakie ollies.
>
> —MILES ORKIN, "Mucho Slingage by the Pool"

Though valuable within a group, slang is often too private or imprecise for academic or business writing.

5c. Colloquial language

COLLOQUIAL LANGUAGE is the everyday spoken language, including expressions such as *go crazy, get along with, a lot, kids* (for *children*), and *stuff* (for possessions or other objects). Dictionaries label this language "informal" or "colloquial."

Colloquial language suits informal writing, and an occasional colloquial word can help you achieve a desired emphasis in otherwise formal writing. But most colloquial language is not precise enough for academic or career writing.

5d. Technical words

All disciplines and professions rely on specialized language that allows the members to communicate precisely and efficiently with each other. Chemists, for instance, have their *phosphatides,* and literary critics have their *subtexts.* Use the terms of a discipline or profession when you are writing within it.

However, when you are writing for a nonspecialist audience, avoid unnecessary technical terms and carefully define the terms you must use.

5e. Indirect and pretentious writing

Small, plain, and direct words are usually preferable to big, showy, or evasive words. Take special care to avoid the following:

- EUPHEMISMS are presumably inoffensive words that substitute for words deemed potentially offensive or too blunt, such as *passed away* for *died* or *misspeak* for *lie.* Use euphemisms only when you know that blunt, truthful words would needlessly hurt or offend members of your audience.
- DOUBLE TALK (at times called DOUBLESPEAK or WEASEL WORDS) is language intended to confuse or to be misunderstood: the *revenue enhancement* that is really a tax, the *biodegradable* bags that still last decades. Double talk has no place in honest writing.
- PRETENTIOUS WRITING is fancy language that is more elaborate than its subject requires. Choose your words for their exactness and economy. The big, ornate word may be tempting, but pass it up. Your readers will be grateful.

PRETENTIOUS   Many institutions of higher education recognize the need for youth at the threshold of maturity to confront the choice of life's endeavor and thus require students to select a field of concentration.

REVISED   Many colleges and universities force students to make decisions about their careers by requiring them to select a major.

5f. Sexist and other biased language

Language can reflect and perpetuate inaccurate and hurtful prejudices toward groups of people, especially racial, ethnic, religious, age, and sexual groups. Because it hurts or alienates, biased language disconnects writer from reader. Unbiased language is a courtesy to the reader. It does not submit to stereotypes, it treats people as individuals, and it labels groups as they wish to be labeled.

Stereotypes of race, ethnicity, and other characteristics

A STEREOTYPE characterizes and judges people simply on the basis of their membership in a group: *Men are uncommunicative. Women are emotional. Liberals want to raise taxes. Conservatives are affluent.*

In your writing, avoid statements about the traits of whole groups that may be true of only some members. Be especially cautious about substituting such statements for the evidence you should be providing instead.

STEREOTYPE	Immigrants live off the taxes of citizens. [Asserts that all immigrants live on public assistance funded by taxes, but many immigrants support themselves and pay taxes.]
REVISED	In 1996 immigrants received $50.8 billion in public assistance and paid $20.3 billion in taxes.

Some stereotypes have become part of the language, but they are still potentially offensive.

STEREOTYPE	The administrators are too blind to see the need for a new gymnasium.
REVISED	The administrators do not understand the need for a new gymnasium.

Sexist language

SEXIST LANGUAGE distinguishes needlessly between men and women in such matters as occupation, ability, behavior, temperament, and maturity. It can wound or irritate readers and indicates the writer's thoughtlessness or unfairness. The following guidelines can help you eliminate sexist language from your writing.

• Avoid demeaning and patronizing language—for instance, identifying women and men differently or trivializing either gender.

SEXIST	Dr. Keith Harold and Lydia Hawkins coauthored the article.
REVISED	Dr. Keith Harold and Dr. Lydia Hawkins coauthored the article.
REVISED	Keith Harold and Lydia Hawkins coauthored the article.
SEXIST	Ladies are entering almost every occupation formerly filled by men.
REVISED	*Women* are entering almost every occupation formerly filled by men.

- Avoid occupational or social stereotypes, assuming that a role or profession is exclusively male or female.

  SEXIST   The considerate doctor commends a nurse when she provides his patients with good care.

  REVISED   The considerate doctor commends a nurse *who provides good care for patients.*

- Avoid using *man* or words containing *man* to refer to all human beings. Some alternatives:

businessman	businessperson
chairman	chair, chairperson
congressman	representative in Congress, legislator
craftsman	craftsperson, artisan
layman	layperson
mankind	humankind, humanity, human beings, people
manpower	personnel, human resources
policeman	police officer
salesman	salesperson, sales representative

  SEXIST   Man has not reached the limits of social justice.

  REVISED   *Humankind* [or *Humanity*] has not reached the limits of social justice.

  SEXIST   The furniture consists of manmade materials.

  REVISED   The furniture consists of *synthetic* materials.

- Avoid using *he* to refer to both genders. (See also pp. 46–47.)

  SEXIST   The newborn child explores his world.

  REVISED   The newborn child explores *his or her* world. [Male and female pronouns.]

  REVISED   Newborn *children* explore *their* world. [Plural.]

  REVISED   The newborn child explores *the* world. [Pronoun avoided.]

Inappropriate labels

Labels for groups of people can be shorthand stereotypes and can be discourteous when they ignore readers' preferences. Although sometimes dismissed as "political correctness," sensitivity in applying labels hurts no one and helps gain your readers' trust and respect.

- Avoid labels that (intentionally or not) disparage the person or group you refer to. A person with emotional problems is not a *mental patient*. A person with cancer is not a *cancer victim*. A person using a wheelchair is not *wheelchair-bound*.

5f

- Use names for racial, ethnic, and other groups that reflect the preferences of each group's members, or at least many of them. Examples of current preferences include *African American* or *black, latino/latina* (for Americans of Spanish-speaking descent), and *disabled* (rather than *handicapped*). But labels change often. To learn how a group's members wish to be labeled, ask them directly, attend to usage in reputable periodicals, or check a recent dictionary.

6
EXACT WORDS

To write clearly and effectively, you will want to find the words that fit your meaning exactly and convey your attitude precisely.

6a. The right word for your meaning

One key to helping readers understand you is to use words according to their established meanings.

- Become acquainted with a dictionary. Consult it whenever you are unsure of a word's meaning.
- Distinguish between similar-sounding words that have widely different meanings.

INEXACT   Older people often suffer *infirmaries* [places for the sick].

EXACT   Older people often suffer *infirmities* [disabilities].

Some words, called HOMONYMS, sound exactly alike but differ in meaning: for example, *principal/principle* or *rain/reign/rein*. (Many homonyms and near-homonyms are listed in the Glossary of Usage, p. 203.)

- Distinguish between words with related but distinct meanings.

INEXACT   Television commercials *continuously* [unceasingly] interrupt programming.

EXACT   Television commercials *continually* [regularly] interrupt programming.

- Distinguish between words that have similar basic meanings but different emotional associations, or CONNOTATIONS.

It is a *daring* plan. [The plan is bold and courageous.]
It is a *reckless* plan. [The plan is thoughtless and risky.]

Many dictionaries list and distinguish such SYNONYMS, words with approximately, but often not exactly, the same meanings.

6b. Concrete and specific words

Clear, exact writing balances abstract and general words, which outline ideas and objects, with concrete and specific words, which sharpen and solidify.

6d

- ABSTRACT WORDS name qualities and ideas: *beautiful, management, culture, freedom, awesome.* CONCRETE WORDS name things we can know by our five senses of sight, hearing, touch, taste, and smell: *sleek, humming, brick, bitter, musty.*
- GENERAL WORDS name classes or groups of things, such as *buildings, weather,* or *birds,* and include all the varieties of the class. SPECIFIC WORDS limit a general class, such as *buildings,* by naming one of its varieties, such as *skyscraper, Victorian courthouse,* or *hut.*

Abstract and general statements need development with concrete and specific details. For example:

VAGUE The size of his hands made his smallness real. [How big were his hands? How small was he?]

EXACT Not until I saw his white, doll-like hands did I realize that he stood a full head shorter than most other men.

6c. Idioms

IDIOMS are expressions in any language that do not fit the rules for meaning or grammar—for instance, *put up with, plug away at, make off with.*

Because they are not governed by rules, idioms usually cause particular difficulty for people learning to speak and write a new language. But even native speakers of English misuse some idioms involving prepositions,° such as *agree on a plan, agree to a proposal,* and *agree with a person* or *charge for a purchase* and *charge with a crime.*

When in doubt about an idiom, consult your dictionary under the main word (*agree* and *charge* in the examples). (See also p. 34 on verbs with particles.)

6d. Trite expressions

TRITE EXPRESSIONS, or CLICHÉS, are phrases so old and so often repeated that they have become stale. Examples include *better late than never, beyond the shadow of a doubt, face the music, green with envy, ladder of success, point with pride, sneaking suspicion,* and *wise as an owl.*

Clichés may slide into your drafts. In editing, be wary of any expression you have heard or used before. Substitute fresh words of your own, or restate the idea in plain language.

7
CONCISENESS

Concise writing makes every word count. Conciseness is not the same as mere brevity: detail and originality should not be cut with needless words. Rather, the length of an expression should be appropriate to the thought.

You may find yourself writing wordily when you are unsure of your subject or when your thoughts are tangled. It's fine, even necessary, to stumble and grope while drafting. But you should straighten out your ideas and eliminate wordiness during revision and editing.

7a. Focusing on the subject and verb

Using the subjects° and verbs° of your sentences for the key actors and actions will reduce words and emphasize important ideas. (See p. 9 for more on this topic.)

> **WORDY** The *occurrence* of the winter solstice, the shortest day of the year, *is* an event occurring about December 22.
>
> **CONCISE** The winter *solstice*, the shortest day of the year, *occurs* about December 22.

Focusing on subjects and verbs will also help you avoid several other causes of wordiness: nouns made from verbs, weak verbs, and the passive voice.° See pages 9–10 for discussion of these topics.

7b. Cutting empty words

Cutting words that contribute nothing to your meaning will make your writing move faster and work harder.

> **WORDY** *As far as I am concerned,* because *of the fact that a situation of* discrimination continues in *the field of* medicine, women have not *at the present time* achieved equality with men.
>
> **CONCISE** Because of continuing discrimination in medicine, women have not yet achieved equality with men.

The italicized parts of the wordy sentence above illustrate several kinds of empty words.

- Some phrases add nothing to meaning:

all things considered	in a manner of speaking
a person by the name of	in my opinion
as far as I'm concerned	last but not least
for all intents and purposes	more or less

- Some abstract or general words, along with other words they require (such as *the* and *of*), pad sentences:

area	element	kind	situation
aspect	factor	manner	thing
case	field	nature	type

- Some word groups mean the same thing as single words:

FOR	SUBSTITUTE
at all times	always
at the present time	now
at this point in time	now
for the purpose of	for
due to the fact that	because
because of the fact that	because
in the event that	if
by means of	by
in the final analysis	finally

7c. Cutting unneeded repetition

Repeating or restating key words from sentence to sentence can link the sentences and emphasize information the reader already knows (see p. 11). But unnecessary repetition weakens sentences and paragraphs.

WORDY   Many unskilled workers *without training in a particular job* are unemployed *and do not have any work*. These *unskilled workers* depend on government aid.

CONCISE   Many unskilled workers are unemployed. *They* depend on government aid.

Be especially alert to phrases that say the same thing twice. In the following examples, only the italicized words are needed:

circle around	important [basic] *essentials*
consensus of opinion	*repeat* again
cooperate together	*return* again
final *completion*	*square* [*round*] in shape
the future to come	surrounding *circumstances*

7d. Reducing clauses and phrases

Modifiers° can be expanded or contracted depending on the emphasis you want to achieve. (Generally, the longer a construction, the more emphasis it has.) When editing your sentences, consider whether any modifiers can be reduced without loss of emphasis or clarity.

WORDY	The Channel Tunnel, *which runs between Britain and France,* bores through *a bed of solid chalk that is twenty-three miles across.*
CONCISE	The Channel Tunnel *between Britain and France* bores through *twenty-three miles of solid chalk.*

7e. Cutting *there is* or *it is*

Sentences beginning *there is* or *it is* (called expletive constructions°) are sometimes useful to emphasize a change in direction, but usually they just add needless words.

WORDY	*There were delays and cost overruns that* plagued the tunnel's builders. *It was a fear of investors that* they would not earn profits once the tunnel opened.
CONCISE	*Delays and cost overruns* plagued the tunnel's builders. *Investors feared* that they would not earn profits once the tunnel opened.

7f. Combining sentences

Often the information in two or more sentences can be combined into one tight sentence.

WORDY	So far, business has been disappointing. Fewer travelers than were expected have boarded the tunnel train. The train runs between London and Paris.
CONCISE	So far, business has been disappointing, with fewer travelers than expected boarding the tunnel train that runs between London and Paris.

II
SENTENCE PARTS AND PATTERNS

Checklist for
Sentence Parts and Patterns

This checklist focuses on the most common and potentially confusing grammatical errors. See the contents inside the back cover for a more detailed guide to this part.

VERBS

✓ Have you used the correct forms of irregular verbs such as *has broken* [not *has broke*]? (See p. 29.)

✓ Have you used the appropriate endings for verbs, such as *he asks* [not *ask*]? (See p. 29.)

✓ Have you used helping verbs where required, as in *she has been* [not *she been*]? (See p. 30.)

✓ Have you matched verbs to their subjects, as in *The list of items is* [not *are*] *long*? (See p. 40.)

PRONOUNS

✓ Do pronouns match the words they refer to, as in *Each of the women had her* [not *their*] *say*? (See p. 45.)

✓ Do pronouns refer clearly to the words they substitute for, avoiding uncertainties such as *Jill thanked Tracy when she* [Jill or Tracy?] *arrived?* (See p. 47.)

✓ Are pronouns consistent, avoiding shifts such as *When one enters college, you meet new ideas?* (See p. 49.)

MODIFIERS

✓ Do modifiers fall close to the words they describe, as in *Trash cans without lids invite animals* [not *Trash cans invite animals without lids*]? (See p. 54.)

✓ Do modifiers clearly modify another word in the sentence, as in *Jogging, she pulled a muscle* [not *Jogging, a muscle was pulled*]? (See p. 56.)

SENTENCE FAULTS

✓ Are your sentences complete, each with a subject and a verb and none a freestanding subordinate clause? For instance, *But first she called the police* [not *But first called the police*]; *New stores open weekly* [not *New stores weekly*]; and *The new cow calved after the others did* [not *The new cow calved. After the others did*]? (See p. 57.)

✓ Have you linked complete sentences (main clauses) with a comma and a coordinating conjunction (*Cars jam the roadways, and they contribute to smog*), with a semicolon (*Many parents did not attend; they did not want to get involved*), or with a semicolon and a conjunctive adverb (*The snow fell heavily; however, it soon melted*)? (See p. 59.)

8
VERB FORMS

Verb forms may give you trouble when the verb is irregular, when you omit certain endings, or when you need to use helping verbs.

8a. *Sing/sang/sung* and other irregular verbs

Most verbs are REGULAR: their past-tense form° and past participle° end in *-d* or *-ed:*

> Today the birds *migrate*. They *soar*. [Plain form° of verb.]
>
> Yesterday the birds *migrated*. They *soared*. [Past-tense form.]
>
> In the past the birds have *migrated*. They have *soared*. [Past participle.]

About two hundred IRREGULAR VERBS in English create their past-tense form and past participle in some way besides adding *-d* or *-ed*. These irregular verbs include *become* (*became/become*), *begin* (*began/begun*), *eat* (*ate/eaten*), *give* (*gave/given*), *rise* (*rose/risen*), and *sing* (*sang/sung*).

> Today the birds *fly*. They *begin* migration. [Plain form.]
>
> Yesterday the birds *flew*. They *began* migration. [Past-tense form.]
>
> In the past the birds have *flown*. They have *begun* migration. [Past participle.]

Check a dictionary under a verb's plain form if you have any doubt about the verb's other forms. If the verb is regular, the dictionary will follow the plain form with the *-d* or *-ed* form. If the verb is irregular, the dictionary will follow the plain form with the past-tense form and then the past participle. If the dictionary gives only one irregular form after the plain form, the past-tense form and past participle are the same (*think, thought, thought*).

8b. *-s* and *-ed* verb endings

Speakers of some English dialects as well as nonnative speakers of English sometimes omit verb endings that are

For Web sites on sentence parts and patterns, see pages 197–98.

required by standard English. One is the *-s* ending on the verb when (1) the subject° is *he, she, it,* or a singular noun° and (2) the verb's action occurs in the present.

> The letter *asks* [not *ask*] for a quick response.
> The company *has* [not *have*] delayed responding.
> The treasurer *doesn't* [not *don't*] have the needed data.
> Delay *is* [not *be*] costly.

A second omitted ending is the *-d* or *-ed* needed when (1) the verb's action occurred in the past (*we bagged*), (2) the verb form functions as a modifier° (*used cars*), or (3) the verb form combines with a form of *be* or *have* (*was supposed, has asked*).

> The company *used to* [not *use to*] be more responsive.
> We *provided* [not *provide*] the *requested* [not *request*] data as soon as we were *asked* [not *ask*].
> We were *supposed* [not *suppose*] to be the best in the industry.

8c. Helping verbs

HELPING VERBS combine with some verb forms to indicate time and other kinds of meanings, as in *can run, might suppose, will open, was sleeping, had been eaten.* The main verb° in these phrases is the one that carries the main meaning (*run, suppose, open, sleeping, eaten*).

Required helping verbs

Some English dialects omit helping verbs required by standard English. In the sentences below, the underlined helping verbs are essential:

> Archaeologists *are conducting* fieldwork all over the world. [Not *Archaeologists conducting.* . . .]
> Many *have been* fortunate in their discoveries. [Not *Many been.* . . .]
> Some *could be* real-life Indiana Joneses. [Not *Some be.* . . .]

In these examples, omitting the helping verb would create an incomplete sentence, or SENTENCE FRAGMENT (p. 57).

Combinations of helping and main verbs   ESL

Helping verbs and main verbs combine in specific ways.

NOTE The main verb in a verb phrase (the one carrying the main meaning) does not change to show a change in subject or time: *she has sung, you had sung.* Only the helping verb may change, as in these examples.

Form of *be* + present participle

Create the progressive tenses° with *be, am, is, are, was, were,* or *been* followed by the main verb's present participle° (ending in *-ing*).

She *is working* on a new book.

Be and *been* require additional helping verbs to form progressive tenses.

can	might	should ⎫		have ⎫		
could	must	will ⎬ *be* working		has ⎬ *been* working		
may	shall	would ⎭		had ⎭		

When forming the progressive tenses, be sure to use the *-ing* form of the main verb.

Note Verbs that express mental states or activities rather than physical actions do not usually appear in the progressive tenses. These verbs include *adore, appear, believe, belong, have, hear, know, like, love, need, see, taste, think, understand,* and *want.*

Faulty   She *is wanting* to understand contemporary ethics.

Revised   She *wants* to understand contemporary ethics.

Form of *be* + past participle

Create the passive voice° with *be, am, is, are, was, were, being,* or *been* followed by the main verb's past participle° (usually ending in *-d* or *-ed* or, for irregular verbs, in *-t* or *-n*).

Her latest book *was completed* in four months.
It *was brought* to the President's attention.

Be, being, and *been* require additional helping verbs to form the passive voice.

have ⎫		am was ⎫		
has ⎬ *been* completed		is were ⎬ *being* completed		
had ⎭		are ⎭		

will *be* completed

Be sure to use the main verb's past participle for the passive voice.

Note Use only transitive verbs° to form the passive voice.

Faulty   A philosophy conference *was occurred* that week. [*Occur* is not a transitive verb.]

Revised   A philosophy conference *occurred* that week.

FORM OF *HAVE* + PAST PARTICIPLE

Four forms of *have* serve as helping verbs: *have, has, had, having*. One of these forms plus the main verb's past participle creates one of the perfect tenses.°

> Some students *have complained* about the laboratory. Others *had complained* before.

Will and other helping verbs sometimes accompany forms of *have* in the perfect tenses.

> Several more students *will have complained* by the end of the week.

FORM OF *DO* + PLAIN FORM

Always with the plain form° of the main verb, three forms of *do* serve as helping verbs: *do, does, did*. These forms have three uses:

- To pose a question: *How <u>did</u> the trial <u>end</u>?*
- To emphasize the main verb: *It <u>did end</u> eventually.*
- To negate the main verb, along with *not* or *never: The judge <u>did not withdraw</u>.*

Be sure to use the main verb's plain form with any form of *do*.

> **FAULTY**   The judge did *remained* in court.
> **REVISED**   The judge did *remain* in court.

MODAL + PLAIN FORM

The MODAL helping verbs include *be able to, be supposed to, can, could, had better, have to, may, might, must, ought to, shall, should, used to, will,* and *would*. The most common meanings (and the verbs conveying the meanings) are these:

- Ability (*can, could, be able to*): *The equipment <u>could</u> detect small vibrations.*
- Possibility (*could, may, might, could/may/might have* + past participle°): *The equipment <u>may have</u> failed.*
- Necessity or obligation (*must, have to, be supposed to*): *The lab <u>must</u> purchase a backup.*
- Permission (*may, can, could*): *The lab <u>may</u> spend the money.*
- Intention (*will, shall, would*): *The lab <u>will</u> spend the money.*
- Request (*could, can, would*): *<u>Could</u> you please obtain a bid?*
- Advisability (*should, had better, ought to, should have* + past participle): *You <u>ought to</u> obtain three bids.*
- Past habit (*would, used to*): *We <u>used to</u> obtain five bids.*

8d. Verb + gerund or infinitive ESL

A GERUND is the *-ing* form of a verb used as a noun (*Smoking kills*). An INFINITIVE is the plain form° of the verb plus *to* (*Try to quit*). Gerunds and infinitives may follow certain verbs but not others. And sometimes the use of a gerund or infinitive with the same verb changes the meaning of the verb.

Either gerund or infinitive

A gerund or an infinitive may follow these verbs with no significant difference in meaning: *begin, can't bear, can't stand, continue, hate, hesitate, like, love, prefer, start.*

The pump began *working*. The pump began *to work*.

Meaning change with gerund or infinitive

With four verbs—*forget, remember, stop,* and *try*—a gerund has quite a different meaning from an infinitive.

The engineer stopped *watching* the pump. [She no longer watched.]

The engineer stopped *to watch* the pump. [She stopped in order to watch.]

Gerund, not infinitive

Do not use an infinitive after these verbs: *admit, adore, appreciate, avoid, consider, deny, detest, discuss, dislike, enjoy, escape, finish, imagine, keep, mind, miss, practice, put off, quit, recall, resent, resist, risk, suggest, tolerate, understand.*

FAULTY   She suggested *to check* the pump.
REVISED   She suggested *checking* the pump.

Infinitive, not gerund

Do not use a gerund after these verbs: *agree, ask, assent, beg, claim, decide, expect, have, hope, manage, mean, offer, plan, pretend, promise, refuse, say, wait, want, wish.*

FAULTY   She decided *checking* the pump.
REVISED   She decided *to check* the pump.

Noun or pronoun + infinitive

Some verbs may be followed by an infinitive alone or by a noun° or pronoun° and an infinitive: *ask, beg, choose, dare, expect, help, need, promise, want, wish, would like.* A noun or pronoun changes the meaning.

She expected *to watch*.
She expected *her workers to watch*.

Some verbs *must* be followed by a noun or pronoun before an infinitive: *admonish, advise, allow, cause, challenge, command, convince, encourage, forbid, force, hire, instruct, order, permit, persuade, remind, require, teach, tell, warn.*

She instructed *her workers to watch.*

Do not use *to* before the infinitive when it comes after one of the following verbs and a noun or pronoun: *feel, have, hear, let, make* ("force"), *see, watch.*

She let her workers *learn* by observation.

8e. Verb + particle ESL

Some verbs consist of two words: the verb itself and a PARTICLE, a preposition° or adverb° that affects the meaning of the verb, as in *Look up the answer* (research the answer) or *Look over the answer* (check the answer). Many of these two-word verbs are defined in dictionaries. (There are some three-word verbs, too, such as *put up with* and *run out of.*)

Some two-word verbs may be separated in a sentence; others may not.

Inseparable two-word verbs

Verbs and particles that may not be separated by any other words include the following: *catch on, get along, give in, go out, grow up, keep on, look into, run into, run out of, speak up, stay away, take care of.*

FAULTY   Children *grow* quickly *up.*
REVISED   Children *grow up* quickly.

Separable two-word verbs

Most two-word verbs that take direct objects° may be separated by the object.

Parents *help out* their children.
Parents *help* their children *out.*

If the direct object is a pronoun,° the pronoun *must* separate the verb from the particle.

FAULTY   Parents *help out* them.
REVISED   Parents *help* them *out.*

The separable two-word verbs include the following: *call off, call up, fill out, fill up, give away, give back, hand in, help out, look over, look up, pick up, point out, put away, put back, put off, take out, take over, try on, try out, turn down.*

9
VERB TENSES

Definitions and examples of the verb tenses appear on pages 224–25. The following are the most common trouble spots.

9a. Uses of the present tense (*sing*)

Most academic and business writing uses the past tense° (*the rebellion occurred*), but the present tense has several distinctive uses:

ACTION OCCURRING NOW
We *define* the problem differently.

HABITUAL OR RECURRING ACTION
Banks regularly *undergo* audits.

A GENERAL TRUTH
The earth *is* round.

DISCUSSION OF LITERATURE, FILM, AND SO ON
Huckleberry Finn *has* adventures we all envy.

FUTURE TIME
Funding *ends* in less than a year.

9b. Uses of the perfect tenses (*have/had/will have sung*)

The perfect tenses° generally indicate an action completed before another specific time or action. The present perfect tense° also indicates action begun in the past and continued into the present.

present perfect
The dancer *has performed* here only once.

past perfect
The dancer *had trained* in Asia before his performance here ten years ago.

future perfect
He *will have performed* here again by next month.

9c. Consistency in tense

Within a sentence, the tenses of verbs and verb forms need not be identical as long as they reflect actual changes in time: *Ramon will graduate from college twenty years after his father arrived in America.* But needless shifts in tense will confuse or distract readers.

INCONSISTENT	Immediately after Booth *shot* Lincoln, Major Rathbone *threw* himself upon the assassin. But Booth *pulls* a knife and *plunges* it into the major's arm.
REVISED	Immediately after Booth *shot* Lincoln, Major Rathbone *threw* himself upon the assassin. But Booth *pulled* a knife and *plunged* it into the major's arm.

9d. Sequence of tenses

The SEQUENCE OF TENSES is the relation between the verb tense in a main clause° and the verb tense in a subordinate clause.°

Past or past perfect tense in main clause

When the verb in the main clause is in the past tense° or past perfect tense,° the verb in the subordinate clause must also be past or past perfect.

The researchers *discovered* that people *varied* widely in their knowledge of public events.
[past] [past]

The variation *occurred* because respondents *had been born* in different decades.
[past] [past perfect]

EXCEPTION Always use the present tense° for a general truth: *Columbus did not know that the earth is round.*

Conditional sentences ESL

A CONDITIONAL SENTENCE usually consists of a subordinate clause beginning *if, when,* or *unless* and a main clause stating the result. The three kinds of conditional sentences use distinctive verbs.

FACTUAL RELATION

For statements that something happens whenever something else happens, use the present tense in both clauses.

When a voter *casts* a ballot, he or she *has* complete privacy.
[present] [present]

If the linked events occurred in the past, use the past tense in both clauses.

When voters *registered* in some states, they *had* to pay a poll tax.
[past] [past]

PREDICTION

For a prediction, use the present tense in the subordinate clause and the future tense° in the main clause.

Unless citizens *regain*[present] faith in politics, they *will*[future] not *vote*.

SPECULATION

For speculating about events that are possible though unlikely, use the past tense in the subordinate clause and *would, could,* or *might* plus the verb's plain form in the main clause.

If voters *had*[past] more confidence, they *would vote*[would + verb] more often.

Use *were* instead of *was* when the subject is *I, he, she, it,* or a singular noun. (See also p. 38.)

If the voter *were*[past] more confident, he or she *would vote*[would + verb] more often.

9d

For events that are impossible now—that are contrary to fact—use the same forms as above (including the distinctive *were* when applicable).

If Lincoln *were*[past] alive, he *might inspire*[might + verb] confidence.

For events that were impossible in the past, use the past perfect tense in the subordinate clause and *would, could,* or *might* plus the present perfect tense° in the main clause.

If Lincoln *had survived*[past perfect] the Civil War, he *might have stabi-*[might + present perfect]*lized* the country.

Indirect quotations ESL

An indirect quotation° usually appears in a subordinate clause, and its verb depends on the verb in the main clause.

When the verb in the main clause is in the present tense, the verb in the indirect quotation (subordinate clause) is in the same tense as the original quotation.

Haworth *says*[present] that Lincoln *is*[present] our noblest national hero. [Quotation: "Lincoln *is* our noblest national hero."]

When the verb in the main clause is in the past tense, the verb in the indirect quotation usually changes tense from the original quotation. Present tense changes to past tense.

An assistant to Lincoln *said*[past] that the President *was*[past] always generous. [Quotation: "The President *is* always generous."]

Past tense and present perfect tense change to past perfect tense. (Past perfect tense does not change.)

Lincoln *said* [past] that events *had controlled* [past perfect] him. [Quotation: "Events *have controlled* me."]

10
VERB MOOD

The MOOD of a verb indicates whether a sentence is a statement or a question (*The theater* needs *help.* Can *you* help *the theater?*), a command (*Help the theater*), or a suggestion, desire, or other nonfactual expression (*I wish I were an actor*).

10a. Consistency in mood

Shifts in mood within a sentence or among related sentences can be confusing. Such shifts occur most frequently in directions.

INCONSISTENT   Dissolve the crystals in the liquid. Then you should heat the solution to 120°C. [The first sentence is a command, the second a statement.]

REVISED   Dissolve the crystals in the liquid. Then *heat* the solution to 120°C. [Consistent commands.]

10b. Subjunctive mood: *I wish I were*

The SUBJUNCTIVE MOOD expresses a suggestion, requirement, or desire, or it states a condition that is contrary to fact (that is, imaginary or hypothetical).

- Suggestion or requirement with the verb *ask, insist, urge, require, recommend,* or *suggest:* use the verb's plain form° with all subjects.

  Rules require that every donation *be* mailed.

- Desire or present condition contrary to fact: use the verb's past-tense form;° for *be,* use the past-tense form *were.*

  If the theater *were* in better shape and *had* more money, its future would be guaranteed.

  I wish I *were* able to donate money.

- Past condition contrary to fact: use the verb's past perfect form° (*had* + past participle).

The theater would be better funded if it *had been* better managed.

NOTE In a sentence expressing a condition contrary to fact, the helping verb° *would* or *could* does not appear in the clause beginning *if: Many people would have helped if they had* [not *would have*] *known.* Notice also that *have*, not *of*, follows *would* or *could: would have* [not *of*] *helped.*

11
VERB VOICE

The VOICE of a verb tells whether the subject° of the sentence performs the action (ACTIVE VOICE) or is acted upon (PASSIVE VOICE).

ACTIVE VOICE	Commercial services *expand* participation on the Internet.
PASSIVE VOICE	Participation on the Internet *is expanded* by commercial services.

11a. Consistency in voice

A shift in voice (and subject) within or between sentences can be awkward or even confusing.

INCONSISTENT	Commercial *services provide* fairly inexpensive Internet access, and *navigation is made* easy by them.
REVISED	Commercial *services provide* fairly inexpensive Internet access, and *they make* navigation easy.

11b. Active voice vs. passive voice

The active voice always names the actor in a sentence (whoever performs the verb's action), whereas the passive voice puts the actor in a phrase after the verb or even omits the actor altogether. Thus the active voice is usually more clear, emphatic, and concise than the passive voice.

WEAK PASSIVE	The *Internet is used* for research by many scholars, and its *expansion* to the general public *has been criticized* by some.
STRONG ACTIVE	Many *scholars use* the Internet for research, and *some have criticized* its expansion to the general public.

The passive voice is useful in two situations: when the actor is unknown and when the actor is unimportant or less important than the object of the action.

> The Internet *was established* in 1969 by the US Department of Defense. The network *has* now *been extended* both nationally and internationally. [In the first sentence the writer wishes to stress the Internet rather than the Department of Defense. In the second sentence the actor is unknown or too complicated to name.]

> After the solution *had been cooled* to 10°C, the acid *was added.* [The person who cooled and added, perhaps the writer, is less important than the facts that the solution was cooled and acid was added. Passive sentences are common in scientific writing.]

12b

12

AGREEMENT OF SUBJECT AND VERB

A subject° and its verb° should agree in number° (singular, plural) and person° (first, second, third).

> More *Japanese Americans live* in Hawaii and California
> subject   verb
> than elsewhere.

> *Daniel Inouye was* the first Japanese American in Congress.
> subject   verb

12a. Words between subject and verb

> A catalog of courses and requirements often *baffles* [not *baffle*] students.

> The requirements stated in the catalog *are* [not *is*] unclear.

Phrases beginning with *as well as, together with, along with,* and *in addition to* do not change the number of the subject.

> The president, as well as the deans, *has* [not *have*] agreed to revise the catalog.

12b. Subjects with *and*

> Frost and Roethke *were* American poets who died in the same year.

Note When *each* or *every* precedes the compound subject, the verb is usually singular.

Each man, woman, and child *has* a right to be heard.

12c. Subjects with *or* or *nor*

When parts of a subject are joined by *or* or *nor*, the verb agrees with the nearer part.

Either the painter or the carpenter *knows* the cost.

The cabinets or the bookcases *are* too costly.

When one part of the subject is singular and the other is plural, the sentence will be awkward unless you put the plural part second.

Awkward   Neither the owners nor the contractor *agrees*.

Improved   Neither the contractor nor the owners *agree*.

12d. *Everyone* and other indefinite pronouns

Indefinite pronouns° include *anybody, anyone, each, everybody, everyone, neither, no one, nothing, one, somebody,* and *something*. They are usually singular in meaning, and they take singular verbs.

Something *smells*.   Neither *is* right.

A few indefinite pronouns such as *all, any, none,* and *some* may take a singular or plural verb depending on whether the word they refer to is singular or plural.

All of the money *is* reserved for emergencies.

All of the funds *are* reserved for emergencies.

12e. *Team* and other collective nouns

A collective noun° such as *team* or *family* takes a singular verb when the group acts as a unit.

The group *agrees* that action is necessary.

But when the group's members act separately, use a plural verb.

The old group *have* gone their separate ways.

12f. *Who, which,* and *that*

When used as subjects, *who, which,* and *that* refer to another word in the sentence. The verb agrees with this other word.

Mayor Garber ought to listen to the people who *work* for her.

Bardini is the only aide who *has* her ear.

Bardini is one of the aides who *work* unpaid. [Of the aides who work unpaid, Bardini is one.]

Bardini is the only one of the aides who *knows* the community. [Of the aides, only one, Bardini, knows the community.]

12g. *News* and other singular nouns ending in -*s*

Singular nouns° ending in -*s* include *athletics, economics, mathematics, news, physics, politics,* and *statistics.*

After so long a wait, the news *has* to be good.

Statistics *is* required of psychology majors.

These words take plural verbs when they describe individual items rather than whole bodies of activity or knowledge.

The statistics *prove* him wrong.

12h. Inverted word order

Is voting a right or a privilege?

Are a right and a privilege the same thing?

There *are* differences between them.

12i. *Is, are,* and other linking verbs

Make a linking verb° agree with its subject, usually the first element in the sentence, not with other words referring to the subject.

The child's sole support *is* her court-appointed guardians.

Her court-appointed guardians *are* the child's sole support.

PRONOUNS

13

PRONOUN FORMS

A noun° or pronoun° changes form to show the reader how it functions in a sentence. These forms—called CASES—are SUBJECTIVE (such as *I, she, they, man*), OBJECTIVE (such as *me, her, them, man*), and POSSESSIVE (such as *my, her, their, man's*). A list of the case forms appears on pages 214–15.

13c

13a. Compound subjects and objects: *she and I* vs. *her and me*

Subjects° and objects° consisting of two or more nouns and pronouns have the same case forms as they would if one pronoun stood alone.

compound subject
She and Ming discussed the proposal.

compound object
The proposal disappointed *her and him*.

To test for the correct form, try one pronoun alone in the sentence. The case form that sounds correct is probably correct for all parts of the compound.

The prize went to [*he, him*] and [*I, me*].
The prize went to *him*.
The prize went to *him and me*.

13b. Subject complements: *it was she*

Both a subject and a subject complement° appear in the same form—the subjective case.

subject
complement
The one who cares most is *she*.

If this construction sounds stilted to you, use the more natural order: <u>*She*</u> *is the one who cares most.*

13c. *Who* vs. *whom*

The choice between *who* and *whom* depends on the use of the word.

Questions

At the beginning of a question use *who* for a subject and *whom* for an object.

43

subject⟶
Who wrote the policy?   object⟵
Whom does it affect?

Test for the correct form by answering the question with the form of *he* or *she* that sounds correct. Then use the same form in the question.

[*Who, Whom*] does one ask?
One asks *her*.
Whom does one ask?

Subordinate clauses

In subordinate clauses° use *who* and *whoever* for all subjects, *whom* and *whomever* for all objects.

subject⟶
Give old clothes to *whoever* needs them.

object⟵
I don't know *whom* the mayor appointed.

Test for the correct form by rewriting the subordinate clause as a sentence. Replace *who* or *whom* with the form of *he* or *she* that sounds correct. Then use the same form in the original subordinate clause.

Few people know [*who, whom*] they should ask.
They should ask *her*.
Few people know *whom* they should ask.

NOTE Don't let expressions such as *I think* and *she says* confuse you when they come between the subject *who* and its verb.

subject⟶
He is the one *who* I think is best qualified.

13d. Other constructions

We or *us* with a noun

The choice of *we* or *us* before a noun depends on the use of the noun.

⟶ object of
preposition
Freezing weather is welcomed by *us* skaters.

subject⟶
We skaters welcome freezing weather.

Pronoun in an appositive

An APPOSITIVE is a word or word group that renames a noun or pronoun. Within an appositive the form of a pronoun depends on the function of the word the appositive renames.

⟶ object of verb
The class elected two representatives, DeShawn and *me*.

Two representatives, DeShawn and *I*, were elected.
(subject — DeShawn and I)

Pronoun after *than* or *as*

After *than* or *as* in a comparison, the form of a pronoun indicates what words may have been omitted. A subjective pronoun must be the subject of the omitted verb:

Some critics like Glass more than *she* [does].
(subject)

An objective pronoun must be the object of the omitted verb:

Some critics like Glass more than [they like] *her*.
(object)

Subject and object of an infinitive

An INFINITIVE is the plain form° of the verb plus *to* (*to swim*). Both its object and its subject are in the objective form.

The school asked *him* to speak.
(subject of infinitive)

Students chose to invite *him*.
(object of infinitive)

Form before a gerund

A GERUND is the *-ing* form of a verb used as a noun (*a runner's breathing*). Generally, use the possessive form of a pronoun or noun immediately before a gerund.

The coach disapproved of *their* lifting weights.

The *coach's* disapproving was a surprise.

14
AGREEMENT OF PRONOUN AND ANTECEDENT

The word a pronoun refers to is its ANTECEDENT.

Homeowners fret over *their* tax bills.
(antecedent) *(pronoun)*

Its amount makes the tax *bill* a dreaded document.
(pronoun) *(antecedent)*

For clarity, a pronoun should agree with its antecedent in person° (first, second, third), number° (singular, plural), and gender° (masculine, feminine, neuter).

14a. Antecedents with *and*

The dean and my adviser have offered *their* help.

NOTE When *each* or *every* precedes the compound antecedent, the pronoun is singular.

Every girl and woman took *her* seat.

14b. Antecedents with *or* or *nor*

When parts of an antecedent are joined by *or* or *nor*, the pronoun agrees with the nearer part.

Tenants or owners must present *their* grievances.

Either the tenant or the owner will have *her* way.

When one subject is plural and the other singular, put the plural subject second to avoid awkwardness.

Neither the owner nor the tenants have made *their* case.

14c. *Everyone, person,* and other indefinite words

Indefinite words do not refer to any specific person or thing. They include indefinite pronouns° (such as *anyone, everybody, everything, no one, somebody*) and generic nouns° (such as *person, individual, child, student*).

Most indefinite words are singular in meaning and take singular pronouns.

Everyone on the women's team now has *her* own locker.

Each of the men still has *his* own locker.

Though they are singular, indefinite words often seem to mean "many" or "all" rather than "one" and are mistakenly referred to with plural pronouns, as in *Everyone has their own locker.* If you find yourself making this error, you have several options for correcting it:

- When you intend the indefinite word to include both masculine and feminine genders, use *he or she* (*him or her, his or her*).

An athlete deserves *his or her* privacy.

Everyone is entitled to *his or her* own locker.

To avoid awkwardness, don't use *he or she* more than once in several sentences. And avoid the combination *he/she*, which many readers do not accept.

- Change the indefinite word to a plural, and use a plural pronoun to match.

Athletes deserve *their* privacy.

All athletes are entitled to *their* own lockers. [Notice that *locker* also changes to *lockers*.]

- Rewrite the sentence to omit the pronoun.

An athlete deserves privacy.
Everyone is entitled to *a* locker.

NOTE All three techniques will help you avoid the so-called generic *he*, using the masculine pronoun to refer to both genders. Although traditional, the generic *he* is now seen as sexist because it appears to exclude females. (See also p. 21.)

14d. *Team* and other collective nouns

Use a singular pronoun with *team, family, group,* or another collective noun° when referring to the group as a unit.

The committee voted to disband *itself.*

When referring to the individual members of the group, use a plural pronoun.

The old group have gone *their* separate ways.

15

REFERENCE OF PRONOUN TO ANTECEDENT

If a pronoun° does not refer clearly to the word it substitutes for (its ANTECEDENT), readers will have difficulty grasping the pronoun's meaning.

15a. Single antecedent

When either of two nouns can be a pronoun's antecedent, the reference will not be clear.

15a

CONFUSING   Emily Dickinson is sometimes compared with Jane Austen, but *she* was quite different.

Revise such a sentence in one of two ways:

• Replace the pronoun with the appropriate noun.

CLEAR   Emily Dickinson is sometimes compared with Jane Austen, but *Dickinson* [or *Austen*] was quite different.

• Avoid repetition by rewriting the sentence. If you use the pronoun, make sure it has only one possible antecedent.

CLEAR   Despite occasional comparison, Emily Dickinson and Jane Austen were quite different.

CLEAR   Though sometimes compared with *her*, Emily Dickinson was quite different from Jane Austen.

15b. Close antecedent

A clause° beginning *who, which,* or *that* should generally fall immediately after the word it refers to.

CONFUSING   Jody found a dress in the attic *that* her aunt had worn.

CLEAR   In the attic Jody found a dress *that* her aunt had worn.

15c. Specific antecedent

A pronoun should refer to a specific noun° or other pronoun.

Vague *this, that, which,* or *it*

This, that, which, or *it* should refer to a specific noun, not to a whole word group expressing an idea or situation.

CONFUSING   The British knew little of the American countryside, and they had no experience with the colonists' guerrilla tactics. *This* gave the colonists an advantage.

CLEAR   The British knew little of the American countryside, and they had no experience with the colonists' guerrilla tactics. This *ignorance and inexperience* gave the colonists an advantage.

15c

Implied nouns

A pronoun cannot refer clearly to a noun that is merely implied by some other word or phrase, such as *news* in *newspaper* or *happiness* in *happy*.

CONFUSING	Cohen's report brought *her* a lawsuit.
CLEAR	Cohen was sued over *her* report.
CONFUSING	Her reports on psychological development generally go unnoticed outside *it.*
CLEAR	Her reports on psychological development generally go unnoticed outside *the field.*

Indefinite *it* and *they*

It and *they* should have definite antecedents.

CONFUSING	In the average television drama *they* present a false picture of life.
CLEAR	The average television *drama* presents a false picture of life.

15d

15d. Consistency in pronouns

Within a sentence or a group of related sentences, pronouns should be consistent. You may shift pronouns unconsciously when you start with *one* and soon find it too stiff.

INCONSISTENT	*One* will find when reading that *your* concentration improves with practice, so that *you* comprehend more in less time.
REVISED	*You* will find when reading that your concentration improves with practice, so that you comprehend more in less time.

(Use *you* in this way only when you mean to address the reader directly, as in giving advice or instructions. Avoid *you* otherwise, especially when the context is not appropriate: *In the twelfth century,* one [or *a person* or *people*, not *you*] *had to struggle simply to survive.*)

Inconsistent pronouns also occur when singular shifts to plural: *Everyone who reads regularly will improve his or her* [not *their*] *speed.* See pages 46–47.

MODIFIERS

16
ADJECTIVES AND ADVERBS

ADJECTIVES modify nouns° (*good child*) and pronouns° (*special someone*). ADVERBS modify verbs° (*see well*), adjectives (*very happy*), other adverbs (*not very*), and whole word groups (*Otherwise, the room was empty*). The only way to tell if a modifier should be an adjective or an adverb is to determine its function in the sentence.

16a. Adjective vs. adverb

Use only adverbs, not adjectives, to modify verbs, adverbs, or other adjectives.

NOT   They took each other *serious*. They related *good*.

BUT   They took each other *seriously*. They related *well*.

16b. Adjective with linking verb: *felt bad*

A modifier after a verb should be an adjective if it describes the subject,° an adverb if it describes the verb. In the first example below, the linking verb° *felt* connects the subject and an adjective describing the subject.

The sailors felt *bad*.
    linking   adjective
    verb

Some sailors fare *badly* in rough weather.
    verb   adverb

Good and *well* are frequently confused after verbs.

Decker trained *well*. [Adverb.]

She felt *well*. Her prospects were *good*. [Adjectives.]

16c. Comparison of adjectives and adverbs

Comparison° allows adjectives and adverbs to show degrees of quality or amount by changing form: *red, redder, reddest; awful, more awful, most awful; quickly, less quickly, least quickly.* A dictionary will list the *-er* and *-est* endings if they can be used. Otherwise, use *more* and *most* or *less* and *least*.

Some modifiers are irregular, changing their spelling for comparison: for example, *good, better, best; many, more, most; badly, worse, worst.*

Comparisons of two or more than two

Use the *-er* form, *more,* or *less* when comparing two items. Use the *-est* form, *most,* or *least* when comparing three or more items.

Of the two tests, the litmus is *better.*
Of all six tests, the litmus is *best.*

Double comparisons

A double comparison combines the *-er* or *-est* ending with the word *more* or *most.* It is redundant.

Chang was the *wisest* [not *most wisest*] person in town.
He was *smarter* [not *more smarter*] than anyone else.

16d

Complete comparisons

A comparison should be complete.

• The comparison should state a relation fully enough to ensure clarity.

UNCLEAR   Car makers worry about their industry more than environmentalists.

CLEAR   Car makers worry about their industry more than environmentalists *do.*

CLEAR   Car makers worry about their industry more than *they worry about* environmentalists.

• The items being compared should in fact be comparable.

ILLOGICAL   The cost of an electric car is greater than a gasoline-powered car. [Illogically compares a cost and a car.]

REVISED   The cost of an electric car is greater than *the cost of* [or *that of*] a gasoline-powered car.

16d. Double negatives

In a DOUBLE NEGATIVE two negative words cancel each other out. Some double negatives are intentional: for instance, *She was* <u>*not*</u> *unhappy* indicates with understatement that she was indeed happy. But most double negatives say the opposite of what is intended: *Jenny did* <u>*not*</u> *feel* <u>*nothing*</u> asserts that Jenny felt other than nothing, or something.

| FAULTY | The IRS *cannot hardly* audit all tax returns. *None* of its audits *never* touch many cheaters. |
| REVISED | The IRS *cannot* audit all tax returns. Its audits *never* touch many cheaters. |

16e. Present and past participles as adjectives ESL

Both present participles° and past participles° may serve as adjectives: *a burning house, a burned house.* As in the examples, the two participles usually differ in the time they indicate.

But some present and past participles—those derived from verbs expressing feeling—can have altogether different meanings. The present participle refers to something that causes the feeling: *That was a frightening storm.* The past participle refers to something that experiences the feeling: *They quieted the frightened horses.* Similar pairs include the following:

annoying/annoyed · pleasing/pleased
boring/bored · satisfying/satisfied
confusing/confused · surprising/surprised
exciting/excited · tiring/tired
exhausting/exhausted · troubling/troubled
interesting/interested · worrying/worried

16f. Articles: *a, an, the* ESL

Articles° usually trouble native English speakers only in the choice of *a* versus *an: a* for words beginning with consonant sounds (*a bridge, a uniform*), *an* for words beginning with vowel sounds, including silent *h*'s (*an apple, an urge, an hour*).

For nonnative speakers, *a, an,* and *the* can be difficult, because many other languages use such words quite differently or not at all. In English, their uses depend on the kinds of nouns they precede and the context they appear in.

Singular count nouns

A COUNT NOUN names something countable and can form a plural: *glass/glasses, mountain/mountains, child/children, woman/women.*

• *A* or *an* precedes a singular count noun when your reader does not already know its identity, usually because you have not mentioned it before.

A scientist in our chemistry department developed *a* process to strengthen metals. [*Scientist* and *process* are being introduced for the first time.]

- *The* precedes a singular count noun that has a specific identity for your reader, usually because (1) you have mentioned it before, (2) you identify it immediately before or after you state it, (3) it is unique (the only one in existence), or (4) it refers to an institution or facility that is shared by the community.

A scientist in our chemistry department developed a process to strengthen metals. *The* scientist patented *the* process. [*Scientist* and *process* were identified in the opening sentence.]

The most productive laboratory is *the* research center in *the* chemistry department. [*Most productive* identifies *laboratory. In the chemistry department* identifies *research center.* And the *chemistry department* is a shared facility.]

The sun rises in *the* east. [*Sun* and *east* are unique.]

Many men and women aspire to *the* presidency. [*Presidency* is a shared institution.]

Plural count nouns

A or *an* never precedes a plural noun. *The* does not precede a plural noun that names a general category. *The* does precede a plural noun that names specific representatives of a category.

Men and *women* are different. [*Men* and *women* name general categories.]

The women formed a team. [*Women* refers to specific people.]

Noncount nouns

A NONCOUNT NOUN names something that is not usually considered countable in English, and so it does not form a plural. Examples include the following:

Abstractions: confidence, democracy, education, equality, evidence, health, information, intelligence, knowledge, luxury, peace, pollution, research, success, supervision, truth, wealth, work

Food and drink: bread, flour, meat, milk, salt, water, wine

Emotions: anger, courage, happiness, hate, love, respect, satisfaction

Natural events and substances: air, blood, dirt, gasoline, gold, hair, heat, ice, oil, oxygen, rain, smoke, wood

Groups: clergy, clothing, equipment, furniture, garbage, jewelry, junk, legislation, mail, military, money, police

Fields of study: architecture, accounting, biology, business, chemistry, engineering, literature, psychology, science

16f

A or *an* never precedes a noncount noun. *The* does precede a noncount noun that names specific representatives of a general category.

> *Vegetation* suffers from drought. [*Vegetation* names a general category.]

> *The* vegetation in the park withered or died. [*Vegetation* refers to specific plants.]

Note Many nouns are sometimes count nouns and sometimes noncount nouns.

> The library has *a room* for readers. [*Room* is a count noun meaning "walled area."]

> The library has *room* for reading. [*Room* is a noncount noun meaning "space."]

Proper nouns

A PROPER NOUN names a particular person, place, or thing and begins with a capital letter: *February, Joe Allen*. *A* or *an* never precedes a proper noun. *The* does occasionally, as with oceans (*the Pacific*), regions (*the Middle East*), rivers (*the Snake*), some countries (*the United States*), and some universities (*the University of Texas*).

> *Garcia* lives in *Boulder,* where he attends *the University of Colorado.*

17
MISPLACED AND DANGLING MODIFIERS

For clarity, modifiers generally must fall close to the words they modify.

17a. Misplaced modifiers

A MISPLACED MODIFIER falls in the wrong place in a sentence. It may be awkward, confusing, or even unintentionally funny.

Clear placement

Confusing   He served steak to the men *on paper plates.*

Revised   He served the men steak *on paper plates.*

Confusing   Many dogs are killed by automobiles and trucks *roaming unleashed.*

REVISED   Many dogs *roaming unleashed* are killed by automobiles and trucks.

Only and other limiting modifiers

LIMITING MODIFIERS include *almost, even, exactly, hardly, just, merely, nearly, only, scarcely,* and *simply.* They should fall immediately before the word or word group they modify.

UNCLEAR   They *only* saw each other during meals.

REVISED   They saw *only* each other during meals.

REVISED   They saw each other *only* during meals.

Infinitives and other grammatical units

Some grammatical units should generally not be split by long modifiers. For example, a long adverb° between subject° and verb° can be awkward and confusing.

AWKWARD   *Kuwait,* after the Gulf War ended in 1991, *began* returning to normal.

REVISED   After the Gulf War ended in 1991, *Kuwait began* returning to normal.

A SPLIT INFINITIVE—a modifier placed between *to* and the verb—can be especially awkward and annoys many readers.

AWKWARD   Forecasters expected temperatures *to* not *rise.*

REVISED   Forecasters expected temperatures not *to rise.*

A split infinitive may sometimes be unavoidable without rewriting, though it may still bother some readers.

Several US industries expect *to* more than *triple* their use of robots.

Order of adjectives   ESL

English follows distinctive rules for arranging two or three adjectives before a noun. (A string of more than three adjectives before a noun is rare.) Adjectives always precede the noun except when they are subject complements,° and they follow this order:

1. Article or other word marking the noun: *a, an, the, this, Mary's*
2. Word of opinion: *beautiful, disgusting, important, fine*
3. Word about measurement: *small, huge, short, towering*

17a

4. Word about shape: *round, flat, square, triangular*
5. Word about age: *old, young, new, ancient*
6. Word about color: *green, white, black, magenta*
7. Word about origin (nationality, religion, etc.): *European, Iranian, Jewish, Parisian*
8. Word about material: *wooden, gold, nylon, stone*

Examples of this order include *a new state law, all recent business reports,* and *the blue litmus paper.*

17b. Dangling modifiers

A DANGLING MODIFIER does not sensibly modify anything in its sentence.

DANGLING *Passing the building,* the vandalism became visible.

Like most dangling modifiers, this one introduces a sentence, contains a verb form (*passing*), and implies but does not name a subject (whoever is passing). Readers assume that this implied subject is the same as the subject of the sentence (*vandalism*). When it is not, the modifier "dangles" unconnected to the rest of the sentence.

Revise dangling modifiers to achieve the emphasis you want.

* Rewrite the dangling modifier as a complete clause with its own stated subject and verb. Readers can accept different subjects when they are both stated.

DANGLING *Passing the building,* the vandalism became visible.

REVISED *As we passed* the building, the vandalism became visible.

* Change the subject of the sentence to a word the modifier properly describes.

DANGLING *Trying to understand the causes,* vandalism has been extensively studied.

REVISED Trying to understand the causes, *researchers have* extensively *studied* vandalism.

18

SENTENCE FRAGMENTS

A SENTENCE FRAGMENT is part of a sentence that is set off as if it were a whole sentence by an initial capital letter and a final period or other end punctuation. Although writers occasionally use fragments deliberately and effectively, readers perceive most fragments as serious errors in standard English. Use the tests below to ensure that you have linked or separated your ideas both appropriately for your meaning and correctly, without creating sentence fragments.

18a

ESL Some languages other than English allow the omission of the subject° or the verb.° Except in commands (*Close the door*), English always requires you to state the subject and verb.

18a. Tests for fragments

A word group punctuated as a sentence should pass *all three* of the following tests. If it does not, it is a fragment and needs to be revised.

Test 1: Find the verb.

Some sentence fragments lack any verb form:°

FRAGMENT	Thousands of new sites on the World Wide Web.
REVISED	Thousands of new sites *have appeared* on the World Wide Web.

The verb in a complete sentence must be able to change form as on the left below. A verb form that cannot change this way (as on the right) cannot serve as a sentence verb.

	COMPLETE SENTENCES	**SENTENCE FRAGMENTS**
SINGULAR	The network *grows*.	The network *growing*.
PLURAL	Networks *grow*.	Networks *growing*.
PRESENT	The network *grows*.	
PAST	The network *grew*.	The network *growing*.
FUTURE	The network *will grow*.	

(See also p. 30 on the use of helping verbs° to prevent sentence fragments.)

Test 2: Find the subject.

The subject of the sentence will usually come before the verb. If there is no subject, the word group is probably a fragment.

FRAGMENT   And has enormous appeal.

REVISED   And *the Web* has enormous appeal.

NOTE Commands, in which the subject *you* is understood, are not sentence fragments: [*You*] *Experiment with the Web.*

Test 3: Make sure the clause is not subordinate.

A SUBORDINATE CLAUSE begins with either a subordinating conjunction° (such as *because, if, when*) or a relative pronoun° (*who, which, that*). Subordinate clauses serve as parts of sentences, not as whole sentences.

FRAGMENT   When the government devised the Internet.

REVISED   The government devised the Internet. [Removing *When* leaves a complete sentence.]

REVISED   When the government devised the Internet, *no expansive computer network existed.* [Adding a new main clause° to the subordinate clause completes the sentence.]

NOTE Questions beginning *who, whom,* or *which* are not sentence fragments: *Who rattled the cage?*

18b. Revision of fragments

Correct sentence fragments in one of the two ways shown above, depending on the importance of the information in the fragment.

- Rewrite the fragment as a complete sentence. The information in the fragment will then have the same importance as that in other complete sentences.

  FRAGMENT   The Web is a recent addition to the Internet. *Which allows users to move easily between sites.*

  REVISED   The Web is a recent addition to the Internet. *It* allows users to move easily between sites.

- Combine the fragment with the appropriate main clause. The information in the fragment will then be subordinated to that in the main clause.

  FRAGMENT   The Web is easy to use. *Loaded with links and graphics.*

  REVISED   The Web, *loaded with links and graphics,* is easy to use.

18b

19

COMMA SPLICES
AND FUSED SENTENCES

When you combine two complete sentences (main clauses°) in one sentence, you need to give readers a clear signal that one clause is ending and the other beginning. In a COMMA SPLICE two main clauses are joined (or spliced) only by a comma, which is usually too weak to signal the link between main clauses.

COMMA SPLICE	The ship was huge, its mast stood eighty feet high.

19a

In a FUSED SENTENCE (or RUN-ON SENTENCE) the clauses are not separated at all.

FUSED SENTENCE	The ship was huge its mast stood eighty feet high.

19a. Main clauses without *and, but, or, nor, for, so, yet*

And, but, or, or another coordinating conjunction° often signals the joining of main clauses. When a sentence with two main clauses lacks this signal (and is thus a comma splice or fused sentence), revise the sentence in one of the following ways:

- Insert a coordinating conjunction when the ideas in the main clauses are closely related and equally important.

COMMA SPLICE	Some laboratory-grown foods taste good, they are nutritious.
REVISED	Some laboratory-grown foods taste good, *and* they are nutritious.

In a fused sentence insert a comma and a coordinating conjunction.

FUSED SENTENCE	Chemists have made much progress they still have a way to go.
REVISED	Chemists have made much progress, *but* they still have a way to go.

- Insert a semicolon between clauses if the relation between the ideas is very close and obvious without a conjunction.

COMMA SPLICE	Good taste is rare in laboratory-grown vegetables, they are usually bland.
REVISED	Good taste is rare in laboratory-grown vegetables; they are usually bland.

- Make the clauses into separate sentences when the ideas expressed are only loosely related.

COMMA SPLICE	Chemistry has contributed to our understanding of foods, many foods such as wheat and beans can be produced in the laboratory.
REVISED	Chemistry has contributed to our understanding of foods. Many foods such as wheat and beans can be produced in the laboratory.

- Subordinate one clause to the other when one idea is less important than the other. The subordinate clause will modify something in the main clause.

COMMA SPLICE	The vitamins are adequate, the flavor and color are deficient.
REVISED	*Even though* the vitamins are adequate, the flavor and color are deficient.

19b. Main clauses related by *however, for example,* and so on

Two kinds of words can describe how one main clause relates to another: conjunctive adverbs,° such as *however, instead, meanwhile,* and *thus;* and other transitional expressions,° such as *even so, for example, in fact,* and *of course.* Two main clauses related by all conjunctive adverbs and most transitional expressions must be separated by a period or by a semicolon. The connecting word or phrase is also generally set off by a comma or commas.

COMMA SPLICE	Most Americans refuse to give up unhealthful habits, consequently our medical costs are higher than those of many other countries.
REVISED	Most Americans refuse to give up unhealthful habits. Consequently, our medical costs are higher than those of many other countries.
REVISED	Most Americans refuse to give up unhealthful habits; consequently, our medical costs are higher than those of many other countries.

To test whether a word or phrase is a conjunctive adverb or transitional expression, try repositioning it in its clause. It can move.

Most Americans refuse to give up unhealthful habits; our medical costs, consequently, are higher than those of many other countries.

III

PUNCTUATION

Checklist for Punctuation

This checklist focuses on the most troublesome punctuation marks and uses, showing correctly punctuated sentences with brief explanations. For the other marks and other uses covered in this part, see the contents inside the back cover.

COMMA

✓ Subways are convenient, *but* they are costly to build. [Comma before *and, but,* or another coordinating conjunction between main clauses. See p. 64.]

✓ Subways are convenient *but* costly. [No comma before *and, but,* or another coordinating conjunction *not* between main clauses. See p. 64.]

✓ *Because of their cost,* new subways are rarely built. [Comma after an introductory element. See p. 64.]

✓ Light rail, *which is less costly,* is often more feasible. [Commas around a nonrestrictive element. See p. 65.]

✓ Those *who favor mass transit* often propose light rail. [No commas arround a restrictive element. See p. 65.]

✓ In a few older cities, commuters can choose from *subways, buses, light rail, and railroads.* [Commas separating items in a series. See p. 66.]

SEMICOLON

✓ She chose not to practice law; she wanted to work with her hands. [Semicolon between main clauses not joined by *and, but,* or another coordinating conjunction. See p. 68.]

✓ She had a law degree; *however,* she became a carpenter. [Semicolon between main clauses joined by a conjunctive adverb or transitional expression. See p. 69.]

COLON

✓ The school has one goal: to train businesspeople. [Colon ending a main clause to introduce information. See p. 70.]

APOSTROPHE

✓ Bill *Smith's* dog saved the life of the *Smiths'* grandchild. [Apostrophe-plus-*s* to show possession by singular words. Apostrophe only to show possession by plural words ending in -*s.* See p. 71.]

✓ *Its* [for *The dog's*] bark warned the family. [No apostrophe for possessive personal pronouns. See p. 72.]

✓ *It's* [for *It is*] an intelligent dog. [Apostrophe for contractions. See p. 72.]

62

20
END PUNCTUATION

End a sentence with one of three punctuation marks: a period, a question mark, or an exclamation point.

20a. Period for most sentences and some abbreviations

STATEMENTS

The airline went bankrupt.
It no longer flies.

MILD COMMANDS

Think of the possibilities.
See page 27.

INDIRECT QUESTIONS°

The article asks how we can improve math education.
It asks what cost we are willing to pay.

ABBREVIATIONS

P.	Ph.D.	Mr.	Feb.
Dr.	e.g.	Mrs.	ft.
St.	i.e.	Ms.	a.m., p.m.

Periods may be omitted from abbreviations of two or more words written in all-capital letters.

MD	BC, AD	USA	IBM	JFK
BA	AM, PM	US	USMC	AIDS

NOTE When a sentence ends in an abbreviation with a period, don't add a second period: *The university offers a well-respected Ph.D.*

20b. Question mark for direct questions°

What is the result?
What is the difference between those proposals?

20c. Exclamation point for strong statements and commands

No! We must not lose this election!
"Oh!" she gasped.

NOTE Use exclamation points sparingly, even in informal writing. They can make writing sound overly dramatic.

20c

For Web sites on punctuation, see page 197.

21

THE COMMA

The comma is the most common punctuation mark inside sentences, helping to separate sentence elements and prevent misreading. The comma's main uses (and misuses) appear below.

21a. Comma with *and, but, or, nor, for, so, yet*

Between main clauses

Use a comma before *and, but, or, nor, for, so,* and *yet* (the coordinating conjunctions°) when they link complete sentences (main clauses°).

Banks offer many services, *but* they could do more.
Many banks offer investment advice, *and* they help small businesses establish credit.

NOTE The comma goes before, not after, the coordinating conjunction.

Not between words, phrases, or subordinate clauses

Generally, do not use a comma before *and, but, or,* and *nor* when they link pairs of words, phrases,° or subordinate clauses°—that is, elements other than main clauses.

NOT One bank *established* special accounts for older depositors, *and counseled* them on investments.
BUT One bank established special accounts for older depositors, and counseled them on investments.

21b. Comma with introductory elements

Use a comma after most elements that begin sentences and are distinct from the main clause.

When a new century nears, futurists multiply.
Fortunately, some news is good.

You may omit the comma after a short introductory element if there's no risk that the reader will run the introductory element and main clause together: *By the year 2000 we may have reduced pollution.*

NOTE The subject° of a sentence is not an introductory element but a part of the main clause. Thus, do not use a comma to separate the subject and its verb.

NOT Some *pessimists, may be* disappointed.
BUT Some pessimists, may be disappointed.

21c. Comma or commas with interrupting and concluding elements

Use a comma or commas to set off elements that provide nonessential information—information that could be deleted without altering the basic meaning of the sentence or leaving it too general.

NOTE When nonessential information falls in the middle of the sentence, be sure to use one comma *before* and one *after* it.

Around nonrestrictive elements

A NONRESTRICTIVE ELEMENT adds information about a word in the sentence but does not limit the word to a particular individual or group. Omitting the italicized element from any sentence below would remove incidental details but would not affect the sentence's basic meaning.

NONRESTRICTIVE MODIFIERS

Hai Nguyen, *who emigrated from Vietnam,* lives in Denver.
His company, *which is ten years old,* studies air and water pollution.
Nguyen's family lives in Baton Rouge and Chicago, *even though he lives in Denver.*

NONRESTRICTIVE APPOSITIVES

APPOSITIVES are words or word groups that rename nouns.

Nguyen's work, *advanced research into air pollution,* keeps him in Denver.
His wife, *Tina Nguyen,* reports for a newspaper in Chicago.

Not around restrictive elements

Do not use commas to set off RESTRICTIVE ELEMENTS, modifiers and appositives containing information essential to the meaning of the sentence. Omitting the italicized element from any sentence below would alter the meaning substantially, leaving the sentence unclear or too general.

RESTRICTIVE MODIFIERS

People *who join recycling programs* rarely complain about the extra work.
The programs *that succeed* are often staffed by volunteers.
Most people recycle *because they believe they have a responsibility to the earth.*

RESTRICTIVE APPOSITIVES

The label *"Recycle"* on products becomes a command.
The activist *Susan Bower* urges recycling.
The book *Efficient Recycling* provides helpful tips.

21c

Around absolute phrases

An ABSOLUTE PHRASE consists usually of the *-ing* form of a verb plus a subject for the verb. The phrase modifies the whole main clause of the sentence.

Health insurance ⌒ *its cost always rising* ⌒ is a concern for many students.

Around transitional or parenthetical expressions

A transitional expression° such as *however, for example,* and *of course* forms a link between ideas. It is nonrestrictive and is usually set off with a comma or commas.

Most students at the city colleges ⌒ *for example* ⌒ have no health insurance.

A parenthetical expression° provides supplementary information not essential for meaning—for instance, *fortunately, to be frank,* and *all in all.* It can be enclosed in parentheses (see p. 78) or, with more emphasis, in commas.

Some schools ⌒ *it seems* ⌒ do not offer group insurance.

NOTE Do not add a comma after a coordinating conjunction° (*and, but,* and so on) or a subordinating conjunction° (*although, because,* and so on). To distinguish between these words and transitional or parenthetical expressions, try moving the word or expression around in its clause. Transitional or parenthetical expressions can be moved; coordinating and subordinating conjunctions cannot.

Around phrases of contrast

Students may focus on the cost of care ⌒ *not their health.*

Around *yes* and *no*

All schools should agree that ⌒ *yes* ⌒ they will provide at least minimal insurance at low cost.

Around words of direct address

Heed this lesson ⌒ *readers.*

21d. Commas with series

Between series items

Use commas to separate the items in lists or series.

The names *Belial* ⌒ *Beelzebub* ⌒ and *Lucifer* sound ominous.

The comma before the last item in a series (before *and*) is optional, but it is never wrong and it is usually clearer.

21d

Not around series

Do not use a comma *before* or *after* a series.

NOT The skills of, *agriculture, herding, and hunting,* sustained the Native Americans.

BUT The skills of⌒agriculture, herding, and hunting⌒sustained the Native Americans.

21e. Comma with adjectives

Between equal adjectives

Use a comma between two or more adjectives° when each one modifies the same word equally. As a test, such adjectives could be joined by *and*.

The *dirty⌒dented* car was a neighborhood eyesore.

Not between unequal adjectives

Do not use a comma between adjectives when one forms a unit with the modified word. As a test, the two adjectives could not sensibly be joined by *and*.

The house overflowed with *ornate⌒electric* fixtures.
Among the junk in the attic was *one⌒lovely* vase.

21f. Commas with dates, addresses, place names, numbers

When they appear within sentences, elements punctuated with commas are also ended with commas.

DATES

July 4⌒ 1776⌒ was the day the Declaration was signed. [Note that commas appear before *and* after the year.]

The United States entered World War II in December⌒ 1941. [No comma is needed between a month or season and a year.]

ADDRESSES AND PLACE NAMES

Use the address 806 Ogden Avenue⌒ Swarthmore⌒ Pennsylvania 19081⌒ for all correspondence. [No comma is needed between the state name and zip code.]

NUMBERS

The new assembly plant cost $7⌒525⌒000.
A kilometer is 3⌒281 feet [*or* 3281 feet].

21g. Commas with quotations

A comma or commas usually separate a quotation from a signal phrase that identifies the source, such as *she said* or *he replied*.

Eleanor Roosevelt said⊙"You must do the thing you think you cannot do."

"Knowledge is power⊙" wrote Francis Bacon.

"You don't need a weatherman⊙" sings Bob Dylan⊙ "to know which way the wind blows."

Do not use a comma when the signal phrase interrupts the quotation between main clauses.° Instead, follow the signal phrase with a semicolon or period.

"That part of my life was over," she wrote⊙"his words had sealed it shut."

"That part of my life was over," she wrote⊙"His words had sealed it shut."

22
THE SEMICOLON

The semicolon separates equal and balanced sentence elements, usually complete sentences (main clauses°).

22a. Semicolon between complete sentences not joined by *and, but, or, nor,* etc.

Between complete sentences

Use a semicolon between complete sentences (main clauses°) that are not connected by *and, but, or, nor, for, so,* or *yet* (the coordinating conjunctions°).

Increased taxes are only one way to pay for programs⊙ cost cutting also frees up money.

Not between main clauses and subordinate elements

Do not use a semicolon between a main clause and a subordinate element, such as a subordinate clause° or a phrase.°

NOT According to African authorities; only about 35,000 Pygmies exist today.

BUT According to African authorities⊙only about 35,000 Pygmies exist today.

NOT Anthropologists have campaigned; for the protection of the Pygmies' habitat.

BUT Anthropologists have campaigned⊙for the protection of the Pygmies' habitat.

22b. Semicolon with *however, for example,* and so on

Use a semicolon between complete sentences (main clauses°) that are related by two kinds of words: conjunctive adverbs,° such as *hence, however, indeed, moreover, therefore,* and *thus;* and other transitional expressions,° such as *after all, for example, in fact,* and *of course.*

Blue jeans have become fashionable all over the world; however, the American originators still wear more jeans than anyone else.

A conjunctive adverb or transitional expression may move around within its clause, so the semicolon will not always come just before the adverb or expression. The adverb or expression itself is usually set off with a comma or commas.

Blue jeans have become fashionable all over the world; the American originators, *however,* still wear more jeans than anyone else.

22c. Semicolons with series

Between series items

Use semicolons (rather than commas) to separate items in a series when the items contain commas.

The custody case involved Amy Dalton, the child; Ellen and Mark Dalton, the parents; and Ruth and Hal Blum, the grandparents.

Not before a series

Do not use a semicolon to introduce a series. (Use a colon or a dash instead.)

NOT   Teachers have heard all sorts of reasons why students do poorly; psychological problems, family illness, too much work, too little time.

BUT   Teachers have heard all sorts of reasons why students do poorly: psychological problems, family illness, too much work, too little time.

23

THE COLON

The colon is mainly a mark of introduction, but it has a few other conventional uses as well.

23

23a. Colon for introduction

At end of main clause

The colon ends a complete sentence (main clause°) and introduces various additions:

Soul food has a deceptively simple definition: the ethnic cooking of African Americans. [Introduces an explanation.]

At least three soul food dishes are familiar to most Americans: fried chicken, barbecued spareribs, and sweet potatoes. [Introduces a series.]

Soul food has one disadvantage: fat. [Introduces an appositive.°]

One soul food chef has a solution: "Instead of using ham hocks to flavor beans, I use smoked turkey wings. The soulful, smoky taste remains, but without all the fat of pork." [Introduces a long quotation.]

Not inside main clause

Do not use a colon inside a main clause, especially after *such as* or a verb.

NOT The best-known soul food dish is: fried chicken. Many Americans have not tasted delicacies such as: chitlins and black-eyed peas.

BUT The best-known soul food dish is fried chicken. Many Americans have not tasted delicacies such as chitlins and black-eyed peas.

23b. Colon with salutations of business letters, titles and subtitles, divisions of time, and biblical citations

SALUTATION OF A BUSINESS LETTER

Dear Ms. Burak:

TITLE AND SUBTITLE

Anna Freud: Her Life and Work

TIME

12:26   6:00

BIBLICAL CITATION

1 Corinthians 3:6–7

24
THE APOSTROPHE

The apostrophe (') appears as part of a word to indicate possession, the omission of one or more letters, or (in a few cases) plural number.

24a. Apostrophe with possessives

The POSSESSIVE form of a word indicates that it owns or is the source of another word: *the dog's hair, everyone's hope.* For nouns° and indefinite pronouns,° such as *everyone,* the possessive form always includes an apostrophe and often an *-s.*

NOTE The apostrophe or apostrophe-plus-*s* is an *addition.* Before this addition, always spell the name of the owner or owners without dropping or adding letters.

Singular words: Add *-'s.*

Bill *Boughton's* skillful card tricks amaze children.
Anyone's eyes would widen.

The *-'s* ending for singular words usually pertains to singular words ending in *-s.*

Sandra *Cisneros's* work is highly regarded.
The *business's* customers filed suit.

However, some writers add only the apostrophe to singular words ending in *-s,* especially when the additional *s* would make the word difficult to pronounce (*Moses'*) or when the name sounds like a plural (*Rivers'*).

Plural words ending in *-s:* Add *-'* only.

Workers' incomes have fallen slightly over the past year.
Many students take several *years'* leave after high school.
The *Murphys'* son lives at home.

Plural words not ending in *-s:* Add *-'s.*

Children's educations are at stake.
We need to attract the *media's* attention.

Compound words: Add *-'s* only to the last word.

The *brother-in-law's* business failed.
Taxes are always *somebody else's* fault.

Two or more owners: Add *-'s* depending on possession.

Zimbale's and *Mason's* comedy techniques are similar.
[Each comedian has his own technique.]
The child recovered despite her *mother and father's* neglect. [The mother and father were jointly neglectful.]

24b. Misuses of the apostrophe

Not with plural nouns°

NOT The unleashed *dog's* belonged to the *Jones'.*
BUT The unleashed *dogs* belonged to the *Joneses.*

Not with singular verbs°

Not   The subway *break's* down less often now.
But   The subway *breaks* down less often now.

Not with possessives of personal pronouns°

Not   The car is *her's*, not *their's*. *It's* color is red.
But   The car is *hers*, not *theirs*. *Its* color is red.

Note: Don't confuse possessive pronouns and contractions: *its, your, their,* and *whose* are possessives. *It's, you're, they're,* and *who's* are contractions. See below.

24c. Apostrophe with contractions

A CONTRACTION replaces one or more letters, numbers, or words with an apostrophe.

it is	it's	cannot	can't
you are	you're	does not	doesn't
they are	they're	were not	weren't
who is	who's	class of 1997	class of '97

Note The four contractions on the left are easily confused with the possessive pronouns° *its, your, their,* and *whose.* To avoid misusing any of these words, search for all of them in your drafts (a word processor can help with this search). Then test for correctness:

• Do you intend the word to contain the sentence verb *is* or *are,* as in *It is a shame, They are to blame, You are right, Who is coming?* Then use an apostrophe: *it's, they're, you're, who's.*
• Do you intend the word to indicate possession, as in *Its tail was wagging, Their car broke down, Your eyes are blue, Whose book is that?* Then don't use an apostrophe.

24d. Apostrophe with plural abbreviations, dates, and words or characters named as words

ABBREVIATIONS

Use the apostrophe to form the plural of most abbreviations containing periods: *Ph.D.'s.* You can omit the apostrophe for the plural of an abbreviation without periods: *CD-ROMs.*

DATES

The apostrophe for the years in a decade is optional: *1990s, 1990's.*

WORDS OR CHARACTERS NAMED AS WORDS

We often refer to a word, letter, or number as the word or character itself, rather than use it for its meaning:

The word <u>but</u> starts with a <u>b</u>.

To make such a word or character plural, add an *-s*. An apostrophe is optional as long as you are consistent.

The sentence has too many <u>but</u>s [or <u>but</u>'s].
Two <u>3</u>s [or <u>3</u>'s] end the zip code.

NOTE The word or character is underlined or italicized (see p. 110), but the added *-s* and any apostrophe are not.

25
QUOTATION MARKS

25a

Quotation marks—either double (" ") or single (' ')—mainly enclose direct quotations from speech and from writing.

This chapter treats the main uses of quotation marks. For when to use quotations from sources in a paper, see pages 132–33. For how to integrate quotations into your own prose, see pages 136–40. For punctuation to use when altering quotations, see pages 78–80.

NOTE Quotation marks *always* come in pairs, one before and one after the quoted material.

25a. Quotation marks with direct quotations

Double quotation marks

A DIRECT QUOTATION reports what someone said or wrote, in the exact words of the original.

"Life," said the psychoanalyst Karen Horney, "remains a very efficient therapist."

NOTE Do not use quotation marks with an INDIRECT QUOTATION, which reports what someone said or wrote but not in the exact words of the original: *Karen Horney remarked that life is a good therapist.*

Single quotation marks

Use single quotation marks to enclose a quotation within a quotation.

"In formulating any philosophy," Woody Allen writes, "the first consideration must always be: What can we know? . . . Descartes hinted at the problem when he wrote, ❛My mind can never know my body, although it has become quite friendly with my leg❜."

Long quotations

Use an indention to set off long quotations from the main body of your text. *Do not use quotation marks with a set-off quotation.*

> In his 1967 study of the lives of unemployed black men, Elliot Liebow observes that "unskilled" construction work requires more experience and skill than is generally assumed.
>
> > ❛A healthy, sturdy, active man of good intelligence requires from two to four weeks to break in on a construction job. . . . It frequently happens that his foreman or the craftsman he services is not willing to wait that long for him to get into condition or to learn at a glance the difference in size between a rough 2 x 8 and a finished 2 x 10❜(62)

25a

(The parenthetical number at the end of the quotation is a source citation.)

The length of a set-off quotation and method of displaying it vary among academic disciplines. Here are the formats recommended by the principal discipline guides:

- *English, foreign languages, and some other humanities* (*MLA Handbook for Writers of Research Papers*, 5th ed.): This is the style illustrated above. Set off four or more lines of poetry and five or more typed lines of prose. Indent the quotation one inch or ten spaces from the left, double-space the quotation, and double-space above and below the quotation.

- *History, art history, and some other humanities* (*The Chicago Manual of Style*, 14th ed., and the student guide adapted from it, Kate L. Turabian's *A Manual for Writers of Term Papers, Theses, and Dissertations*, 6th ed.): Set off poetry quotations of more than two lines. Set off prose quotations of two or more sentences that run eight or more lines. (You may set off shorter quotations to emphasize or compare them.) Indent any displayed quotation four spaces from the left, single-space the quotation, and double-space above and below it.

- *Psychology and some other disciplines* (*Publication Manual of the American Psychological Association*, 4th ed.):

Set off quotations of forty or more words. For student papers, indent the quotation five spaces from the left, single-space the quotation, and double-space above and below the quotation.

- *Life sciences, physical sciences, and mathematics* (*Scientific Style and Format: The CBE Manual for Authors, Editors, and Publishers,* 6th ed.): This guide specifies only that long quotations be set off and indented, so any of the formats above is appropriate.

Dialogue

When quoting a conversation, put the speeches in double quotation marks and begin a new paragraph for each speaker.

> "What shall I call you? Your name?" Andrews whispered rapidly, as with a high squeak the latch of the door rose.
> "Elizabeth," she said. "Elizabeth."
>
> —GRAHAM GREENE, *The Man Within*

25c

25b. Quotation marks with titles of works

Do not use quotation marks for the titles of your own papers. Within your text, however, use quotation marks to enclose the titles of works that are published or released within larger works (see below). Use underlining (italics) for all other titles (see p. 109).

SONG	**ESSAY**
"Satisfaction"	"Joey: A 'Mechanical Boy'"
SHORT STORY	**EPISODE OF A TELEVISION OR RADIO PROGRAM**
"The Gift of the Magi"	"The Mexican Connection" (on <u>60 Minutes</u>)
SHORT POEM	
"Her Kind"	**SUBDIVISION OF A BOOK**
ARTICLE IN A PERIODICAL	"The Mast Head" (Chapter
"Does 'Scaring' Work?"	35 of <u>Moby-Dick</u>)

NOTE Some academic disciplines do not require quotation marks for titles within source citations. See pages 169–76 (APA style) and 178–84 (CBE style).

25c. Quotation marks with words used in a special sense

On movie sets movable "wild walls" make a one-walled room seem four-walled on film.

Avoid using quotation marks to express irony—that is, to indicate that you are using a word with a different or even opposite meaning than usual. Instead of *Americans "justified" their treatment of the Indians,* say what you mean straightforwardly, perhaps *Americans <u>attempted to justify</u> their treatment of the Indians.*

NOTE Use underlining or italics to highlight words you are defining. (See p. 110.)

25d. Quotation marks with other punctuation

Commas and periods: Inside quotation marks

Jonathan Swift wrote a famous satire, "A Modest Proposal**,"** in 1729.

"Swift's 'A Modest Proposal**,'**" wrote one critic, "is so outrageous that it cannot be believed**."**

EXCEPTION When a parenthetical source citation immediately follows a quotation, place any comma or period *after* the citation: *One critic calls the essay "outrageous" (Olms 26)***.**

Colons and semicolons: Outside quotation marks

A few years ago the slogan in elementary education was "learning by playing**";** now educators focus on basic skills.

We all know the meaning of "basic skills**":** reading, writing, and arithmetic.

Dashes, question marks, and exclamation points: Inside quotation marks only if part of the quotation

When a dash, exclamation point, or question mark is part of the quotation, place it *inside* quotation marks. Don't use any other punctuation, such as a period or comma.

"But must you**—"** Marcia hesitated, afraid of the answer.

"Go away**!"** I yelled.

Did you say, "Who is she**?"** [When both your sentence and the quotation would end in a question mark or exclamation point, use only the mark in the quotation.]

When a dash, question mark, or exclamation point applies only to the larger sentence, not to the quotation, place it *outside* quotation marks—again, with no other punctuation.

Betty Friedan's question in 1963**—"**Who knows what women can be**?"—**encouraged others to seek answers.

Who said, "Now cracks a noble heart**"?**

25d

26

OTHER MARKS

The other marks of punctuation are the dash, paren-theses, the ellipsis mark, brackets, and the slash.

26a. Dash or dashes: Shifts and interruptions

The dash (—) punctuates sentences. In contrast, the hy-phen (-) punctuates words. Form a dash with two hyphens (--)—no extra space before, after, or between the hyphens. Or use the character called an em-dash on your word processor.

Shifts in tone or thought

The novel—if one can call it that—appeared in 1994.
If the book had a plot—but a plot would be too conven-tional.

Nonessential elements

You may use dashes instead of commas to set off and emphasize elements that are not essential to the meaning of your sentence (see p. 65). Be sure to use a pair of dash-es when the element interrupts the sentence.

The qualities Monet painted—sunlight, rich shadows, deep colors—abounded near the rivers and gardens he used as subjects.

Introductory series and concluding series and explanations

Shortness of breath, skin discoloration, persistent indiges-tion, the presence of small lumps—all these may signify cancer. [Introductory series.]
The patient undergoes a battery of tests—CAT scan, bron-choscopy, perhaps even biopsy. [Concluding series.]
Many patients are disturbed by the CAT scan—by the need to keep still for long periods in an exceedingly small space. [Concluding explanation.]

You could use a colon (p. 70) instead of a dash in the last two examples. The dash is more informal.

26b. Parentheses: Nonessential elements

Parentheses always come in pairs, one before and one after the punctuated material.

Parenthetical expressions

Parentheses de-emphasize PARENTHETICAL EXPRESSIONS—explanatory or supplemental words or phrases. (Commas emphasize these expressions more and dashes still more.)

The population of Philadelphia (now about 1.6 million) has declined since 1950.

Don't put a comma before a parenthetical expression enclosed in parentheses. Punctuation after the parenthetical expression should be placed outside the closing parenthesis.

> **NOT** Philadelphia's population compares with Houston's, (about 1.6 million.)

> **BUT** Philadelphia's population compares with Houston's (about 1.6 million).

Labels for lists within text

26c

Outside the Middle East, the countries with the largest oil reserves are (1) Venezuela (63 billion barrels), (2) Russia (57 billion barrels), and (3) Mexico (51 billion barrels).

Do not use parentheses for such labels when you set a list off from your text.

26c. Ellipsis mark: Omissions from quotations

The ellipsis mark consists of three spaced periods (. . .). It generally indicates an omission from a quotation, as illustrated in the following excerpts from this quotation about environmentalism:

ORIGINAL QUOTATION

"At the heart of the environmentalist world view is the conviction that human physical and spiritual health depends on sustaining the planet in a relatively unaltered state. Earth is our home in the full, genetic sense, where humanity and its ancestors existed for all the millions of years of their evolution. Natural ecosystems—forests, coral reefs, marine blue waters—maintain the world exactly as we would wish it to be maintained. When we debase the global environment and extinguish the variety of life, we are dismantling a support system that is too complex to understand, let alone replace, in the foreseeable future."   —EDWARD O. WILSON, "Is Humanity Suicidal?"

1. OMISSION OF THE MIDDLE OF A SENTENCE

"Natural ecosystems . . . maintain the world exactly as we would wish it to be maintained."

**2. OMISSION OF THE END OF A SENTENCE, WITHOUT SOURCE
CITATION**

"Earth is our home. . . ." [The sentence period, closed up to
the last word, precedes the ellipsis mark.]

3. OMISSION OF THE END OF A SENTENCE, WITH SOURCE CITATION

"Earth is our home . . ." (Wilson 27). [The sentence period
follows the source citation.]

4. OMISSION OF THE BEGINNING OF A SENTENCE

" . . . [H]uman physical and spiritual health depends on
sustaining the planet in a relatively unaltered state." [The
brackets indicate a change in capitalization from the original.]

5. OMISSION OF PARTS OF TWO SENTENCES

"At the heart of the environmentalist world view is the conviction that human physical and spiritual health depends
on sustaining the planet . . . where humanity and its ancestors existed for all the millions of years of their evolution."

26c

6. OMISSION OF ONE OR MORE SENTENCES

"At the heart of the environmentalist world view is the
conviction that human physical and spiritual health depends on sustaining the planet in a relatively unaltered
state. . . . When we debase the global environment and extinguish the variety of life, we are dismantling a support
system that is too complex to understand, let alone replace, in the foreseeable future."

7. USE OF A WORD OR PHRASE

Wilson describes the earth as "our home." [No ellipsis
mark needed.]

Note these features of the examples:

- Use an ellipsis mark when it is not otherwise clear that
you have left out material from the source, as when the
words you quote form a complete sentence that is different in the original (examples 1–5). You don't need
an ellipsis mark at the beginning or end of a word or
phrase because it will already be obvious that you
omitted something (example 7).
- After a grammatically complete sentence, an ellipsis
mark usually follows a sentence period and a space
(examples 2 and 6). The exception occurs when a parenthetical source citation follows the quotation (example 3), in which case the sentence period falls after the
citation.

If you omit one or more lines of poetry or paragraphs of prose from a quotation, use a separate line of ellipsis marks across the full width of the quotation to show the omission.

26d. Brackets: Changes in quotations

Brackets have highly specialized uses in mathematical equations, but their main use for all kinds of writing is to indicate that you have altered a quotation to fit it into your sentence, clarify it, or correct it. (See also p. 137.)

"[T]hat Texaco station [just outside Chicago] is one of the busiest in the nation," said a company spokesperson.

26e. Slash: Options, breaks in poetry lines, and electronic addresses

OPTIONS

Some teachers oppose pass/fail courses.

BREAKS IN POETRY LINES

When you run two lines of poetry into your text, separate them with a slash surrounded by space.

Many readers have sensed a reluctant turn away from death in Frost's lines "The woods are lovely, dark and deep, / But I have promises to keep."

ELECTRONIC ADDRESSES

Slashes divide the parts of most electronic addresses—for instance, *http://www.stanford.edu/depts/spd/spc.html.* (See also p. 121.)

IV

FORM AND APPEARANCE

Checklist for
Form and Appearance

This checklist covers the main considerations in designing documents and adjusting the forms of words (spelling and the hyphen, capitals, underlining or italics, abbreviations, numbers). For a detailed guide to this part, see the contents inside the back cover.

✓ Have you used the elements of document design—such as type, margins, headings, and illustrations—to produce a clear and attractive document? (See pp. 83–88.)

✓ Will the design of your document meet the expectations of readers in the discipline, field, or medium in which you are writing? (See pp. 89–101.)

✓ Are all your words spelled correctly? Don't rely on your spelling checker to answer this question. (See pp. 101–06.)

✓ Have you used capital letters appropriately for proper nouns and adjectives and for the titles of works and persons? (See pp. 106–08.)

✓ Have you used underlining or italics primarily for the titles of works published separately from other works? Does your use of underlining or italics in source citations conform to your discipline's or instructor's requirements? (See pp. 108–10.)

✓ Have you used abbreviations appropriately for the discipline or field you are writing in? (See pp. 110–12.)

✓ Have you expressed numbers in numerals or words appropriately for the discipline or field you are writing in? (See pp. 112–14.)

27

DOCUMENT DESIGN

Legible, consistent, and attractive papers and correspondence serve your readers and reflect well on you. This chapter shows the basics of formatting any document clearly and effectively (27a), provides guidelines for academic papers in various disciplines (27b), and discusses formats for business correspondence such as job-application letters, résumés, memos, and electronic mail (27c).

27a. Clear and effective documents

Your papers, reports, and correspondence must of course be neat and legible. That means, at a minimum, a readable typeface, adequate margins, and very few, if any, corrections. But you can do more to make your work accessible and attractive, especially if you work on a computerized word processor. You can use paper, type, white space, headings, lists, tables, and figures to put your ideas across efficiently and forcefully.

Paper

Unless your project demands otherwise, use 8½″ × 11″ white bond paper of at least sixteen-pound weight, and use the same type of paper throughout a project. Type or print on only one side of each sheet. If your printer uses fanfold paper, remove the rows of holes along the sides and separate the pages at the folds before submitting the final document.

Type

PRINT QUALITY

Type or print all documents. (Handwriting may be acceptable in some academic assignments, but always check with your instructor before submitting a handwritten paper.) Use black type, making sure that the typewriter's or printer's ribbon or cartridge is fresh enough to produce a dark impression. If you use a dot-matrix printer (which forms characters out of tiny dots), make sure the tails on letters such as *j*, *p*, and *y* fall below the line of type, as they do here.

27a

For Web sites on form and appearance, see page 198.

TEXT SPACING

Academic papers are generally double-spaced; business writing is often single-spaced. See pages 89–94 and 94–100, respectively, for more on the spacing of lines.

TEXT TYPE

The type for the text of your document should be at least 10 or 12 points, as illustrated by these type samples:

`12-point Courier`   12-point Times Roman
`10-point Courier`   10-point Times Roman

Use one space between words and after most punctuation, including the punctuation at the ends of sentences. (See p. 77 for how to make dashes, and see p. 78 for the special spacing with ellipsis marks, which show omissions from quotations.) Use handwriting to make symbols that are not on your keyboard.

HIGHLIGHTED TYPE

Within the text use <u>underlining</u>, *italics*, or **boldface** to emphasize key words or sentences. (See Chapter 30.) For academic research writing, ask your instructor whether he or she prefers underlining or italics with source citations.

Many readers consider the constant use of type embellishments to be distracting. Vary type selectively to enhance your meaning, not just to decorate your work.

LONG QUOTATIONS

Set off long quotations according to the guidelines for various disciplines on pages 74–75.

SOURCE CITATIONS

To cite sources for your work, follow one of the systems discussed on pages 140–95, as appropriate for the field you're writing in.

CORRECTIONS

Business correspondence should be error-free, without visible corrections. Academic writing permits some corrections on the final version. Make any corrections *neatly*, either on a typewriter or by hand in black ink. If a page has more than a few errors, retype or reprint it.

White space, headings, and lists

The white space on a page eases crowding, highlights elements, and focuses readers' attention.

PARAGRAPH BREAKS

An indention at the beginning of a paragraph (in double-spaced copy) or extra space between paragraphs

27a

(in single-spaced copy) gives readers a break and shows that you have divided ideas into manageable chunks.

MARGINS

Use minimum one-inch margins on all sides of every page. Use a larger left margin if you plan to bind the document on the left. An uneven right margin is almost always acceptable. If your word processor or typewriter will produce an even (or justified) right margin, use the feature only if it does not sometimes leave wide spaces between words.

HEADINGS

Headings are signposts. In a long or complex document, they break the text into manageable chunks and orient readers.

When you use headings, follow these guidelines:

- Use one, two, or three levels of headings depending on the needs of your material and the length of your document. Some level of heading every two or so pages will help keep readers on track.
- Create an outline of your document in order to plan where headings should go. Reserve the first level of heading for the main points (and sections) of your document. Use a second and perhaps a third level of heading to mark subsections of supporting information.
- Keep headings as short as possible while making them specific about the material that follows.
- Word headings consistently—for instance, all questions (*What Is the Scientific Method?*), all phrases° with -*ing* words (*Understanding the Scientific Method*), or all phrases with nouns (*The Scientific Method*).
- Indicate the relative importance of headings with type size, positioning, and highlighting, such as capital letters, underlining, or boldface.

27a

FIRST-LEVEL HEADING

<u>Second-Level Heading</u>

Third-Level Heading

A word processor provides more type styles and sizes than a typewriter.

FIRST-LEVEL HEADING

Second-Level Heading

Third-Level Heading

- Keep the appearance simple: most reports or papers shouldn't need more than two type styles or two or three type sizes (including the body type). Except in promotional pieces, avoid extra-large letters and unusual styles of type (such as outline and shadow type).

- Don't break a page immediately after a heading. Push the heading to the next page.

NOTE Document format in psychology and some other social sciences requires a particular treatment of headings. See pages 92–93.

LISTS

Whenever your document contains a list of related items—for example, the steps in a process or the elements in a proposal—consider setting the items off and marking them with numbers or bullets (centered dots, used in the list below about tables and figures). A list is easier to read than a paragraph and adds white space to the page. Most word-processing programs can format a numbered or bulleted list automatically.

Tables and figures

27a

Tables and figures (graphs, charts, diagrams, photographs) can often make a point for you more efficiently and effectively than words can. Tables and figures present data, make comparisons, show changes, explain processes, and represent what something looks like, among other uses.

Follow these guidelines for any table or figure:

- Focus on a purpose for your table or figure—a reason for including it and a point you want it to make. Otherwise, readers may find it irrelevant or confusing.
- Provide a source note whenever the data or the entire table or figure is someone else's independent material (see p. 134). Each discipline has a slightly different style for such source notes; those in the table opposite and the figures on page 88 reflect the style of the social sciences. See also Chapters 39–42.
- Number tables and figures separately (Table 1, Table 2, etc.; Figure 1, Figure 2, etc.).
- Refer to each table or figure (for instance, "See Figure 2") at the point(s) in the text where readers will benefit by consulting it.
- Unless your document includes many tables and/or figures, place each one on a page by itself immediately after the page that refers to it.
- Many computer programs can create tables, graphs, charts, and other illustrations when you supply the raw data. If you use many tables and figures in your writing, you may want to learn computerized graphics.

Many organizations and academic disciplines have preferred styles for tables and figures that differ from those given here. When in doubt about how to prepare and place tables and figures, ask your instructor or supervisor.

TABLES

Tables usually summarize raw data, displaying the data concisely and clearly.

- Above the table, provide a self-explanatory title. Readers should see what the table shows without having to refer to the body of your document.
- Provide self-explanatory headings for horizontal rows and vertical columns. Use abbreviations only if you are certain readers will understand them.
- Lay out rows and columns for maximum clarity. In the sample below, for instance, lines divide the table into parts, headings align with their data, and numbers align vertically down columns.

Table 1

Computers, Telephones, and Televisions per 1,000 People (1994)

Location	Computers	Telephones	Televisions
Worldwide	37	152	174
United States	365	965	900
Europe	93	508	419
Japan	105	645	625
Former Soviet republics	14	145	335

27a

Note: From 8th Annual Computer Industry Almanac (p. 38), by K. P. Juliussen and E. Juliussen, 1995, Incline Village, NV: Computer Industry Almanac.

FIGURES

Figures often recast data into visual form. They include the three kinds shown on the next page: pie charts (showing percentages making up a whole), bar graphs (showing comparative data), and line graphs (showing change). Figures also include photographs, drawings, diagrams, and other graphics.

- Below the figure, provide a self-explanatory caption or legend. Readers should see what the figure shows without having to refer to the body of your document.
- Provide self-explanatory labels for all parts of the figure.

- Draw the figure to reflect its purpose and the visual effect you want it to have. For instance, shortening the horizontal date scale in Figure 3 below emphasizes the dramatic upward movement of the line over time.

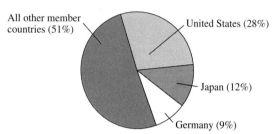

Figure 1. Member countries' assessments to United Nations budget of $1.1 billion in 1994. From "The U.N. at 50," by R. Mylan, 1995, October 18, Newsweek, p. 17.

27a

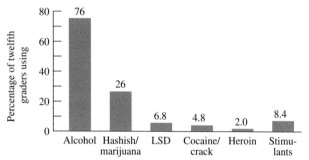

Figure 2. Use of alcohol, compared with other drugs, among twelfth graders (1993). Data from Monitoring the Future Study, 1994, Ann Arbor, MI: University of Michigan Press.

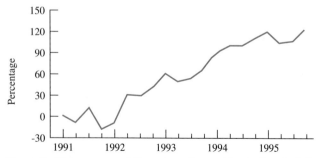

Figure 3. Five-year cumulative return for equities in Standard & Poor's 500 Index, 1991–1995.

27b. Academic papers

The principles of document design discussed in section 27a apply generally to academic writing, but most disciplines require specific variations to suit the needs of their research and writing.

MLA format: English, foreign languages, and some other humanities

The style guide for English and some other humanities is the *MLA Handbook for Writers of Research Papers,* 5th ed. (1999), published by the Modern Language Association. This guide recommends a document format like the one discussed in section 27a for paper, type, margins, and illustrations. The samples below show details of this format.

Number all pages, starting with 1 for the first page and continuing in sequence through any endnotes and the list of works cited. Add your last name just before each page number, as illustrated by "Perez" in the samples.

FIRST PAGE OF PAPER

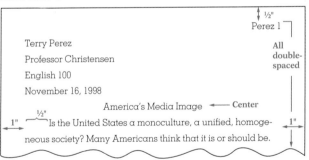

LATER PAGE OF PAPER

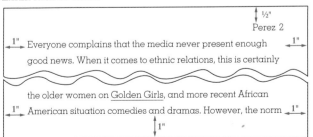

NOTE For MLA format for long quotations set off from the text, see page 74. For MLA format for source citations, see pages 146–48.

Chicago format: History, art history, philosophy, and some other humanities

The Chicago Manual of Style, 14th ed. (1993), serves as a style guide for history, art history, philosophy, and some other humanities. A guide for students adapted from *The Chicago Manual* is Kate L. Turabian, *A Manual for Writers of Term Papers, Theses, and Dissertations,* 6th ed., revised by John Grossman and Alice Bennett (1996).

Both of these books recommend a document format that resembles the one discussed in section 27a. For spacing and arranging elements, use the MLA format illustrated on the previous page, with the following exceptions:

• Provide a title page (not numbered) with at least the full title of the paper, your name, and the date. As in the example below, you may also include other infor-

TITLE PAGE

27b

INDIAN NATIONALISM IN INDIAN ART
AFTER WORLD WAR I ← Double-space

REYNA P. DIXON

ART HISTORY 236
MS. PARIKH ← Double-space
DECEMBER 16, 1998

mation requested by your instructor, such as the course title and the instructor's name. Use all-capital letters, and center everything horizontally and vertically on the page. Double-space between adjacent lines, adding extra space where shown in the example.

- Number text pages with a number only, consecutively from the first page through the entire paper. On the first page of the paper and the first page of any endnotes and the bibliography, place the page number at the bottom of the page, centered (see p. 158). On all other pages, place the number at the top, either centered or at the right margin, and double-space to the text below.
- Capitalize the title on the first text page, and triple-space beneath it.

NOTE See page 74 for Chicago format for long quotations set off from the text. And see pages 157–59 for Chicago format for source citations.

APA format: Psychology and some other social sciences

The style guide for psychology, educational psychology, and some other social sciences is the *Publication Manual of the American Psychological Association,* 4th ed. (1994).

The APA guide outlines a structure as well as a format for many kinds of student papers:

1. The title page includes the full title, your name, the course title, the instructor's name, and the date. Include a shortened form of the title along with the page number at the top of this and all other pages. Number the title page 1. The APA allows either the layout below or one like that opposite for Chicago style, with the addition of the shortened title and page number.

TITLE PAGE

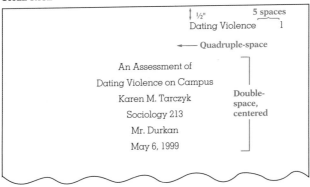

27b

2. The first section, labeled "Abstract," summarizes (in about 100 words) your subject, research method, findings, and conclusions. Put the abstract on a page by itself.

ABSTRACT

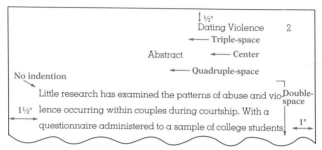

3. The body of the paper begins with a restatement of the paper's title and then an introduction (not labeled). The introduction concisely presents the problem you researched, your research method, the relevant background (such as related studies), and the purpose of your research.

FIRST PAGE OF BODY

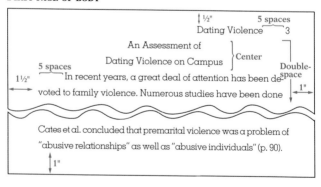

4. The next section, labeled "Method," provides a detailed discussion of how you conducted your research, including a description of the research subjects, any materials or tools you used (such as questionnaires), and the procedure you followed. In the illustration on the facing page, the label "Method" is a first-level heading, formatted as in the sample. When you need second- and third-level headings in addition, use these formats, always double-spacing:

First-Level Heading

Second-Level Heading

    Third-level heading. Run this heading into the text

paragraph.

LATER PAGE OF BODY

                                Dating Violence   4

All the studies indicate a problem that is being ne-

glected. My objective was to gather data on the extent and

nature of premarital violence and to discuss possible inter-

pretations.

                       Method ←——**Double-space**

I conducted a survey of 200 students (134 females, 66

males) at a large state university in the northeastern United

States. The sample consisted of students enrolled in an intro-

5. The "Results" section (labeled with a first-level heading) summarizes the data you collected, explains how you analyzed them, and presents them in detail, often in tables, graphs, or charts.
6. The "Discussion" section (labeled with a first-level heading) interprets the data and presents your conclusions. (When the discussion is brief, you may combine it with the previous section under the heading "Results and Discussion.")
7. The "References" section, beginning a new page, includes all your sources. See pages 169–76.

    Number all pages consecutively, from the title page through the references.

    NOTE See pages 74–75 for the APA format for long quotations set off from the text. And see pages 169–70 for APA format for source citations.

CBE format: Life sciences, physical sciences, and mathematics

    The style guide for the life sciences and often for the physical sciences and mathematics is *Scientific Style and Format: The CBE Manual for Authors, Editors, and Publishers*, 6th ed. (1994), published for the Council of Biology Editors. For student papers (as opposed to those planned for publication), use a structure and format like that shown for APA style (beginning p. 91). (You may omit the shortened title before the page number.)

27b

Note For CBE format for long quotations set off from the text, see page 75. For CBE format for source citations, see page 178.

27c. Business correspondence

The essential document format discussed in section 27a applies to most business writing, with important additions for headings and other elements. This section discusses business letters (using the example of the job-application letter), résumés, business memos, and electronic mail.

Job application letter

In any letter to a businessperson, you are addressing someone who wants to see quickly why you are writing and how to respond to you. For a job application, see the sample on the next page and use the following guidelines.

CONTENT

- Think of the letter as an interpretation of your résumé for a particular job, not as a detailed account of the entire résumé. Instead of reciting your job history, highlight and reshape only the relevant parts.
- Announce at the outset what job you seek and how you heard about it.
- Include any special reason you have for applying, such as a specific career goal.
- Summarize your qualifications for this particular job, including relevant facts about education and employment and emphasizing notable accomplishments. Mention that additional information appears in an accompanying résumé.
- At the end of the letter, mention that you are available for an interview at the convenience of the addressee, or specify when you will be available (for instance, when your current job or classes leave you free).

FORMAT

- For any business correspondence, use either unlined white paper measuring 8½″ × 11″ or what is called letterhead stationery with your address printed at the top of the sheet.
- Type the letter single-spaced with double-space between elements and paragraphs. Use only one side of a sheet.
- The salutation of a letter greets the addressee. Whenever possible, address your letter to a specific person.

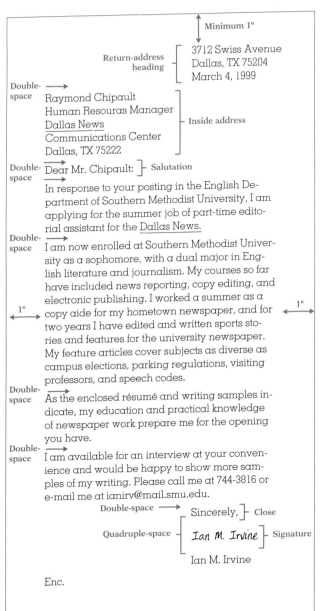

Minimum 1"

Return-address heading

3712 Swiss Avenue
Dallas, TX 75204
March 4, 1999

Double-space →

Raymond Chipault
Human Resouras Manager
Dallas News
Communications Center
Dallas, TX 75222

Inside address

Double-space → Dear Mr. Chipault: ─ Salutation

In response to your posting in the English Department of Southern Methodist University, I am applying for the summer job of part-time editorial assistant for the Dallas News.

Double-space →

I am now enrolled at Southern Methodist University as a sophomore, with a dual major in English literature and journalism. My courses so far have included news reporting, copy editing, and electronic publishing. I worked a summer as a copy aide for my hometown newspaper, and for two years I have edited and written sports stories and features for the university newspaper. My feature articles cover subjects as diverse as campus elections, parking regulations, visiting professors, and speech codes.

1" ← →

1" ← →

27c

Double-space →

As the enclosed résumé and writing samples indicate, my education and practical knowledge of newspaper work prepare me for the opening you have.

Double-space →

I am available for an interview at your convenience and would be happy to show more samples of my writing. Please call me at 744-3816 or e-mail me at ianirv@mail.smu.edu.

Double-space → Sincerely, ─ Close

Quadruple-space → *Ian M. Irvine* ─ Signature

Ian M. Irvine

Enc.

(Call the company or department to ask whom to address.) If you can't find a person's name, then use a job title (*Dear Human Resources Manager*) or a general salutation (*Dear Smythe Shoes*).

- For the letter's close, choose an expression that reflects the formality of the situation: *Respectfully, Cordially,* and *Sincerely* are more formal than *Best wishes* or *Regards.*
- The envelope should show your name and address in the upper-left corner and the addressee's name, title, and address in the center. Use an envelope that will accommodate the letter once it is folded horizontally in thirds.

Résumé

For the résumé that accompanies your letter of application, you can use the sample on the next page and the guidelines below.

- Provide the following, in table form: your name and address, career objective, education, employment history, any special skills or awards, and information about how to obtain your references.
- Use headings to mark the various sections of the résumé, spacing around them and within sections so that important information stands out.
- Usage varies on capital letters in résumés. Keep in mind that passages with many capitals can be hard to read. Definitely use capitals for proper nouns (pp. 107–08), but consider dropping them for job titles, course names, department names, and the like.
- Limit your résumé to one page so that it can be quickly reviewed. However, if your experience and education are extensive, a two-page résumé is preferable to a single cramped, unreadable page.

Employers often need an electronic copy of a résumé so that they can add it to a computerized database of applicants. They may scan a paper copy to convert it to an electronic file, or they may request electronic copy from you in the first place. If you think a potential employer may use an electronic version of your résumé, follow these additional guidelines:

- Keep the design simple so that the résumé can be read accurately by a scanner or transmitted accurately by electronic mail. Avoid images, unusual type, more than one column, vertical or horizontal lines, and other embellishments.

27c

Ian M. Irvine

3712 Swiss Avenue
Dallas, TX 75204
214-744-3816
ianirv@mail.smu.edu

Position desired	Part-time editorial assistant.
Education	*Southern Methodist University,* 1997 to present. Current standing: sophomore. Major: English literature and journalism. Journalism courses: news reporting, copy editing, electronic publishing, communications arts, broadcast journalism.
	Abilene (Texas) Senior High School, 1993–1997. Graduated with academic, college-preparatory degree.
Employment history	1997 to present. Reporter, *Daily Campus*, student newspaper of Southern Methodist University. Write regular coverage of baseball, track, and soccer teams. Write feature stories on campus policies and events. Edit sports news, campus listings, features.
	Summer 1998. Copy aide, *Abilene Reporter-News*. Routed copy, ran errands, and assisted reporters with research.
	Summer 1997. Painter, Longhorn Painters, Abilene. Prepared and painted exteriors and interiors of houses.
Special skills	Fluent in Spanish. Proficient in Internet research and word processing.
References	Available upon request: Placement Office Southern Methodist University Dallas, TX 75275

27c

- Use concise, concrete words to describe your experience—words like *managed* (not *had responsibility for*) or *reporter* (not *staff member responsible for reporting*). An employer may use such concise, concrete words to search a résumé database for people with particular skills and experiences.

NOTE For more extensive help with cover letters, résumés, and other elements of a job search, see the Web sites listed on page 198.

Business memo

Unlike business letters, which address people in other organizations, business memos (short for memorandums) address people within the same organization. A memo can be quite long, but more often it deals briefly with a specific topic, such as an answer to a question, a progress report, or an evaluation. Both the content and the format of a memo aim to get to the point and dispose of it quickly, as indicated in the following guidelines and the sample on the next page.

27c

CONTENT

- State your reason for writing in the first sentence, perhaps outlining a problem, making a request, referring to a request that prompted the memo, or briefly summarizing new findings. Do not, however, waste words with expressions like "The purpose of this memo is. . . ."
- Devote the first paragraph to a succinct presentation of your solution, recommendation, answer, or evaluation. The first paragraph should be short, and by its end your reader should know precisely what to expect from the rest of the memo: the details and reasoning that support your conclusion.
- Deliver the support in the body of the memo. The paragraphs may be numbered or bulleted so that the main divisions of your message are easy to see. In a long memo, you may need headings (see pp. 85–86).
- Suit your style and tone to your audience. For instance, you'll want to address your boss or a large group of readers more formally than you would a coworker who is also a friend.
- Whatever your style and tone, write concisely. Keep your sentences short and your language simple, using technical terms only when your readers will understand them. Provide only the information that readers need to know.

Bigelow Wax Company

TO: Aileen Rosen, Director of Sales
FROM: Patricia Phillips, Territory 12 *PP*
DATE: February 12, 1999
SUBJECT: 1998 sales of Quick Wax in Territory 12

Since it was introduced in January of 1998, Quick Wax has been unsuccessful in Territory 12 and has not affected the sales of our Easy Shine. Discussions with customers and my own analysis of Quick Wax suggest three reasons for its failure to compete with our product.

1. Quick Wax has not received the promotion necessary for a new product. Advertising—primarily on radio—has been sporadic and has not developed a clear, consistent image for the product. In addition, the Quick Wax sales representative in Territory 12 is new and inexperienced; he is not known to customers, and his sales pitch (which I once overheard) is weak. As far as I can tell, his efforts are not supported by phone calls or mailings from his home office.

2. When Quick Wax does make it to the store shelves, buyers do not choose it over our product. Though priced competitively with our product, Quick Wax is poorly packaged. The container seems smaller than ours, though in fact it holds the same eight ounces. The lettering on the Quick Wax package (red on blue) is difficult to read, in contrast to the white-on-green lettering on the Easy Shine package.

3. Our special purchase offers and my increased efforts to serve existing customers have had the intended effect of keeping customers satisfied with our product and reducing their inclination to stock something new.

Copies: L. Goldberger, Director of Marketing
　　　　　L. MacGregor, Customer Service Manager

27c

FORMAT

- The memo has no return address, inside address, salutation, or close. Instead, as shown in the sample memo on the previous page, the heading typically consists of the company's name, the addressee's name, the writer's name, the date, and a subject description or title.
- Type the body of the memo as you would the body of a business letter: single-spaced, double-spaced between paragraphs, and no paragraph indentions.
- Never sign a business memo, but do initial your name in the heading.
- If copies of the memo need to be sent to people not listed in the "To" line, list those people two spaces below the last line.

Electronic mail

Postings by electronic mail tend to be more offhand and informal than standard business letters on paper. E-mail can communicate very effectively with a little care.

CONTENT AND STRUCTURE

- An e-mail posting announces itself in the reader's list of incoming mail, which may be extensive. Give your posting a subject heading that accurately describes the contents, so that your reader knows what priority to assign it.
- Because an e-mail reader must scroll through a posting—and so cannot review two or more screens at once—make your posting as short as possible.
- Also because of scrolling, a posting will be more effective if it is tightly structured, with a clear forecast of its contents and a clear division into parts. Use short paragraphs, and insert blank lines between paragraphs. For long messages, consider using headings to break up the text and direct your reader's attention.
- Because many e-mail users cannot display a posting while they are responding to it, your postings should center on one or two points. Then the reader has a better chance of responding to your whole message.
- You can respond to someone else's posting by copying parts of it into your own message. But copy only the *relevant* parts, not the entire posting, so that your reader can focus on what you have to say.

ETIQUETTE

Because it is sometimes anonymous as well as immediate, e-mail has been subject to abuses. Its users have developed some basic courtesies:

- The headings in an e-mail message are usually dictated by the network, but you can still address your reader(s) by name and sign off with your own name.
- Most e-mailers consider the medium more immediate than print mail and expect quick responses to their messages.
- E-mail, like faxes, may be broadcast to many recipients at once with a few keystrokes. Avoid flooding your correspondents with irrelevant postings: target your messages only to those who can actually use them.
- Don't forward a posting you have received unless you know the writer does not mind.
- E-mail sometimes seems more free and impersonal than telephone conversations or print mail. But that's no justification for flaming, or attacking, correspondents. Address them respectfully and politely, as you would on paper.

REVISION

- Take the time to read your posting before sending it. You may see ways to tighten your message, clarify your points, or moderate your tone.
- Errors in grammar, punctuation, and spelling will interfere with your message. Proofread before sending.

28a

28
SPELLING AND THE HYPHEN

Spelling, including using the hyphen, is a skill you can acquire by paying attention to words and by developing three habits:

- Carefully proofread your writing.
- Cultivate a healthy suspicion of your spellings.
- Habitually check a dictionary when you doubt a spelling.

28a. Spelling checkers

The spelling checkers for computerized word processors can help you find and track spelling errors in your papers. But their usefulness is limited, mainly because they can't spot the very common error of confusing words with similar spellings, such as the following:

accept (to receive)	affect (to influence)
except (other than)	effect (a result)

board (a plane of wood)
bored (uninterested)

brake (to stop)
break (to smash)

cite (to quote an authority)
sight (the ability to see)
site (a place)

forth (forward)
fourth (after *third*)

hear (to perceive by ear)
here (in this place)

its (possessive of *it*)
it's (contraction of *it is*)

no (the opposite of *yes*)
know (to be certain)

passed (past tense of *pass*)
past (after; a time gone by)

principal (most important;
the head of a school)
principle (a basic truth or
law)

scene (where an action
occurs)
seen (past participle of *see*)

stationary (unmoving)
stationery (writing paper)

their (possessive of *they*)
there (opposite of *here*)
they're (contraction of *they
are*)

to (toward)
too (also)
two (following *one*)

weather (climate)
whether (*if,* or introducing
a choice)

who's (contraction of *who
is*)
whose (possessive of *who*)

your (possessive of *you*)
you're (contraction of *you
are*)

28b

A spelling checker cannot replace your own careful proofreading.

28b. Spelling rules

We often misspell syllables rather than whole words. The following rules focus on troublesome syllables.

ie and *ei*

Follow the familiar jingle: *i* before *e* except after *c* or when pronounced "ay" as in *neighbor* and *weigh.*

i BEFORE *e*	believe	thief
e BEFORE *i*	receive	ceiling
ei PRONOUNCED "AY"	freight	vein

EXCEPTIONS Remember some common exceptions with this sentence: *The weird foreigner neither seizes leisure nor forfeits height.*

Silent final *e*

Drop a silent final *e* when adding an ending that begins with a vowel. Keep the *e* if the ending begins with a consonant.

advise + able = advisable   care + ful = careful

EXCEPTIONS Keep the final *e* before a vowel to prevent confusion or mispronunciation: *dyeing, changeable.* Drop the *e* before a consonant when another vowel comes before the *e: argument, truly.*

Final *y*

When adding to a word ending in *y*, change *y* to *i* when it follows a consonant. Keep the *y* when it follows a vowel, precedes *-ing*, or ends a proper name.

beauty, beauties   day, days
worry, worried   study, studying
supply, supplier   Minsky, Minskys

Consonants

When adding an ending to a one-syllable word that ends in a consonant, double the consonant if it follows a single vowel. Otherwise, don't double the consonant.

slap, slapping   pair, paired

For words of more than one syllable, double the final consonant when it follows a single vowel and ends a stressed syllable once the new ending is added. Otherwise, don't double the consonant.

submit, submitted   despair, despairing
refer, referred   refer, reference

Plurals

Most nouns form plurals by adding *s* to the singular form. Nouns ending in *s, sh, ch,* or *x* add *es* to the singular.

boy, boys   kiss, kisses
table, tables   lurch, lurches
Murphy, Murphys   tax, taxes

Nouns ending in a vowel plus *o* add *s.* Nouns ending in a consonant plus *o* add *es.*

ratio, ratios   hero, heroes

Form the plural of a compound noun by adding *s* to the main word in the compound. The main word may not fall at the end.

passersby   breakthroughs
fathers-in-law   city-states

Some English nouns that come from other languages form the plural according to their original language.

28b

analysis, analyses	medium, media
crisis, crises	phenomenon, phenomena
criterion, criteria	piano, pianos

American vs. British spellings `ESL`

American and British or Canadian spellings differ in ways such as the following.

AMERICAN	BRITISH
color, humor	colour, humour
theater, center	theatre, centre
canceled, traveled	cancelled, travelled
judgment	judgement
realize, analyze	realise, analyse
defense, offense	defence, offence

28c. Commonly misspelled words

You can reduce spelling errors by mastering a list like the one below. Try to memorize six to seven words at a time, pronouncing each one aloud and writing it out. Look words up in a dictionary if you are unsure of their pronunciation or meaning.

28c

absence	beginning	desperate
accidentally	believe	develop
accommodate	benefited	dictionary
accumulate	bureaucracy	disappear
achieve	business	disappoint
acknowledge	calendar	disastrous
acquire	cemetery	dissatisfied
across	changeable	eighth
actually	characteristic	eligible
address	column	embarrass
aggravate	commitment	emphasize
all right	committed	entirely
a lot	committee	environment
altogether	competition	especially
amateur	conceive	exaggerate
among	conquer	exhaust
analyze	conscience	existence
answer	conscious	familiar
apparent	courteous	fascinate
appearance	criticism	February
appropriate	criticize	foreign
argument	curiosity	forty
ascend	decision	friend
athlete	definitely	government
attendance	describe	grammar
audience	description	guidance
basically	despair	harass

height	permissible	schedule
humorous	physical	secretary
immediately	playwright	seize
incredible	politician	separate
inevitably	practically	siege
intelligence	precede	similar
interest	preference	sincerely
irrelevant	preferred	sophomore
irresistible	prejudice	succeed
knowledge	primitive	surprise
laboratory	privilege	temperature
leisure	proceed	thorough
license	professor	throughout
maintenance	prominent	tragedy
mathematics	pronunciation	transferred
misspelled	quiet	truly
necessary	receive	unnecessary
noticeable	recommend	usable
occasionally	reference	usually
occur	referred	vacuum
occurrence	religious	vengeance
omitted	repetition	villain
originally	restaurant	Wednesday
paralleled	rhythm	weird
performance	roommate	whether

28d

28d. The hyphen

Use the hyphen to form compound words and to divide words at the ends of lines.

Compound words

Compound words may be written as a single word (*breakthrough*), as two words (*decision makers*), or as a hyphenated word (*cross-reference*). Check a dictionary for the spelling of a compound word. Except as explained below, any compound not listed in the dictionary should be written as two words.

Sometimes a compound word comes from combining two or more words into a single adjective.° When such a compound adjective precedes a noun, a hyphen forms the words clearly into a unit.

> She is a well-known actor.
> Some Spanish-speaking students work as translators.

When a compound adjective follows the noun, the hyphen is unnecessary.

> The actor is well-known.
> Many students are Spanish-speaking.

The hyphen is also unnecessary in a compound modifier containing an *-ly* adverb, even before the noun: *clearly defined terms.*

Fractions and compound numbers

Hyphens join the parts of fractions: *three-fourths, one-half.* And the whole numbers *twenty-one* to *ninety-nine* are always hyphenated.

Prefixes and suffixes

Do not use hyphens with prefixes except as follows:

- With the prefixes *self-, all-,* and *ex-: self-control, all-inclusive, ex-student.*
- With a prefix before a capitalized word: *un-American.*
- With a capital letter before a word: *T-shirt.*
- To prevent misreading: *de-emphasize, re-create a story.*

The only suffix that regularly requires a hyphen is *-elect,* as in *president-elect.*

Word division

Use a hyphen to divide a word from one line to the next, following these rules:

- Divide words only between syllables—for instance, *win-dows,* not *wi-ndows.* Check a dictionary for correct syllable breaks.
- Never divide a one-syllable word.
- Leave at least two letters on the first line and three on the second line. If a word cannot be divided to follow this rule (for instance, *a-bus-er*), don't divide it.

NOTE Most word-processing programs divide words automatically at appropriate breaks when you instruct them to do so.

29

CAPITAL LETTERS

The following conventions and a dictionary can help you decide whether to capitalize a particular word. In general, capitalize only when a rule or the dictionary says you must. This guideline applies to electronic mail and other online communications: messages written in all-capitals or with no capitals are hard to read.

NOTE The social, natural, and applied sciences require specialized capitalization for terminology, such as *Condi-*

tions A and B or *Escherichia coli.* Consult one of the style guides listed on pages 140–41 for the requirements of the discipline you are writing in.

29a. First word of a sentence

Every writer should own a good dictionary.

29b. Proper nouns and adjectives

PROPER NOUNS name specific persons, places, and things: *Shakespeare, California, World War I.* PROPER ADJECTIVES are formed from some proper nouns: *Shakespearean, Californian.* Capitalize all proper nouns and proper adjectives but not the articles (*a, an, the*) that precede them.

SPECIFIC PERSONS AND THINGS

Stephen King   Boulder Dam

SPECIFIC PLACES AND GEOGRAPHICAL REGIONS

New York City   the Northeast, the South

But: northeast of the city, going south

DAYS OF THE WEEK, MONTHS, HOLIDAYS

Monday   Yom Kippur
May   Christmas

But: winter, spring, summer, fall

HISTORICAL EVENTS, DOCUMENTS, PERIODS, MOVEMENTS

the Vietnam War   the Renaissance
the Constitution   the Romantic Movement

GOVERNMENT OFFICES OR DEPARTMENTS AND INSTITUTIONS

House of Representatives   Polk Municipal Court
Department of Defense   Northeast High School

POLITICAL, SOCIAL, ATHLETIC, AND OTHER ORGANIZATIONS AND THEIR MEMBERS

B'nai B'rith   Democratic Party, Democrats
Rotary Club   Atlanta Falcons
League of Women Voters   Chicago Symphony Orchestra

RACES, NATIONALITIES, AND THEIR LANGUAGES

Native American   Germans
African American   Swahili
Caucasian   Italian

But: blacks, whites

29b

RELIGIONS, THEIR FOLLOWERS, AND TERMS FOR THE SACRED

Christianity, Christians	God
Catholicism, Catholics	Allah
Judaism, Orthodox Jew	the Bible (*but* biblical)
Islam, Muslims	the Koran

COMMON NOUNS AS PARTS OF PROPER NOUNS

Main Street	Lake Superior
Central Park	Ford Motor Company
Pacific Ocean	Madison College

But: the ocean, college course, the company

29c. Titles and subtitles of works

Within your text, capitalize all the words in a title and subtitle *except* the following: articles (*a, an, the*), *to* in infinitives,° and connecting words (prepositions° and conjunctions°) of fewer than five letters. Capitalize even these short words when they are the first or last word in a title or when they fall after a colon or semicolon.

"Once More to the Lake"	*Management: A New Theory*
A Diamond Is Forever	"Courtship Through the Ages"
"Knowing Whom to Ask"	*File Under Architecture*
Learning from Las Vegas	*An End to Live For*

NOTE Some academic disciplines require a different treatment of titles within source citations, such as capitalizing only the first words of some or all titles. See pages 169–76 (APA style), 178–84 (CBE style), and 190–95 (Columbia online style for the sciences).

29d. Titles of persons

Before a person's name, capitalize his or her title. After the name, do not capitalize the title.

Professor Otto Osborne	Otto Osborne, a professor
Doctor Jane Covington	Jane Covington, a doctor

30
UNDERLINING (ITALICS)

Underlining and *italic type* indicate the same thing: the word or words are being distinguished or emphasized. In business the almost universal use of computerized word processors makes both forms of highlighting possible, and italics may be preferred. In schools the use of italics is less common, and many disciplines continue to require underlining for works in source citations. Consult your instructor before you use italic type.

NOTE If you underline two or more words in a row, underline the space between the words, too: <u>Criminal Statistics: Misuses of Numbers.</u>

30a. Titles of works

Do not underline the title of your own paper unless it contains an element (such as a book title) that requires underlining.

Within your text, underline the titles of works, such as books and periodicals, that are published, released, or produced separately from other works. (See below.) Use quotation marks for all other titles, such as short stories and articles in periodicals. (See p. 75.)

BOOK
<u>War and Peace</u>

PLAY
<u>Hamlet</u>

PAMPHLET
<u>The Truth About Alcoholism</u>

LONG MUSICAL WORK
The Beatles' <u>Revolver</u>
But: Symphony in C

WORK OF VISUAL ART
Michelangelo's <u>David</u>

LONG POEM
<u>Paradise Lost</u>

PERIODICAL
<u>Philadelphia Inquirer</u>

PUBLISHED SPEECH
Lincoln's <u>Gettysburg Address</u>

TELEVISION OR RADIO PROGRAM
<u>60 Minutes</u>

MOVIE
<u>Psycho</u>

EXCEPTIONS Legal documents, the Bible, and their parts are generally not underlined.

We studied the Book of Revelation in the New English Bible.

NOTE Some academic disciplines do not require underlining or italics for some or all titles within source citations. See pages 178–84 on CBE style.

30b. Ships, aircraft, spacecraft, trains

<u>Challenger</u>   <u>Orient Express</u>   <u>Queen Elizabeth 2</u>
<u>Apollo XI</u>   <u>Montrealer</u>   <u>Spirit of St. Louis</u>

30b

30c. Foreign words

Underline a foreign expression that has not been absorbed into our language. A dictionary will say whether a word is still considered foreign to English.

The scientific name for the brown trout is <u>Salmo trutta</u>. [The Latin scientific names for plants and animals are always underlined.]

The Latin <u>De gustibus non est disputandum</u> translates roughly as "There's no accounting for taste."

30d. Words or characters named as words

Underline words or characters (letters or numbers) that are referred to as themselves rather than used for their meanings.

Some people pronounce <u>th</u>, as in <u>thought</u>, with a faint <u>s</u> or <u>f</u> sound.

The word <u>syzygy</u> refers to a straight line formed by three celestial bodies, as in the alignment of the earth, sun, and moon.

30e. Online alternatives

Electronic mail and other forms of online communication generally do not allow conventional highlighting such as underlining or italics for the purposes described above. The program may not be able to produce the highlighting or may reserve it for a special function. (On World Wide Web sites, for instance, underlining indicates a link to another site.)

To distinguish book titles and other elements that usually require underlining or italics, type an underscore before and after the element: *Measurements coincide with those in* _Joule's Handbook_. You can also emphasize words with asterisks before and after: *I *will not* be able to attend.*

Don't use all-capital letters for emphasis; they yell too loudly. (See also pp. 100–01.)

31
ABBREVIATIONS

The following guidelines on abbreviations pertain to the text of a nontechnical document. All academic disciplines use abbreviations in source citations, and much technical writing, such as in the sciences and engineering, uses many abbreviations in the document text. See Chapters 39–43 on source citations. Consult one of the style guides listed on pages 140–41 for the in-text requirements of the discipline you are writing in.

NOTE Usage varies, but writers increasingly omit periods from abbreviations of two or more words written in all-capital letters: *US, BA, USMC.* See page 63.

31a. Titles before and after proper names

BEFORE THE NAME	AFTER THE NAME
Dr. James Hsu	James Hsu, MD
Mr., Mrs., Ms., Hon.,	DDS, DVM, Ph.D.,
St., Rev., Msgr., Gen.	Ed.D., OSB, SJ, Sr., Jr.

Do not use abbreviations such as *Rev., Hon., Prof., Rep., Sen., Dr.,* and *St.* (for *Saint*) unless they appear before a proper name.

31b. Familiar abbreviations

Abbreviations using initials are acceptable in most writing as long as they are familiar to readers.

INSTITUTIONS	LSU, UCLA, TCU
ORGANIZATIONS	CIA, FBI, YMCA, AFL-CIO
CORPORATIONS	IBM, CBS, ITT
PEOPLE	JFK, LBJ, FDR
COUNTRIES	USA

NOTE If a name or term (such as *operating room*) appears often in a piece of writing, then its abbreviation (*OR*) can cut down on extra words. Spell out the full term at its first appearance, indicate its abbreviation in parentheses, and then use the abbreviation.

31c. *BC, AD, AM, PM, no.,* and $

Use certain abbreviations only with specific dates or numbers.

44 BC	11:26 AM (*or* a.m.)	no. 36 (*or* No. 36)
AD 1492	8:05 PM (*or* p.m.)	$7.41

The abbreviation BC ("before Christ") always follows a date, whereas AD (*anno Domini,* Latin for "in the year of the Lord") precedes a date.

NOTE BCE ("before the common era") and CE ("common era") are increasingly replacing BC and AD, respectively. Both follow the date: *44 BCE, 1492 CE.*

31c

31d. Latin abbreviations

Generally, use the common Latin abbreviations (without underlining) only in source citations and comments in parentheses.

i.e.	*id est:* that is
cf.	*confer:* compare
e.g.	*exempli gratia:* for example
et al.	*et alii:* and others
etc.	*et cetera:* and so forth
NB	*nota bene:* note well

He said he would be gone a fortnight (i.e., two weeks).
Bloom et al., editors, *Anthology of Light Verse*

31e. Words usually spelled out

In most academic, general, and business writing, certain words should always be spelled out. (In source citations and in technical writing, however, these words are more often abbreviated.)

NOTE Always spell out *and* (rather than using &) unless the symbol appears in a business name.

UNITS OF MEASUREMENT

Mount Everest is 29,028 *feet* [not *ft.*] high.

GEOGRAPHICAL NAMES

The publisher is in *Massachusetts* [not *Mass.* or *MA*].

NAMES OF DAYS, MONTHS, AND HOLIDAYS

The truce was signed on *Tuesday* [not *Tues.*], *April* [not *Apr.*] 16. It was ratified by *Christmas* [not *Xmas*].

NAMES OF PEOPLE

Robert [not *Robt.*] Frost wrote accessible poems.

COURSES OF INSTRUCTION

The writer teaches *political science* [not *poli. sci.*].

32
NUMBERS

This chapter addresses the use of numbers (numerals versus words) in the text of a document. All disciplines use many more numerals in source citations (see Chapters 39–43).

32a. Numerals vs. words

Use numerals for numbers that require more than two words to spell out.

The leap year has *366* days.
The population of Minot, North Dakota, is about *32,800*.

In nontechnical academic writing, spell out numbers of one or two words.

The voyage lasted *sixty* days
The ball game drew *forty-two thousand* people. [A hyphenated number may be considered one word.]

In much business writing, use numerals for all numbers over ten (*five reasons, 11 participants*). In technical academic and business writing, such as in science and engineering, use numerals for all numbers over ten, and use numerals for zero through nine when they refer to exact measurements (*2 liters, 1 hour*). (Technical usage does vary from discipline to discipline. Consult one of the style guides listed on pp. 140–41 for more details.)

NOTE Use a combination of numerals and words for round numbers over a million: *26 million, 2.45 billion*. And use either all numerals or all words when several numbers appear together in a passage, even if convention would require a mixture.

32b

32b. Commonly used numerals

Use numerals for certain kinds of information, even when the numbers could be spelled out in one or two words.

DAYS AND YEARS

June 18, 1985   AD 12
2001   456 BC

PAGES, CHAPTERS, VOLUMES, ACTS, SCENES, LINES

Chapter 9, page 123
Hamlet, Act 5, Scene 3
Statistics, Volume 2

ADDRESSES

355 Stonewall Avenue
Washington, DC 20036

EXACT AMOUNTS OF MONEY

$3.5 million $4.50

DECIMALS, PERCENTAGES, AND FRACTIONS

22.5   3½
48% (*or* 48 percent)

SCORES AND STATISTICS

a ratio of 8 to 1   21 to 7

THE TIME OF DAY

9:00 PM   3:45 AM

32c. Beginnings of sentences

For clarity, spell out any number that begins a sentence. If the number requires more than two words, reword the sentence so that the number falls later and can be expressed as a numeral.

FAULTY   *103* visitors asked for refunds.

AWKWARD   *One hundred three* visitors asked for refunds.

REVISED   Of the visitors, *103* asked for refunds.

32c

V

USING AND DOCUMENTING SOURCES

Checklist for
Using and Documenting Sources

This checklist covers the main considerations in using and documenting sources. For a detailed guide to this part, see the contents inside the back cover.

✓ Formulate a question about your topic that can guide your research. (See p. 117.)

✓ Set goals for your sources: primary vs. secondary, scholarly vs. popular, older vs. newer, impartial vs. biased. (See pp. 117–19.)

✓ Develop keywords that describe your topic for searching electronic sources—the Internet, CD-ROMs, the library's catalog. (See pp. 119–20.)

✓ Use the appropriate sources to answer your research question, choosing from reference works, the Internet (including the World Wide Web), periodicals, government publications, books, and your own original research. (See pp. 120–26.)

✓ Keep a working bibliography of likely sources, recording all the information that you need to find and acknowledge each one. (See pp. 126–27.)

✓ Read and use your sources critically. Evaluate both print and online sources for their relevance and reliability. (See pp. 127–30.) Synthesize sources to find their relationships and to support your own ideas. (See pp. 130–31.)

✓ When taking notes from sources, use summary, paraphrase, or direct quotation depending on the significance of the source's ideas or wording. (See pp. 131–33.)

✓ Do not plagiarize, either deliberately or accidentally, by presenting the words or ideas of others as your own. (See pp. 133–36.)

✓ Integrate source material smoothly and clearly into your own text. (See pp. 136–40.)

✓ Document your sources, using the style appropriate for your discipline or field. (See Chapter 38 for a list of style guides. See Chapters 39–42 for explanations of MLA, Chicago, APA, and CBE styles. See Chapter 43 for an explanation of the Columbia style for online sources, which can supplement other styles.)

33

DEVELOPING A RESEARCH STRATEGY

Research writing gives you a chance to work like a detective solving a case. The mystery is the answer to a question you care about. The search for the answer leads you to consider what others think about your subject, to build on that information, and ultimately to become an expert in your own right.

33a. Topic, question, and thesis

Seek a research subject that interests you and that you care about. Starting with your own views will motivate you, and you will be a participant in a dialogue when you begin examining sources.

Consider what you already know about your topic, what you don't know, and what kinds of information you'll need in order to write about it. This thinking can lead you to a RESEARCH QUESTION, a prompt that focuses and guides your work with sources. Try to narrow the question so that you can answer it in the time and space you have available. The question *What are the most effective weight-loss techniques?* is quite broad: whole books have been written on the subject. In contrast, the question *How well do liquid diets work?* or *How safe are the new weight-loss drugs?* is much narrower. Each question also requires more than a simple "Yes" or "No" answer, so that answering, even tentatively, demands thought about pros and cons, causes and effects.

As you read and write, your question will probably evolve to reflect your increasing knowledge of the subject. Eventually its answer will become the THESIS of your paper, the main idea that all the paper's evidence supports. (See also p. 3.)

33b. Search goals

For many research topics, you'll want to consult a mix of sources, as described below. You can discover or infer most of this information from listings in directories, indexes, bibliographies, and catalogs.

Primary and secondary sources

As much as possible, you should rely on PRIMARY SOURCES, or firsthand accounts: historical documents

For Web sites on using and documenting sources, see pages 198–202.

(letters, speeches, and so on), eyewitness reports, works of literature, reports on experiments or surveys conducted by the writer, or your own interviews, experiments, observations, or correspondence.

In contrast, SECONDARY SOURCES report and analyze information drawn from other sources, often primary ones: a reporter's summary of a controversial issue, a historian's account of a battle, a critic's reading of a poem, a psychologist's evaluation of several studies. Secondary sources may contain helpful summaries and interpretations that direct, support, and extend your own thinking. However, most research-writing assignments expect your own ideas to go beyond those in such sources.

Scholarly and popular sources

The scholarship of acknowledged experts is essential for depth, authority, and specificity. The general-interest views and information of popular sources can help you apply more scholarly approaches to daily life.

- Check the publisher. Is it a scholarly journal (such as *Education Forum*) or a publisher of scholarly books (such as Harvard University Press), or is it a popular magazine (such as *Time* or *Newsweek*) or a publisher of popular books (such as Little, Brown)?
- Check the author. Have you seen the name elsewhere, which might suggest that the author is an expert?
- Check the title. Is it technical, or does it use a general vocabulary?

33b

Older and newer sources

Check the publication date. For most subjects a combination of older, established sources (such as books) and current sources (such as newspaper articles or interviews) will provide both background and up-to-date information. Only historical subjects or very current subjects require an emphasis on one extreme or another.

Impartial and biased sources

Seek a range of viewpoints. Sources that attempt to be impartial can offer an overview of your subject and trustworthy facts. Sources with clear biases can offer a diversity of opinion. Of course, to discover bias, you may have to read the source carefully (see p. 127); but even a bibliographical listing can be informative.

- Check the author. You may have heard of the author as a respected researcher (thus more likely to be objective) or as a leading proponent of a certain view (less likely to be objective).

- Check the title. It may reveal something about point of view. (Consider these contrasting titles: "Drink Your Way to Weight Loss" versus "Nutritional Characteristics of Commercial Liquid Diet Products.")

Sources with helpful features

Does the source have a bibliography (which might direct you to other sources) or an index (which can help you find what you want) or illustrations (which could clarify important concepts)?

34
FINDING SOURCES

You can find sources through your library, your computer, or your own independent research. This chapter explains the basics of an electronic search (below), outlines the kinds of sources available to you (p. 120), and offers guidelines for keeping a working bibliography (p. 126).

34a. Electronic searches

During any research project, you will consult computerized sources: the library's catalog of holdings; indexes, bibliographies, and other references on CD-ROM; and text archives, periodicals, discussion groups, and other sources on the Internet.

To search these resources, you'll need KEYWORDS that describe your topic. The computer then finds sources that match your keywords, using one of two methods:

- Databases such as the library's catalog and periodical indexes usually index sources by authors, titles, and publication years and also by keywords that describe the contents of sources. To search you need to use keywords that both capture your topic *and* match the database's directory of terms. The directory for the library's catalog and some other databases is *Library of Congress Subject Headings,* or *LCSH*.
- For the Internet, which has no overall index like *LCSH*, search engines can help you locate sources. You can use some search engines without keywords by following a series of subject directories. But more powerful search engines can match your keywords with sources that contain those words anywhere—not just in the author's name and the title but also in the full text. The more accurately and specifically your keywords state your topic, the more likely such search engines are to

34a

return appropriate sources. (See p. 122 for more on search engines.)

You can refine your keywords in ways now standard, with some variations, among most databases and search engines. When in doubt about whether or how to use any of the following devices, consult the "Help" section of the resource you are using.

- Use the word *not* or the symbol – ("minus") to narrow your search by excluding irrelevant words: for instance, *(weight control) not exercise.*
- Use the word *and* or the symbol + to narrow your search by indicating that all the terms should appear in the source or its listing: for example, *(weight control) and (liquid diets).*
- Use the word *or* to broaden your search: for example, *dieting or (weight loss) or (weight control).*
- Use quotation marks or parentheses (as in the examples above) to indicate that you want to search for the entire phrase, not the separate words.
- To indicate that you will accept different versions of the same word, use a so-called wild card, such as *, in place of the optional letters: for example, *wom*n* includes both *woman* and *women*. (Some systems use ?, :, or + for a wild card instead of *.)
- Be sure to spell your keywords correctly. Some search tools will look for close matches or approximations, but correct spelling gives you the best chance of finding relevant sources.

34b

You may have to use trial and error in developing your keywords. Because different databases have different directories and many search tools have no directory at all, you should count occasionally on running dry (turning up few or no sources) or hitting uncontrollable gushers (turning up hundreds or thousands of mostly irrelevant sources). But the process is not busywork—far from it. Besides leading you eventually to worthwhile sources, it can also teach you a great deal about your subject: how you can or should narrow it, how it is and is not described by others, what others consider interesting or debatable about it, what the major arguments are.

34b. Kinds of sources

A wide range of sources can help you answer your research question and ultimately support your thesis. This section discusses reference works and the Internet (both on the next page), periodicals (p. 124), government publications (p. 125), books (p. 125), and your own sources, such as interviews (p. 125).

Reference works

Reference works (often available on CD-ROM or over the Internet) include encyclopedias, dictionaries, digests, bibliographies, indexes, handbooks, atlases, and almanacs. Your research *must* go beyond these sources, but they can help you decide whether your topic really interests you, can help you develop your keywords for electronic searches, and can direct you to more detailed sources.

Ask a librarian to give you a starting reference for your subject. The librarian can also tell you which works are available on CD-ROM, over the Internet, or in print.

The Internet

The Internet, linking millions of computers around the world, has a number of distinct advantages for researchers and also one sizable disadvantage. It is current, it is much larger than any single library, and it offers chances to converse with others who are interested in your topic. However, Internet sources are not as reliable as printed sources because they do not necessarily undergo the same process of review and publication. See pages 128–30 for advice on evaluating online sources.

NOTE Internet search programs let you find sources even if you don't know their addresses (called UNIFORM RESOURCE LOCATORS, or URLs). But you'll need the address to return directly to the source and to document the source if you want to use it in your final paper. Here is a translation of the address *http://www.nyu.edu/urban/leaders.html:*

- The initials *http* (for HyperText Transfer Protocol) specify the type of access at a particular location.
- The letters *www.nyu.edu* name the computer that houses the particular source: *nyu* stands for New York University; *edu* indicates that it is an educational institution.
- The rest of the address—*/urban/leaders.html*—specifies the location and name of the source.

THE WORLD WIDE WEB

Through the World Wide Web, you can travel from document to document and even from computer to computer by clicking on highlighted words or images that provide HYPERTEXT LINKS, instructions that tell the computer to find the new material specified. You can also experience sound, images, video, and animation.

34b

To find sources on the Web, you use a search engine that outlines content in a series of directories or that conducts keyword searches. Choose a search engine that uses directories when you haven't yet refined your topic or you want a general overview. (Yahoo is the most popular example.) Choose a search engine that uses keywords when you have refined your topic and seek specific information. (Examples include HotBot and AltaVista.) See page 120 on refining your keywords for a Web search.

You can reach most search engines through the address *http://www.search.com;* for a particular engine, you can usually substitute its name (in small letters) for *search*. Spend the time to get to know a search engine by using its "Help" feature, which will tell you crucial information such as how to format keyword searches and how to interpret the results of a search. Search engines generally list HITS, or sites that match your search criteria, in an order depending on the following: the number of times your search terms appear within a document; whether the terms appear at the beginning, middle, or end of a document; or whether the terms appear in the title or the address of the document.

When searching the Web, keep in mind that some sites are archives and some are not. Archives, usually labeled as such, do not change except with additions. But other sites, such as those for newspapers and magazines, frequently replace old material with new. If you think you'll want to use something in such a site, you should consult it right away. If it seems useful, you should download it to your own computer or take notes from it.

34b

ELECTRONIC MAIL

With electronic mail (e-mail), you can send messages to and receive them from most people who use the Internet, as long as you know their addresses. Doing research, for instance, you might carry on an e-mail conversation with a teacher at your school or with other students. Or you might interview an expert in another state to follow up on a scholarly article he or she published. (See pp. 125–26 on conducting interviews, and see pp. 100–01 for advice on e-mail format and etiquette.)

WEB FORUMS

Many Web sites are devoted to discussions of particular issues. Open to everyone, these forums organize postings into THREADS, or groups of contributions and replies on the same topic. You can visit the site and reach the postings through hypertext links, or you may be able to subscribe so that all postings come to you automatically by e-mail.

Web forums are often listed in the subject directories of search engines, and the site *http://www.forumone.com* offers a large index of forums. When you find a forum that interests you, see if it has a compilation of frequently asked questions (FAQs), which will list the topics covered (and *not* covered) by the group and will answer common questions. Spend some time reading the forum's messages before sending any questions or comments of your own. Reading but not participating (called LURKING) will verify whether the forum is relevant to your topic (and vice versa).

NEWSGROUPS

Like Web forums, newsgroups are open, ongoing discussions organized into threads. Unlike Web forums, newsgroups are not Web sites and are not subscription-based, so you must visit the group to follow the discussion. Newsgroups appear over the Usenet network, and the first letters of their addresses indicate their general subject—for instance, *comp* for computers and technology, *soc* for social issues, *biz* for business.

You can reach potentially relevant groups through the subject directories of Web search engines, through the keywords *list of newsgroups*, or through the address *http://www.dejanews.com*. As with Web forums, look for the newsgroup's frequently asked questions (FAQs) and lurk awhile before jumping into the discussion.

LISTSERVS

Listservs are subscription-based discussion groups: messages from each contributor are usually sent (by e-mail) to all other contributors. The focus of listservs tends to be scholarly or technical: discussions center on building knowledge within the community of subscribers. The discussion on a listserv may thus be more reliable than that on a Web forum or newsgroup. If you find a listserv relevant to your topic, the discussion might orient you to current issues and debates and might lead you to a particular person who can answer your questions. However, listservs are more difficult than other discussion groups to search because you must subscribe to each one, and you may have more difficulty extracting information from a continuing exchange among specialists.

You can find lists of listservs through the subject directories of Web search engines, through the keywords *list of listservs* (not *listserves*), or through an index such as the one at *http://www.nova.edu/Inter-Links/listserv.html*. You'll probably find separate addresses for subscribing to a list (using your e-mail account) and for contributing to it.

34b

Once you have your subscription, take some time getting acclimated: read the list's FAQs and its archives of past messages to ensure that your comments or questions will contribute to the discussion.

SYNCHRONOUS COMMUNICATION

With synchronous (or simultaneous) communication, you and others can correspond in real time, as you might talk on the phone. The programs include IRC (Internet Relay Chat), MUDs (multiuser domains), and MOOs (multiuser domains, object-oriented).

Though used mainly for social purposes, such as games and conversations, synchronous programs are also employed in education and research, as for class discussions, collaborative projects, interviews, and academic debates. Your instructors may ask you to use synchronous communication for coursework or research and will provide the software and instructions you need to get started.

Periodicals

Periodicals—journals, magazines, and newspapers—are invaluable sources of both current and specialized information. Journals contain specialized information intended for readers in a particular field: *American Anthropologist, Journal of Black Studies, Journal of Chemical Education.* Magazines are nonspecialist publications intended for diverse readers: *Newsweek, The New Yorker, Rolling Stone.*

Various indexes to periodicals—many available on CD-ROM or online—provide information on the articles in journals, magazines, and newspapers. The following are a few of the most widely used indexes:

- *InfoTrac:* more than fifteen hundred business, government, technical, and general-interest publications.
- *Humanities Index:* journals in language and literature, history, philosophy, and other humanities.
- *MLA International Bibliography of Books and Articles on the Modern Languages and Literatures:* books and periodicals on literature, linguistics, and languages.
- *New York Times Index:* articles in the most comprehensive US newspaper.
- *Social Sciences Index:* journals in economics, psychology, political science, and other social sciences.
- *General Science Index:* journals in biology, chemistry, physics, and other sciences.
- *Readers' Guide to Periodical Literature:* over a hundred popular magazines.

Searching electronic periodical indexes is discussed under electronic searches on pages 119–20.

Government publications

Government publications provide a vast array of data, public records, and other historical and contemporary information. For US government publications, consult the *Monthly Catalog of US Government Publications*, available on computer. Many federal, state, and local government agencies post important publications—legislation, reports, press releases—on their own Web sites. You can find lists of sites for various federal agencies by using the keywords *United States federal government* with a search engine.

Books

Most academic libraries store their book catalogs on computer; however, older volumes—say, those acquired more than ten years ago—may still be cataloged in bound volumes or on film.

You can search an electronic catalog for authors' names, titles, or keywords describing your subject. As much as possible, the keywords should match words in *Library of Congress Subject Headings,* a multivolume work that lists the headings under which the Library of Congress catalogs books. See pages 119–20 for more on keyword searches.

Your own sources

Academic writing will often require you to conduct primary research for information of your own. For instance, you may need to analyze a poem, conduct an experiment, survey a group of people, or interview an expert.

An interview can be especially helpful for a research project because it allows you to ask questions precisely geared to your topic. You can conduct an interview in person, over the telephone, or online using electronic mail (see p. 122) or a form of synchronous communication (see opposite). A personal interview is preferable if you can arrange it, because you can hear the person's tone and see his or her expressions and gestures.

Here are a few guidelines for interviews:

- Prepare a list of open-ended questions to ask—perhaps ten or twelve for a one-hour interview. Do some research for these questions to discover background on the issues and your subject's published views on the issues.
- Give your subject time to consider your questions, and listen to your subject's answers so that you can ask appropriate follow-up questions.
- Take care in interpreting answers, especially if you are online and thus can't depend on facial expressions, gestures, and tone of voice to convey the subject's attitudes.

34b

- For in-person and telephone interviews, keep careful notes or, if you have the equipment and your subject agrees, tape-record the interview. For online interviews, save the discussion in a file of its own.
- Before you quote your subject in your paper, check with him or her to ensure that the quotations are accurate.

34c. Working bibliography

As you find sources that you think you can use, keep track of them in a working bibliography, a file that contains all the information you need to obtain them and, eventually, to acknowledge them in your paper.

FOR A BOOK

Library call number
Name(s) of author(s), editor(s), translator(s), or others listed
Title and subtitle
Publication data: (1) place of publication; (2) publisher's name; (3) date of publication
Other important data, such as edition or volume number

FOR A PERIODICAL ARTICLE

Name(s) of author(s)
Title and subtitle of article
Title of periodical
Publication data: (1) volume number and issue number (if any) in which the article appears; (2) date of issue; (3) page numbers on which article appears

FOR ELECTRONIC SOURCES

Name(s) of author(s), editor(s), or compiler(s)
Title and subtitle of source
Title and subtitle of any longer work the source appears in, such as periodical, CD-ROM, or online site
Publication data if source is also published in print
Electronic publication data: (1) date of release or online posting; (2) name of sponsor, publisher, or vendor of the online site or CD-ROM; (3) medium (CD-ROM or online); (4) format of online source (e-mail, listserv, Web page, etc.)
Date you consulted the source
Electronic address

FOR OTHER SOURCES

Name(s) of author(s) or others listed, such as a government department or a recording artist
Title of the work
Format, such as unpublished letter or live performance

Publication or production data: (1) publisher's or producer's name; (2) date of publication, release, or production; (3) identifying numbers (if any)

35

EVALUATING AND SYNTHESIZING SOURCES

Research writing is much more than finding sources and reporting their contents. The challenge and interest come from *selecting* appropriate sources and *interacting* with them through CRITICAL READING. To read critically, you analyze a text, identifying its main ideas, evidence, bias, and other relevant elements; you evaluate its usefulness and quality; and you relate it to other texts and to your own ideas.

35a. Evaluation of sources

For most projects you will seek the mix of sources described on pages 117–19. But not all the sources in your working bibliography will contribute to this mix. Some may prove irrelevant to your topic; others may prove unreliable.

In evaluating sources you need to consider how they come to you. The print sources you find through the library (including books and articles that are also released electronically) have been previewed for you by their publishers and by the library's staff. They still require your critical reading, but you can have some confidence in the information they contain. With online sources, however, you can't assume similar previewing, so your critical reading must be especially rigorous.

35a

Print sources

To evaluate print sources, look at dates, titles, summaries, introductions, headings, and author biographies. Try to answer the following questions about each source.

EVALUATE RELEVANCE.

• Does the source devote some attention to your topic?
• Where in the source are you likely to find relevant information or ideas?
• Is the source appropriately specialized for your needs? Check the source's treatment of a topic you know

something about, to ensure that it is neither too superficial nor too technical.

• How important is the source likely to be for your writing?

EVALUATE RELIABILITY.

• How up to date is the source? If the publication date is not recent, be sure that other sources will give you more current views.

• Is the author an expert in the field? Look for an author biography, or look up the author in a biographical reference.

• What is the author's bias? Check biographical information or the author's own preface or introduction. Consider what others have written about the author or the source. (To find such commentary, ask your librarian for citation indexes or book review indexes.)

• Whatever his or her bias, does the author reason soundly, provide adequate evidence, and consider opposing views?

Online sources

To a great extent, the same critical reading that serves you with print sources will help you evaluate online sources, too (see above). But online sources can range from scholarly works to corporate promotions, from government-sponsored data to the self-published rantings of crackpots. To evaluate an online source, you'll first need to figure out what it is.

CHECK THE ELECTRONIC ADDRESS.

Look for an abbreviation that tells you where the source originates: *edu* (educational institution), *gov* (government body), *org* (nonprofit organization), *mil* (military), or *com* (commercial organization). With a source coming from *compex.com,* you should assume that the contents reflect the company's commercial purposes (although the information may still be helpful). With a source coming from *harvard.edu,* you can assume that the contents are more scholarly and objective (although you should still evaluate the information yourself).

DETERMINE AUTHORSHIP OR SPONSORSHIP.

Many sites list the person(s) or group(s) responsible for the site. A Web site may provide links to information about or other work by an author or group, but if not you can refer to a biographical dictionary or conduct a keyword search of the Web (see p. 120). You should also look for mentions of the author or group in your other sources.

35a

Often you will not be able to trace authors or sponsors or even identify them at all. For instance, someone passionate about the rights of adoptees might maintain a Web site devoted to the subject but not identify himself or herself as the author. In such a case, you'll need to evaluate the quality of the information and opinions by comparing them with sources you know to be reliable.

GAUGE PURPOSE.

Inferring the purpose of an online source can help you evaluate its reliability. Some sources may seem intent on selling ideas or products. Others may seem to be building knowledge—for instance, by acknowledging opposing views either directly or through links to other sites. Still others may seem determined to scare readers with shocking statistics or anecdotes.

WEIGH THE CONTRIBUTIONS TO DISCUSSION GROUPS.

You need to read individuals' contributions to discussion groups especially critically because they are unfiltered and unevaluated. Even on a listserv (p. 123), whose subscribers are likely to be professionals in the field, you may find wrong or misleading data and skewed opinions. With the more accessible Web forums (p. 122) and newsgroups (p. 123), you should view postings with considerable skepticism.

You can try to verify a contribution to a discussion group by looking at other contributions, which may help you confirm or refute the questionable posting, and by communicating directly with the author to ask about his or her background and publications. If you can't verify the information from a discussion group and the author doesn't respond to your direct approach, you should probably ignore the source.

CHECK FOR REFERENCES OR LINKS TO RELIABLE SOURCES.

An online source may offer as support the titles of sources that you can trace and evaluate—articles in periodicals, other Internet sources, and so on. A Web site may include links to these other sources.

Be aware, however, that online sources may refer you only to other sources that share the same bias. When evaluating both the original source and its references, look for a fair treatment of opposing views.

EVALUATE THE SOURCE AS A WHOLE.

For Web sites especially, consider both the look and readability of the site and the nature of its links. Is the site thoughtfully designed, or is it cluttered with irrelevant

35a

material and graphics? Is it carefully written or difficult to understand? Do the links help clarify the purpose of the site—perhaps leading to scholarly sources or, in contrast, to frivolous or indecent sites?

BACK UP INTERNET SOURCES.

Always consider Internet sources in the context of other sources so that you can distinguish singular, untested views from more mainstream views that have been subject to verification.

35b. Synthesis of sources

When you begin to locate the differences and similarities among sources, you move into the most significant part of research writing: forging relationships for your own purpose. This SYNTHESIS is an essential step in reading sources critically and in creating new knowledge.

RESPOND TO SOURCES.

Write down what your sources make you think. Do you agree or disagree with the author? Do you find his or her views narrow, or do they open up new approaches for you? Is there anything in the source that you need to research further before you can understand it? Does the source prompt questions that you should keep in mind while reading other sources?

CONNECT SOURCES.

When you notice a link between sources, jot it down. Do two sources differ in their theories or their interpretations of facts? Does one source illuminate another—perhaps commenting or clarifying or supplying additional data? Do two or more sources report studies that support a theory you've read about or an idea of your own?

HEED YOUR OWN INSIGHTS.

Apart from ideas prompted by your sources, you are sure to come up with independent thoughts: a conviction, a point of confusion that suddenly becomes clear, a question you haven't seen anyone else ask. These insights may occur at unexpected times, so it's good practice to keep a notebook handy to record them.

USE SOURCES TO SUPPORT YOUR OWN IDEAS.

As your research proceeds, the responses, connections, and insights you form through synthesis will lead you to answer your starting research question with a statement of your thesis (see p. 117). They will also lead you to the main ideas supporting your thesis—conclusions you have drawn from your synthesis of sources, forming the main divisions of your paper. When drafting the paper, make sure each paragraph focuses on an idea of your own, with the support for the idea coming from your sources. In this way, your paper will synthesize others' work into something wholly your own.

36
TAKING NOTES
AND AVOIDING PLAGIARISM

Taking notes from sources is not a mechanical process of copying from periodicals or downloading from Web sites. Rather, you assess and organize the information in your sources, and you record the information so that you can cite your sources completely and honestly.

36a. Notes: Summary, paraphrase, direct quotation

You can take notes by hand, on computer, by photocopying, or by downloading. Whatever system of note taking you use, make sure that each note has all the bibliographic information you'll need to cite the source in your paper if you decide to use the note. (See pp. 126–27 for a list of information.)

36a

NOTE See Chapter 37 for advice on integrating summaries, paraphrases, and direct quotations into your own sentences. See Chapters 38–43 for advice on documenting any material you borrow from another source.

Summary

When you SUMMARIZE, you condense an extended idea or argument into a sentence or more in your own words. Summary is most useful when you want to record the gist of an author's idea without the background or supporting evidence. Here, for example, is a passage summarized in a sentence.

ORIGINAL

Generalizing about male and female styles of management is a tricky business, because stereotypes have traditionally been used to keep women down. Not too long ago it was a widely accepted truth that women were unstable, indecisive, temperamental and manipulative and weren't good team members because they'd never played football. In fighting off these prejudices many women simply tried to adopt masculine traits in the office.

—ANN HUGHEY and ERIC GELMAN, "Managing the Woman's Way," *Newsweek*, page 47

SUMMARY

Rather than be labeled with the sexist stereotypes that prevented their promotions, many women adopted masculine qualities (Hughey and Gelman 47).

Paraphrase

When you PARAPHRASE, you follow much more closely the author's original presentation, but you still restate it in your own words. Paraphrase is most useful when you want to reconstruct an author's line of reasoning but don't feel the original words merit direct quotation. Here is a paraphrase of the first sentence in the passage by Hughey and Gelman beginning on the previous page.

PARAPHRASE

Hughey and Gelman point out that the risk of stereotyping, which has served as a tool to block women from management, makes it difficult to characterize a feminine management style (47).

When paraphrasing, avoid trying to "translate" the source word for word, line for line. Instead, read the passage several times and then put it aside while trying to write the gist of it. Check your effort against the original to be sure you have captured the source author's meaning without using his or her words or sentence structures.

For an example of a poor and revised paraphrase, see page 135.

36a

Direct quotation

If your purpose is to analyze a particular work, such as a short story or historical document, then you will use many direct quotations from the work. But otherwise you should quote from sources only in the following circumstances:

• The quotation supports or adds context to your own ideas or data.
• The author's original satisfies one of these requirements:

The language is unusually vivid, bold, or inventive.
The quotation cannot be paraphrased without distortion or loss of meaning.
The words themselves are at issue in your interpretation.

The quotation represents and emphasizes the view of an important expert.

The quotation is a graph, diagram, or table.

- The quotation is as short as possible.

It includes only material relevant to your point.

It is edited to eliminate examples and other unneeded material. (See the note below.)

When taking a quotation from a source, copy the material *carefully.* Take down the author's exact wording, spelling, capitalization, and punctuation. Proofread every direct quotation *at least twice,* and be sure you have supplied big quotation marks so that later you won't confuse the direct quotation with a paraphrase or summary.

NOTE As long as you do not distort the original author's meaning and you use appropriate punctuation, you can make changes in quotations for clarity and conciseness. See pages 136–37 on integrating quotations into your own sentences.

36b. Plagiarism

PLAGIARISM (from a Latin word for "kidnapper") is the presentation of someone else's ideas or words as your own. Whether deliberate or accidental, plagiarism is a serious and often punishable offense.

- *Deliberate* plagiarism includes copying a sentence from a source and passing it off as your own, summarizing someone else's ideas without acknowledging your debt, or buying a term paper and handing it in as your own.
- *Accidental* plagiarism includes forgetting to place quotation marks around another writer's words, omitting a source citation because you are not aware of the need for it, or carelessly copying a source when you mean to paraphrase.

36b

ESL More than in many other cultures, teachers in the United States value students' original thinking and writing. In some other cultures, for instance, students may be encouraged to copy the words of scholars without acknowledgment, to demonstrate their mastery of or respect for the scholars' work. But in the United States any use of another's words or ideas without a source citation is plagiarism and is unacceptable. When in doubt about the guidelines in this section, ask your instructor for advice.

What not to acknowledge

YOUR INDEPENDENT MATERIAL

You are not required to acknowledge your own observations, thoughts, compilations of facts, or experimental results, expressed in your own words and format.

COMMON KNOWLEDGE

You need not acknowledge common knowledge: the standard information of a field of study as well as folk literature and commonsense observations.

If you do not know a subject well enough to determine whether a piece of information is common knowledge, make a record of the source. As you read more about the subject, the information may come up repeatedly without acknowledgment, in which case it is probably common knowledge. But if you are still in doubt when you finish your research, always acknowledge the source.

What to acknowledge

You must always acknowledge other people's independent material—that is, any facts or ideas that are not common knowledge or your own. The source may be anything, including a book, an article, a movie, an interview, a microfilmed document, a downloaded image, or an anonymous newsgroup posting. You must acknowledge not only ideas or facts themselves but also the language and format in which the ideas or facts appear, if you use them. The wording, sentence structures, arrangement of ideas, and special graphics (such as a diagram) created by another writer belong to that writer just as his or her ideas do.

36b

NOTE For general guidelines on acknowledging sources, see pages 140–41. See also Chapters 39–43 on, respectively, MLA, Chicago, APA, CBE, and Columbia online styles.

COPIED LANGUAGE: QUOTATION MARKS AND A SOURCE CITATION

The following example baldly plagiarizes the original quotation from Jessica Mitford's *Kind and Usual Punishment*, page 9. Without quotation marks or a source citation, the example matches Mitford's wording (underlined) and closely parallels her sentence structure:

ORIGINAL The character and mentality of the keepers may be of more importance in understanding prisons than the character and mentality of the kept.

PLAGIARISM But the character of prison officials (the keepers) is more important in understanding prisons than the character of prisoners (the kept).

To avoid plagiarism, the writer can paraphrase and cite the source (see the last example below) or use Mitford's actual words *in quotation marks* and *with a source citation* (here, in MLA style):

REVISION
(QUOTATION)
According to one critic of the penal system, "The character and mentality of the keepers may be of more importance in understanding prisons than the character and mentality of the kept" (Mitford 9).

PARAPHRASE OR SUMMARY: ORIGINAL WORDS AND A SOURCE CITATION

The next example changes Mitford's sentence structure, but it still uses her words (underlined) without quotation marks and without a source citation:

PLAGIARISM
In understanding prisons, we should know more about the character and mentality of the keepers than of the kept.

To avoid plagiarism, the writer can use quotation marks and cite the source (see above) or *use his or her own words* and still *cite the source* (because the idea is Mitford's, not the writer's):

REVISION
(PARAPHRASE)
One critic of the penal system maintains that we may be able to learn more about prisons from the psychology of the prison officials than from that of the prisoners (Mitford 9).

ONLINE SOURCES

In general, you should acknowledge online sources when you would any other source: whenever you use someone else's independent material in any form. But online sources may present additional challenges as well:

- Keep in mind that online sources may change from one day to the next or even be removed entirely. Be sure to record complete source information as noted on page 126 each time you consult the source. Without the source information, you *may not* use the source.
- A World Wide Web site may include links to other sites that are copyrighted in their own right and require your acknowledgment. The fact that one person has used a second person's work does not release you from the responsibility to acknowledge the second work.
- If you want to use online material in something you publish online, such as your own site on the World Wide Web, then you may need to seek permission from the copyright holder in addition to citing the source.

36b

- You may have to do additional research to discover the author of an online source such as a listserv or newsgroup posting, whether for your citation or for reuse permission. See page 129 for advice on tracing online authors.

Checklist for avoiding plagiarism

The following checklist can help you avoid plagiarism:

- What type of source are you using: your own independent material, common knowledge, or someone else's independent material? You must acknowledge someone else's material.
- If you are quoting someone else's material, is the quotation exact? Have you inserted quotation marks around quotations run into the text? Have you shown omissions with ellipsis marks and additions with brackets?
- If you are paraphrasing or summarizing someone else's material, have you used your own words and sentence structures, not the source author's? Does your paraphrase or summary employ quotation marks when you resort to the author's exact language? Have you represented the author's meaning without distortion?
- Is each use of someone else's material acknowledged in your text? Are all your source citations complete and accurate?
- Does your list of works cited include all the sources you have drawn from in writing your paper?

37
INTEGRATING SOURCES INTO YOUR TEXT

The evidence of others' information and opinions should back up, not dominate, your own ideas. To synthesize evidence, you need to smooth the transitions between your ideas and words and those of your sources, and you need to give the reader a context for interpreting the borrowed material.

NOTE Integrating quotations into your text may involve several conventions discussed elsewhere:

- For guidelines on when to quote from sources, see pages 132–33.
- For the punctuation of signal phrases such as *he insists*, see pages 67–68.

- For guidelines on when to run quotations into your text and when to display them separately from your text, see pages 74–75.
- For the use of brackets ([ ]) to indicate changes in or additions to quotations, see below and page 80.
- For the use of the ellipsis mark (. . .) to indicate omissions from quotations, see pages 78–80.

37a. Introduction of borrowed material

Integrate all quotations, paraphrases, and summaries smoothly into your own sentences, adding words as necessary to mesh structures.

AWKWARD   One editor disagrees with this view and "a good reporter does not fail to separate opinions from facts" (Lyman 52).

REVISED   One editor disagrees with this view, maintaining that "a good reporter does not fail to separate opinions from facts" (Lyman 52).

To mesh your own and your source's words, you may sometimes need to make a substitution or addition to the quotation, signaling your change with brackets:

WORDS ADDED

"The tabloids [of England] are a journalistic case study in bad reporting," claims Lyman (52).

VERB FORM CHANGED

A bad reporter, Lyman implies, is one who "[fails] to separate opinions from facts" (52). [The bracketed verb replaces *fail* in the original.]

CAPITALIZATION CHANGED

"[T]o separate opinions from facts" is a goal of good reporting (Lyman 52). [In the original, *to* is not capitalized.]

NOUN SUPPLIED FOR PRONOUN

The reliability of a news organization "depends on [reporters'] trustworthiness," says Lyman (52). [The bracketed noun replaces *their* in the original.]

NOTE The examples above and those following use the MLA style of source documentation. See pages 140–41 on this and other documentation styles.

37b. Interpretation of borrowed material

Even when it does not conflict with your own sentence structure, borrowed material will be ineffective if you merely dump it in readers' laps without explaining how you intend it to be understood. In the following passage, we must figure out for ourselves that the writer's sentence and the quotation state opposite points of view.

DUMPED Many news editors and reporters maintain that it is impossible to keep personal opinions from influencing the selection and presentation of facts. "True, news reporters, like everyone else, form impressions of what they see and hear. However, a good reporter does not fail to separate opinions from facts" (Lyman 52).

REVISED Many news editors and reporters maintain that it is impossible to keep personal opinions from influencing the selection and presentation of facts. Yet not all authorities agree with this view. One editor grants that "news reporters, like everyone else, form impressions of what they see and hear." But, he insists, "a good reporter does not fail to separate opinions from facts" (Lyman 52).

Signal phrases

In the revised passage above, the words *One editor grants* and *he insists* are SIGNAL PHRASES: they tell readers who the source is and what to expect in the quotations that follow. Signal phrases usually contain (1) the source author's name (or a substitute for it, such as *One editor* and *he*) and (2) a verb that indicates the source author's attitude or approach to what he or she says. In the passage above, *grants* implies concession and *insists* implies argument. Below are some verbs to use in signal phrases.

AUTHOR IS NEUTRAL	AUTHOR INFERS OR SUGGESTS	AUTHOR ARGUES	AUTHOR IS UNEASY OR DISPARAGING
comments	analyzes	claims	belittles
describes	asks	contends	bemoans
explains	assesses	defends	complains
illustrates	believes	disagrees	condemns
mentions	concludes	holds	deplores
notes	considers	insists	deprecates
observes	finds	maintains	derides
points out	predicts		laments
records	proposes	**AUTHOR AGREES**	warns
relates	reveals		
reports	shows	accepts	
says	speculates	admits	
sees	suggests	agrees	
thinks	supposes	concedes	
writes		concurs	
		grants	

Vary your signal phrases to suit your interpretation of borrowed material and also to keep readers' interest. A signal phrase may precede, interrupt, or follow the borrowed material:

SIGNAL PHRASE PRECEDES

Lyman insists that "a good reporter does not fail to separate opinions from facts" (52).

SIGNAL PHRASE INTERRUPTS

"However," Lyman insists, "a good reporter does not fail to separate opinions from facts" (52).

SIGNAL PHRASE FOLLOWS

"[A] good reporter does not fail to separate opinions from facts," Lyman insists (52).

Background information

You can add information to a quotation to integrate it into your text and inform readers why you are using it. Often, you may want to provide the author's name in the text:

AUTHOR NAMED

Harold Lyman grants that "news reporters, like everyone else, form impressions of what they see and hear." But, Lyman insists, "a good reporter does not fail to separate opinions from facts" (52).

If the source title contributes information about the author or the context of the quotation, you can provide it in the text:

TITLE GIVEN

Harold Lyman, in his book *The Conscience of the Journalist*, grants that "news reporters, like everyone else, form impressions of what they see and hear." But, Lyman insists, "a good reporter does not fail to separate opinions from facts" (52).

Finally, if the quoted author's background and experience reinforce or clarify the quotation, you can provide these credentials in the text:

CREDENTIALS GIVEN

Harold Lyman, a newspaper editor for more than forty years, grants that "news reporters, like everyone else, form impressions of what they see and hear." But, Lyman insists, "a good reporter does not fail to separate opinions from facts" (52).

You need not name the author, source, or credentials in your text when you are simply establishing facts or weaving together facts and opinions from varied sources.

In the following passage, the information is more important than the source, so the name of the source is confined to a parenthetical acknowledgment:

> To end the abuses of the British, many colonists were urging three actions: forming a united front, seceding from Britain, and taking control of their own international trade and diplomacy (Wills 325–36).

38

DOCUMENTING SOURCES

Every time you borrow the words, facts, or ideas of others, you must DOCUMENT the source—that is, supply a reference (or document) telling readers that you borrowed the material and where you borrowed it from. (For when to document sources, see pp. 133–36.)

Editors and teachers in most academic disciplines require special documentation formats (or styles) in their scholarly journals and in students' papers. All the styles use a citation in the text that serves two purposes: it signals that material is borrowed, and it refers readers to detailed information about the source so that they can locate both the source and the place in the source where the borrowed material appears. The detailed source information appears either in footnotes or at the end of the paper.

Aside from these essential similarities, the disciplines' documentation styles differ markedly in citation form, arrangement of source information, and other particulars. Each discipline's style reflects the needs of its practitioners for certain kinds of information presented in certain ways. For instance, the currency of a source is important in the social and natural sciences, where studies build on and correct each other; thus in-text citations in these disciplines usually include a source's date of publication. In the humanities, however, currency is less important, so in-text citations do not include date of publication.

The disciplines' documentation formats are described in style guides, including those in the following list. This book presents the styles of the guides that are marked *.

NOTE For online sources you can supplement these styles with Columbia online style. See Chapter 43.

HUMANITIES

Chicago Manual of Style. 14th ed. 1993. (See pp. 157–66.)
*Gibaldi, Joseph. *MLA Handbook for Writers of Research Papers*. 5th ed. 1999. (See pp. 142–57.)

*Gibaldi, Joseph. *MLA Style Manual and Guide to Scholarly Publishing.* 2nd ed. 1998. (See pp. 142–57.)
*Turabian, Kate L. *A Manual for Writers of Term Papers, Theses, and Dissertations.* 6th ed. Rev. John Grossman and Alice Bennett. 1996. (See pp. 157–66.)

SOCIAL SCIENCES

American Anthropological Association. "Style Guide and Information for Authors." *American Anthropologist* (1977): 774–79.
*American Psychological Association. *Publication Manual of the American Psychological Association.* 4th ed. 1994. (See pp. 166–76.)
American Sociological Association. "Editorial Guidelines." Inside front cover of each issue of *American Sociological Review.*
Linguistics Society of America. "LSA Style Sheet." Printed every December in *LSA Bulletin.*

SCIENCES AND MATHEMATICS

American Chemical Society. *ACS Style Guide: A Manual for Authors and Editors.* 2nd ed. 1997.
American Institute of Physics. *Style Manual for Guidance in the Preparation of Papers.* 4th ed. 1990.
American Mathematical Society. *A Manual for Authors of Mathematical Papers.* Rev. ed. 1990.
American Medical Association. *Manual of Style.* 8th ed. 1989.
Bates, Robert L., Rex Buchanan, and Marla Adkins-Heljeson, eds. *Geowriting: A Guide to Writing, Editing, and Printing in Earth Science.* 5th ed. 1992.
*Council of Biology Editors. *Scientific Style and Format: The CBE Manual for Authors, Editors, and Publishers.* 6th ed. 1994. (See pp. 176–84.)

38

Ask your instructor or supervisor which style you should use. If no style is required, use the guide above that's most appropriate for the discipline you're writing in. Do follow one system for citing sources—and one system only—so that you provide all the necessary information in a consistent format.

NOTE Various computer programs can help you format your source citations in the style of your choice. Such a program will prompt you for needed information (author's name, book title, date of publication, and so on) and will arrange, capitalize, underline, and punctuate the information as required by the style. The program will remove some tedium from documenting sources, but it can't substitute for your own care and attention in giving your sources accurate and complete acknowledgment.

39

MLA DOCUMENTATION STYLE

Widely used in English, foreign languages, and other humanities, the MLA documentation style originates with the Modern Language Association. It appears in *MLA Style Manual and Guide to Scholarly Publishing*, 2nd ed. (1998), and in the corresponding student manual, *MLA Handbook for Writers of Research Papers*, 5th ed. (1999). The MLA's Web site, at *http://www.mla.org/main_stl.htm*, offers occasional updates and answers to frequently asked questions about MLA style.

In MLA style, brief parenthetical citations in the text (39a) direct readers to a list of works cited at the end of the text (39b).

39a. MLA parenthetical citations

Citation formats

The in-text citations of sources must include just enough information for the reader to locate (1) the appropriate source in your list of works cited and (2) the place in the source where the borrowed material appears. Usually, you can meet both these requirements by providing

MLA Parenthetical Citations

1. Author named in your text *143*
2. Author not named in your text *143*
3. A work with two or three authors *143*
4. A work with more than three authors *143*
5. A work with numbered paragraphs or screens instead of pages *143*
6. An entire work or a work with no page or other numbers *143*
7. A multivolume work *144*
8. A work by an author of two or more cited works *144*
9. An unsigned work *144*
10. A government publication or a work with a corporate author *144*
11. A source referred to by another source *144*
12. A literary work *144*
13. The Bible *145*
14. An electronic source *145*
15. More than one work *145*

the author's last name and the page(s) in the source on which the borrowed material appears.

Note Examples 1 and 2 show the two ways of writing in-text citations. In examples 3–13 any citation with the author named in the text could be written instead with the author named in parentheses, or vice versa. The choice depends on how you want to introduce and interpret your sources (see pp. 137–40).

1. Author named in your text

One researcher, Carol Gilligan, concludes that "women impose a distinctive construction on moral problems, seeing moral dilemmas in terms of conflicting responsibilities" (105).

2. Author not named in your text

One researcher concludes that "women impose a distinctive construction on moral problems, seeing moral dilemmas in terms of conflicting responsibilities" (Gilligan 105).

3. A work with two or three authors

As Frieden and Sagalyn observe, "The poor and the minorities were the leading victims of highway and renewal programs" (29).

One text discusses the "ethical dilemmas in public relations practice" (Wilcox, Ault, and Agee 125).

**39a
MLA**

4. A work with more than three authors

Give all authors' names, or give only the first author's name followed by "et al." (the abbreviation for the Latin meaning "and others"). Do the same in your list of works cited.

Lopez, Salt, Ming, and Reisen observe that it took the combined forces of the Americans, Europeans, and Japanese to break the rebel siege of Beijing in 1900 (362).

5. A work with numbered paragraphs or screens instead of pages

According to Palfrey, twins raised apart report similar feelings (pars. 6-7).

6. An entire work or a work with no page or other numbers

Almost 20 percent of commercial banks have been audited for the practice (Friis).

7. A MULTIVOLUME WORK

If you name more than one volume in your list of works cited, give the volume you're acknowledging in your text citation (here, volume 5).

After issuing the Emancipation Proclamation, Lincoln said,

"What I did, I did after very full deliberations, and under a very

heavy and solemn sense of responsibility" (5: 438).

If you name only one volume in your list of works cited, give only the page number in your text citation.

8. A WORK BY AN AUTHOR OF TWO OR MORE CITED WORKS

Give the title of the particular work you're citing, shortening it in a parenthetical citation unless it's already brief (the full title of *Arts*, below, is *The Arts and Human Development*).

At about age seven, most children begin to use appropriate gestures to reinforce their stories (Gardner, Arts 144-45).

9. AN UNSIGNED WORK

Use the title (or a brief version of it) in place of an author's name. This citation has no page number because the entire source is only a page.

"The Right to Die" notes that a death-row inmate may demand his own execution to achieve a fleeting notoriety.

10. A GOVERNMENT PUBLICATION OR A WORK WITH A CORPORATE AUTHOR

One study found that teachers of secondary social studies are receiving more training in methods but less in the discipline itself (Lorenz Research 64).

11. A SOURCE REFERRED TO BY ANOTHER SOURCE

George Davino maintains that "even small children have vivid ideas about nuclear energy" (qtd. in Boyd 22).

12. A LITERARY WORK

For novels that may be available in many editions, cite part, chapter, or other numbers as well as page number.

Toward the end of James's novel, Maggie suddenly feels "the intimate, the immediate, the familiar, as she hadn't had them for so long" (535; pt. 6, ch. 41).

For verse plays and poems that are divided into parts, omit a page number and instead cite the part (here act 3, scene 4) and line number(s) (here 147).

Later in <u>King Lear</u> Shakespeare has the disguised Edgar say, "The prince of darkness is a gentleman" (3.4.147).

13. THE BIBLE

Abbreviate any book title longer than four letters, and then give chapter and verse(s).

According to the Bible, at Babel God "did . . . confound the language of all the earth" (Gen. 11.9).

14. AN ELECTRONIC SOURCE

Many electronic sources can be cited just as printed sources are. For a source with no named author, see model 9. For a source that uses paragraph or some other numbers instead of page numbers, see model 5. For a source with no numbering, just give the author's name, either in parentheses, as in model 6, or in the text:

Michael Tourville, for one, believes that Europe's new single currency will quickly strengthen the continent's large and technologically advanced companies.

15. MORE THAN ONE WORK

Two recent articles point out that a computer badly used can be less efficient than no computer at all (Gough and Hall 201; Richards 162).

39a
MLA

Footnotes or endnotes in special circumstances

Footnotes or endnotes may supplement parenthetical citations when you cite several sources at once, when you comment on a source, or when you provide information that does not fit easily in the text. Signal a footnote or endnote in your text with a numeral raised above the appropriate line. Then write a note with the same numeral.

TEXT

At least five subsequent studies have confirmed these results.[1]

NOTE

[1] Abbott and Winger 266-68; Casner 27; Hoyenga 78-79; Marino 36; Tripp, Tripp, and Walk 179-83.

If the note appears as a footnote, place it at the bottom of the page on which the citation appears, set it off from the text with quadruple spacing, and single-space the note itself. If the note appears as an endnote, place it in numerical order with the other endnotes on a page between the text and the list of works cited; double-space all the endnotes.

39b. MLA list of works cited

At the end of your paper, a list titled "Works Cited" includes all the sources you quoted, paraphrased, or sum-

---

marized in your paper. The format of the list's first page is illustrated on the next page.

ARRANGEMENT Arrange your sources in alphabetical order by the last name of the author (the first author if there is more than one). If an author is not given in the source, alphabetize the source by the first main word of the title (excluding *A, An,* or *The*).

SPACING AND INDENTION Double-space all entries. Type the first line of each entry at the left margin, and indent all subsequent lines one-half inch or five spaces.

39b
MLA

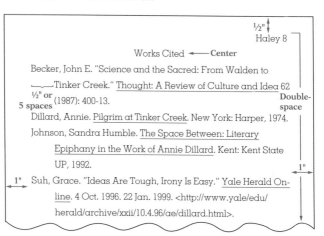

AUTHORS List the author's name last-name first. If there are two or more authors, list all names after the first in normal order. Separate the names with commas.

TITLES Give full titles, capitalizing all important words (see p. 109). For periodical titles, omit any initial *A, An*, or *The*. Underline the titles of books and periodicals; place titles of periodical articles in quotation marks.

PUBLICATION INFORMATION Provide the publication information after the title. For books, give place of publication, publisher's name, and date. (Shorten publishers' names—for instance, *Little* for Little, Brown and *Harvard UP* for Harvard University Press.) For periodical articles, give the volume or issue number, date, and page numbers.

PUNCTUATION Separate the main parts of an entry with periods followed by one space.

Books

1. A BOOK WITH ONE AUTHOR

Gilligan, Carol. In a Different Voice: Psychological Theory and Women's Development. Cambridge: Harvard UP, 1982.

2. A BOOK WITH TWO OR THREE AUTHORS

Frieden, Bernard J., and Lynne B. Sagalyn. Downtown, Inc.: How America Rebuilds Cities. Cambridge: MIT, 1989.

Wilcox, Dennis L., Phillip H. Ault, and Warren K. Agee. Public Relations: Strategies and Tactics. 4th ed. New York: Harper, 1995.

39b
MLA

3. A BOOK WITH MORE THAN THREE AUTHORS

Give all authors' names, or give only the first author's name followed by "et al." (the abbreviation for the Latin meaning "and others"). Do the same in your in-text citations of the source.

Lopez, Geraldo, Judith P. Salt, Anne Ming, and Henry Reisen.
China and the West. Boston: Little, 1990.

Lopez, Geraldo, et al. China and the West. Boston: Little, 1990.

4. TWO OR MORE WORKS BY THE SAME AUTHOR(S)

Gardner, Howard. The Arts and Human Development. New York:
Wiley, 1973.

---. The Quest for Mind: Piaget, Lévi-Strauss, and the Structuralist Movement. New York: Knopf, 1973.

5. A BOOK WITH AN EDITOR

Ruitenbeek, Hendrick, ed. Freud as We Knew Him. Detroit:
Wayne State UP, 1973.

6. A BOOK WITH AN AUTHOR AND AN EDITOR

Mumford, Lewis. The City in History. Ed. Donald L. Miller. New
York: Pantheon, 1986.

7. A TRANSLATION

Alighieri, Dante. The Inferno. Trans. John Ciardi. New York: NAL,
1971.

39b
MLA

8. A BOOK WITH A CORPORATE AUTHOR

Lorenz Research, Inc. Research in Social Studies Teaching. Baltimore: Arrow, 1997.

9. AN ANONYMOUS BOOK

The Dorling Kindersley World Reference Atlas. London: Dorling,
1994.

10. THE BIBLE

The Bible. King James Version.
The New English Bible. London: Oxford UP and Cambridge UP,
1970.

11. A LATER EDITION

Bollinger, Dwight L. Aspects of Language. 2nd ed. New York:
Harcourt, 1975.

12. A REPUBLISHED BOOK

James, Henry. The Golden Bowl. 1904. London: Penguin, 1966.

13. A BOOK WITH A TITLE IN ITS TITLE

Eco, Umberto. Postscript to The Name of the Rose. Trans. William
Weaver. New York: Harcourt, 1983.

14. A WORK IN MORE THAN ONE VOLUME

Using two or more volumes:

Lincoln, Abraham. The Collected Works of Abraham Lincoln.
Ed. Roy P. Basler. 8 vols. New Brunswick: Rutgers UP, 1953.

Using only one volume:

Lincoln, Abraham. The Collected Works of Abraham Lincoln.
Ed. Roy P. Basler. Vol. 5. New Brunswick: Rutgers UP, 1953.
8 vols.

15. A WORK IN A SERIES

Bergman, Ingmar. The Seventh Seal. Mod. Film Scripts Ser. 12.
New York: Simon, 1968.

39b
MLA

16. AN ANTHOLOGY

Barnet, Sylvan, et al., eds. An Introduction to Literature. 11th ed.
New York: Longman, 1997.

17. A SELECTION FROM AN ANTHOLOGY

Chekhov, Anton. "Misery." Trans. Constance Garnett. An Introduction to Literature. Ed. Sylvan Barnet et al. 11th ed. New
York: Longman, 1997. 58-61.

A reprinted scholarly article:

Reekmans, Tony. "Juvenal on Social Change." Ancient Society 2
(1971): 117-61. Rpt. in Private Life in Rome. Ed. Helen West.
Los Angeles: Coronado, 1981. 124-69.

18. TWO OR MORE SELECTIONS FROM THE SAME ANTHOLOGY

Auden, W. H. "The Unknown Citizen." Barnet et al. 687-88.

Barnet, Sylvan, et al., eds. <u>An Introduction to Literature</u>. 11th ed.
New York: Longman, 1997.

Miller, Arthur. <u>Death of a Salesman</u>. Barnet et al. 1163-1231.

19. AN INTRODUCTION, PREFACE, FOREWORD, OR AFTERWORD

Donaldson, Norman. Introduction. <u>The Claverings</u>. By Anthony
Trollope. New York: Dover, 1977. vii-xv.

20. AN ARTICLE IN A REFERENCE WORK

"Reckon." <u>Merriam-Webster's Collegiate Dictionary</u>. 10th ed. 1993.

Mark, Herman F. "Polymers." <u>The New Encyclopaedia Britannica: Macropaedia</u>. 15th ed. 1991.

Periodicals: Journals, magazines, newspapers

**21. AN ARTICLE IN A JOURNAL WITH CONTINUOUS PAGINATION
THROUGHOUT THE ANNUAL VOLUME**

Lever, Janet. "Sex Differences in the Games Children Play."
<u>Social Problems</u> 23 (1976): 478-87.

**22. AN ARTICLE IN A JOURNAL THAT PAGES ISSUES SEPARATELY OR
THAT NUMBERS ONLY ISSUES, NOT VOLUMES**

Dacey, June. "Management Participation in Corporate Buy-
Outs." <u>Management Perspectives</u> 7.4 (1998): 20-31.

23. AN ARTICLE IN A MONTHLY OR BIMONTHLY MAGAZINE

Tilin, Andrew. "Selling the Dream." <u>Worth</u> Sept. 1997: 94-100.

24. AN ARTICLE IN A WEEKLY OR BIWEEKLY MAGAZINE

Stevens, Mark. "Low and Behold." <u>New Republic</u> 24 Dec. 1990: 27-33.

25. AN ARTICLE IN A DAILY NEWSPAPER

Lewis, Peter H. "Many Updates Cause Profitable Confusion."
<u>New York Times</u> 21 Jan. 1999, natl. ed.: D1+.

26. AN UNSIGNED ARTICLE

"The Right to Die." <u>Time</u> 11 Oct. 1976: 101.

27. AN EDITORIAL OR LETTER TO THE EDITOR

"Bodily Intrusions." Editorial. <u>New York Times</u> 29 Aug. 1990, late
ed.: A20.

Dowding, Michael. Letter. <u>Economist</u> 5-11 Jan. 1985: 4.

**39b
MLA**

152 • MLA documentation

28. A REVIEW

Dunne, John Gregory. "The Secret of Danny Santiago." Rev. of
    Famous All over Town, by Danny Santiago. New York
    Review of Books 16 Aug. 1984: 17-27.

29. AN ABSTRACT OF A DISSERTATION

Steciw, Steven K. "Alterations to the Pessac Project of Le Cor-
    busier." Diss. U of Michigan, 1986. DAI 46 (1986): 565C.

30. AN ABSTRACT OF AN ARTICLE

Lever, Janet. "Sex Differences in the Games Children Play." So-
    cial Problems 23 (1976): 478-87. Psychological Abstracts 63
    (1976): item 1431.

Electronic sources

Electronic sources include those available on CD-ROM
and those available online, such as through the Internet.
Online sources require two special pieces of information:

- Give the date when you consulted the source as well as
  the date when the source was posted online. The posting date comes first, with other publication information. Your access date falls near the end of the entry,
  just before the electronic address.
- Give the source's exact electronic address, enclosed in
  angle brackets (< >). Place the address at the end of the
  entry. If you must break an address from one line to the
  next, do so *only* after a slash, and do not hyphenate.

Try to locate all the information required in the following models, so that your readers can trace your sources
with minimal difficulty. However, if you search for and still
cannot find some information, then give what you can find.

NOTE You can supplement or replace MLA style for online sources with Columbia online style (Chapter 43).
However, there are differences between the two styles
(described on pp. 185–86), so ask your instructor which
one you should use.

31. A SOURCE ON A PERIODICAL CD-ROM

A source also published in print (the final date is the CD-
ROM's publication date):

Lewis, Peter H. "Many Updates Cause Profitable Confusion."
    New York Times 21 Jan. 1999, natl. ed.: D1+. New York
    Times Ondisc. CD-ROM. UMI-ProQuest. Mar. 1999.

A source not published in print:

"Vanguard Forecasts." <u>Business Outlook</u>. CD-ROM. Information
Access. Mar. 1998.

32. A SOURCE ON A NONPERIODICAL CD-ROM

Shelley, Mary Wollstonecraft. <u>Frankenstein</u>. <u>Classic Library</u>.
CD-ROM. Alameda: Andromeda, 1993.

33. AN ONLINE BOOK

A book published independently:

James, Henry. <u>The Turn of the Screw</u>. New York: Scribner's,
1908-09. 4 Mar. 1998 <http://www.americanliterature.com/
TS/TSINDX.HTML>.

A book within a scholarly project:

Austen, Jane. <u>Emma</u>. Ed. Ronald Blythe. Harmondsworth: Penguin, 1972. <u>Oxford Text Archive</u>. 1994. Oxford U. 15 Dec.
1997 <ftp://ota.ox.ac.uk/pub/ota/public/english/Austen/
emma.1519>.

34. AN ARTICLE IN AN ONLINE JOURNAL

Palfrey, Andrew. "Choice of Mates in Identical Twins." <u>Modern
Psychology</u> 4.1 (1996): 12 pars. 25 Feb. 1997 <http://
www.liasu.edu/modpsy/palfrey4(1).htm>.

35. AN ONLINE ABSTRACT

Palfrey, Andrew. "Choice of Mates in Identical Twins." <u>Modern
Psychology</u> 4.1 (1996): 12 pars. Abstract. 25 Feb. 1997
<http://www.liasu.edu/modpsy/abstractpalfrey4(1).htm>.

36. AN ARTICLE IN AN ONLINE NEWSPAPER

Still, Lucia. "On the Battlefields of Business, Millions of Casualties." <u>New York Times on the Web</u> 3 Mar. 1996. 17 Aug. 1996
<http://www.nytimes.com/specials/downsize/03down1.html>.

37. AN ARTICLE IN AN ONLINE MAGAZINE

Palevitz, Barry A., and Ricki Lewis. "Death Raises Safety Issues
for Primate Handlers." <u>Scientist</u> 2 Mar. 1998: 1+. 27 Mar.
1998 <http://www.the-scientist.library.upenn.edu/yr1998/
mar/palevitz_p1_980302.html>.

**39b
MLA**

154 • MLA documentation

38. AN ONLINE REVIEW

Detwiler, Donald S., and Chu Shao-Kang. Rev. of Important Documents of the Republic of China, ed. Tan Quon Chin. Journal of Military History 56.4 (1992): 669-84. 16 Sept. 1997 <http://www.jstor.org/fcgi-bin/jstor/viewitem.fcg/08993718/96p0008x>.

39. AN ONLINE SCHOLARLY PROJECT OR DATABASE

Scots Teaching and Research Network. Ed. John Corbett. 2 Feb. 1998. U of Glasgow. 5 Mar. 1998 <http://www.arts.gla.ac.uk/www/comet/starn.htm>.

40. A SHORT WORK FROM AN ONLINE SCHOLARLY PROJECT OR DATABASE

Barbour, John. "The Brus." Scots Teaching and Research Network. Ed. John Corbett. 2 Feb. 1998. U of Glasgow. 5 Mar. 1998 <http://www.arts.gla.ac.uk/www/comet/starn/poetry/brus/contents.htm>.

41. A PERSONAL OR PROFESSIONAL ONLINE SITE

Lederman, Leon. Topics in Modern Physics--Lederman. 10 Oct. 1997. 12 Dec. 1998 <http://www-ed.fnal.gov/samplers/hsphys/people/lederman.html>.

39b
MLA

42. A WORK FROM AN ONLINE SUBSCRIPTION SERVICE

"China--Dragon Kings." The Encyclopedia Mythica. America Online. 6 Jan. 1999. Path: Research and Learn; Encyclopedia; More Encyclopedias; Encyclopedia Mythica.

43. ELECTRONIC MAIL

Millon, Michele. "Re: Grief Therapy." E-mail to the author. 4 May 1999.

44. A POSTING TO A LISTSERV

Reference to the original posting:

Tourville, Michael. "European Currency Reform." 6 Jan. 1998. Online posting. International Finance Discussion List. 8 Jan. 1998 <finance-dl@weg.isu.edu>.

Reference to an archive:

Tourville, Michael. "European Currency Reform." 6 Jan.
1998. Online posting. International Finance Archive.
2 Feb. 1998 <http://www.weg.isu.edu/finance-dl/
46732>.

45. A POSTING TO A NEWSGROUP OR FORUM

A newsgroup:

Cramer, Sherry. "Recent Investment Practices." 26 Mar. 1997.
Online posting. 3 Apr. 1997
<news:biz.investment.current.2700>.

A forum:

Franklin, Melanie. Online posting. 25 Jan. 1999. The Creative
Process: An Artist's Diary. 27 Jan. 1999. <http://forums/
nytimes/com/webin/WebX?14@^182943@.eea3ea7>.

46. AN ONLINE GRAPHIC, VIDEO, OR AUDIO FILE

Hamilton, Calvin J. "Components of Comets." Diagram. Space
Art. 1997. 20 Dec. 1998 <wysisiwyg://94/http://spaceart.com/
solar/eng/comet.htm>.

47. A SYNCHRONOUS COMMUNICATION

Bruckman, Amy. MediaMOO Symposium: Virtual Worlds for
Business? 20 Jan. 1998. MediaMOO. 26 Feb. 1998
<http://www.cc.gatech.edu/Amy.Bruckman/MediaMOO/
cscw-symposium-98.html>.

**39b
MLA**

48. SOFTWARE

Project Scheduler 8000. Ver. 4.1. Orlando: Scitor, 1999.

Other sources

49. A GOVERNMENT PUBLICATION

Stiller, Ann. Historic Preservation and Tax Incentives. US Dept. of
the Interior. Washington: GPO, 1996.

Hawaii. Dept. of Education. Kauai District Schools, Profile 1998-99.
Honolulu: Hawaii Dept. of Education, 1998.

United States. Cong. House. Committee on Ways and Means.
    Medicare Payment for Outpatient Physical and Occupa-
    tional Therapy Services. 102nd Cong., 1st sess. Washing-
    ton: GPO, 1991.

50. A MUSICAL COMPOSITION OR WORK OF ART

Fauré, Gabriel. Sonata for Violin and Piano no. 1 in A major, op. 15.

Sargent, John Singer. Venetian Doorway. Metropolitan Museum
    of Art, New York. Sargent Watercolors. By Donelson F.
    Hoopes. New York: Watson, 1976. 31.

51. A FILM OR VIDEO RECORDING

Spielberg, Steven, dir. Schindler's List. Perf. Liam Neeson and
    Ben Kingsley. Universal, 1993.

Serenade. Chor. George Balanchine. Perf. San Francisco Ballet.
    Dir. Hilary Bean. 1981. Videocassette. PBS Video, 1987.

52. A TELEVISION OR RADIO PROGRAM

Kenyon, Jane, and Donald Hall. "A Life Together." Bill Moyers'
    Journal. PBS. WNET, New York. 17 Dec. 1993.

53. A PERFORMANCE

The English Only Restaurant. By Silvio Martinez Palau. Dir.
    Susana Tubert. Puerto Rican Traveling Theater, New York.
    27 July 1997.

Ozawa, Seiji, cond. Boston Symphony Orch. Concert. Symphony
    Hall, Boston. 25 Apr. 1998.

54. A SOUND RECORDING

Siberry, Jane. "Caravan." Maria. Reprise, 1995.

Brahms, Johannes. Concerto no. 2 in B-flat, op. 83. Perf. Artur
    Rubinstein. Cond. Eugene Ormandy. Philadelphia Orch.
    RCA, 1992.

55. A PUBLISHED LETTER

Buttolph, Mrs. Laura E. Letter to Rev. and Mrs. C. C. Jones. 20
    June 1857. In The Children of Pride: A True Story of Georgia
    and the Civil War. Ed. Robert Manson Myers. New Haven:
    Yale UP, 1972. 334.

39b
MLA

56. A PERSONAL LETTER

Packer, Ann E. Letter to the author. 15 June 1998.

57. A LECTURE OR ADDRESS

Carlone, Dennis. "Architecture for the City of 2000." Tenth Symposium on Urban Issues. Cambridge City Hall, Cambridge. 22 Oct. 1998.

58. AN INTERVIEW

Graaf, Vera. Personal interview. 19 Dec. 1998.

Christopher, Warren. Interview. Frontline. PBS. WGBH, Boston. 13 Feb. 1998.

59. A MAP OR OTHER ILLUSTRATION

Women in the Armed Forces. Map. Women in the World: An International Atlas. By Joni Seager and Ann Olson. New York: Touchstone, 1992. 44-45.

40
CHICAGO DOCUMENTATION STYLE

In history, art history, and many other disciplines, writers rely on *The Chicago Manual of Style*, 14th ed. (1993), or the student reference adapted from it, *A Manual for Writers of Term Papers, Theses, and Dissertations*, by Kate L. Turabian, 6th ed., revised by John Grossman and Alice Bennett (1996). *The Chicago Manual* has a Web site, *http://www.press.uchicago.edu/Misc/Chicago/cmosfaq.html*, that answers frequently asked questions about Chicago style.

Both *The Chicago Manual* and *A Manual for Writers* detail two documentation styles. One, used mainly by scientists and social scientists, closely resembles the style of the American Psychological Association, covered in the next chapter. The other style, used more in the humanities, calls for footnotes or endnotes and an optional bibliography. This style is described below.

40a. Chicago notes and list of works cited

In the Chicago note style, a raised numeral in the text refers the reader to source information in endnotes or

40a

Chic

footnotes. In these notes, the first citation of each source contains all the information readers need to find the source. Thus your instructor may consider a list of works cited optional because it provides much the same information. Ask your instructor whether you should use footnotes or endnotes and whether you should include a list of works cited.

Whether providing footnotes or endnotes, use single spacing for each note and double spacing between notes. With footnotes, separate the notes from the text with a short line, as shown in the following sample:

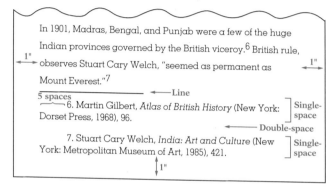

With endnotes, use the format below for a list of works cited, substituting the heading "**NOTES**" and numbered entries as for footnotes.

For the list of sources at the end of the paper, use the format below. Arrange the sources alphabetically by the authors' last names.

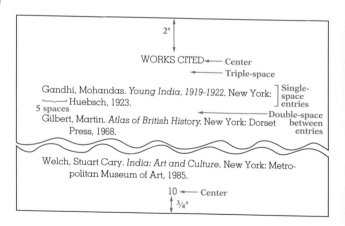

The examples below illustrate the essentials of a note and a works-cited entry.

NOTE

> 6. Martin Gilbert, *Atlas of British History* (New York: Dorset Press, 1968), 96.

WORKS-CITED ENTRY

> Gilbert, Martin. *Atlas of British History.* New York: Dorset Press, 1968.

Notes and works-cited entries share certain features:

- Italicize or underline the titles of books and periodicals (ask your instructor for his or her preference).
- Enclose in quotation marks the titles of parts of books or articles in periodicals.
- Do not abbreviate publishers' names, but omit "Inc.," "Co.," and similar abbreviations.
- Do not use "p." or "pp." before page numbers.

Notes and works-cited entries also differ in important ways:

NOTE	**WORKS-CITED ENTRY**
Start with a number (typed on the line and followed by a period) that corresponds to the note number in the text.	Do not begin with a number.
Indent the first line five spaces.	Indent the second and subsequent lines five spaces.
Give the author's name in normal order.	Begin with the author's last name.
Use commas between elements such as author's name and title.	Use periods between elements, followed by one space.
Enclose publication information in parentheses, with no preceding punctuation.	Precede the publication information with a period, and don't use parentheses.
Include the specific page number(s) you borrowed from, omitting "p." or "pp."	Omit page numbers except for parts of books or articles in periodicals.

**40a
Chic**

Many computerized word-processing programs will automatically position footnotes at the bottoms of appropriate pages. Some will automatically number notes and even renumber them if you add or delete one or more.

40b. Chicago models

In the following models for common sources, notes and works-cited entries appear together for easy reference. Be sure to use the numbered note form for notes and the unnumbered works-cited form for works-cited entries.

Chicago Note and Works-Cited Models

Books

1. A BOOK WITH ONE, TWO, OR THREE AUTHORS

1. Carol Gilligan, *In a Different Voice: Psychological Theory and Women's Development* (Cambridge: Harvard University Press, 1982), 27.

Gilligan, Carol. *In a Different Voice: Psychological Theory and Women's Development*. Cambridge: Harvard University Press, 1982.

1. Dennis L. Wilcox, Phillip H. Ault, and Warren K. Agee, *Public Relations: Strategies and Tactics*, 4th ed. (New York: HarperCollins, 1995), 182.

Wilcox, Dennis L., Phillip H. Ault, and Warren K. Agee. *Public Relations: Strategies and Tactics*. 4th ed. New York: HarperCollins, 1995.

2. A BOOK WITH MORE THAN THREE AUTHORS

2. Geraldo Lopez and others, *China and the West* (Boston: Little, Brown, 1990), 461.

Lopez, Geraldo, Judith P. Salt, Anne Ming, and Henry Reisen. *China and the West*. Boston: Little, Brown, 1990.

3. A BOOK WITH AN EDITOR

3. Hendrick Ruitenbeek, ed., *Freud as We Knew Him* (Detroit: Wayne State University Press, 1973), 64.

Ruitenbeek, Hendrick, ed. *Freud as We Knew Him*. Detroit: Wayne State University Press, 1973.

4. A BOOK WITH AN AUTHOR AND AN EDITOR

4. Lewis Mumford, *The City in History*, ed. Donald L. Miller (New York: Pantheon, 1986), 216-17.

Mumford, Lewis. *The City in History*. Edited by Donald L. Miller. New York: Pantheon, 1986.

40b
Chic

5. A TRANSLATION

5. Dante Alighieri, *The Inferno*, trans. John Ciardi (New York: New American Library, 1971), 51.

Alighieri, Dante. *The Inferno*. Translated by John Ciardi. New York: New American Library, 1971.

6. AN ANONYMOUS WORK

6. *The Dorling Kindersley World Reference Atlas* (London: Dorling Kindersley, 1994), 150-51.

The Dorling Kindersley World Reference Atlas. London: Dorling Kindersley, 1994.

7. A LATER EDITION

7. Dwight L. Bollinger, *Aspects of Language*, 2d ed. (New York: Harcourt Brace Jovanovich, 1975), 20.

Bollinger, Dwight L. *Aspects of Language*. 2d ed. New York: Harcourt Brace Jovanovich, 1975.

8. A WORK IN MORE THAN ONE VOLUME

Citation of one volume without a title:

8. Abraham Lincoln, *The Collected Works of Abraham Lincoln*, ed. Roy P. Basler (New Brunswick: Rutgers University Press, 1953), 5:426-28.

Lincoln, Abraham. *The Collected Works of Abraham Lincoln*. Edited by Roy P. Basler. Vol. 5. New Brunswick: Rutgers University Press, 1953.

Citation of one volume with a title:

8. Linda B. Welkin, *The Age of Balanchine*, vol. 3 of *The History of Ballet* (New York: Columbia University Press, 1969), 56.

Welkin, Linda B. *The Age of Balanchine*. Vol. 3 of *The History of Ballet*. New York: Columbia University Press, 1969.

9. A SELECTION FROM AN ANTHOLOGY

9. Rosetta Brooks, "Streetwise," in *The New Urban Landscape*, ed. Richard Martin (New York: Rizzoli, 1990), 38-39.

Brooks, Rosetta. "Streetwise." In *The New Urban Landscape*, ed. Richard Martin, 37-60. New York: Rizzoli, 1990.

10. A WORK IN A SERIES

10. Ingmar Bergman, *The Seventh Seal*, Modern Film Scripts Series, no. 12 (New York: Simon and Schuster, 1968), 27.

Bergman, Ingmar. *The Seventh Seal*. Modern Film Scripts Series, no. 12. New York: Simon and Schuster, 1968.

11. AN ARTICLE IN A REFERENCE WORK

The abbreviation "s.v." in the examples stands for the Latin *sub verbo*, "under the word."

11. *Merriam-Webster's Collegiate Dictionary*, 10th ed., s.v. "reckon."

Merriam-Webster's Collegiate Dictionary, 10th ed., s.v. "reckon."

11. Mark F. Herman, "Polymers," in *The New Encyclopaedia Britannica: Macropaedia*, 16th ed.

Herman, Mark F. "Polymers." In *The New Encyclopaedia Britannica: Macropaedia*, 16th ed.

40b
Chic

Periodicals: Journals, magazines, newspapers

12. AN ARTICLE IN A JOURNAL WITH CONTINUOUS PAGINATION THROUGHOUT THE ANNUAL VOLUME

12. Janet Lever, "Sex Differences in the Games Children Play," *Social Problems* 23 (1976): 482.

Lever, Janet. "Sex Differences in the Games Children Play." *Social Problems* 23 (1976): 478-87.

13. AN ARTICLE IN A JOURNAL THAT PAGES ISSUES SEPARATELY

13. June Dacey, "Management Participation in Corporate Buy-Outs," *Management Perspectives* 7, no. 4 (1998): 22.

Dacey, June. "Management Participation in Corporate Buy-Outs." *Management Perspectives* 7, no. 4 (1998): 20-31.

14. AN ARTICLE IN A POPULAR MAGAZINE

14. Mark Stevens, "Low and Behold," *New Republic*, 24 December 1990, 28.

Stevens, Mark. "Low and Behold." *New Republic*, 24 December 1990, 27-33.

15. AN ARTICLE IN A NEWSPAPER

15. Peter H. Lewis, "Many Updates Cause Profitable Confusion," *New York Times*, 21 January 1999, national ed., D5.

Lewis, Peter H. "Many Updates Cause Profitable Confusion." *New York Times*, 21 January 1999, national ed., D1, D5.

16. A REVIEW

16. John Gregory Dunne, "The Secret of Danny Santiago," review of *Famous All over Town*, by Danny Santiago, *New York Review of Books*, 16 August 1984, 25.

Dunne, John Gregory. "The Secret of Danny Santiago." Review of *Famous All over Town*, by Danny Santiago. *New York Review of Books*, 16 August 1984, 17-27.

40b
Chic

Electronic sources

The Chicago Manual offers some models for documenting electronic sources, and *A Manual for Writers* updates these and adds a few more. For other electronic sources and simpler formats, you can use Columbia online style for the humanities, discussed in Chapter 43. Pages 186–87 show how to adapt Columbia style to Chicago style. There are differences between the two styles (see p. 187), so ask your instructor which style you should use for online sources.

NOTE Since Chicago style does not specify how to break electronic addresses in notes and works-cited entries, follow MLA style (p. 152): break only after slashes, and do not hyphenate.

17. A SOURCE ON A PERIODICAL CD-ROM

A source also published in print:

17. Peter H. Lewis, "Many Updates Cause Profitable Confusion," *New York Times*, 21 January 1999, national ed., D5. *New York Times Ondisc* [CD-ROM], UMI-ProQuest, March 1999.

Lewis, Peter H. "Many Updates Cause Profitable Confusion." *New York Times*, 21 January 1999, national ed., D1, D5. *New York Times Ondisc* [CD-ROM]. UMI-ProQuest, March 1999.

A source not published in print:

17. "Vanguard Forecasts," *Business Outlook* [CD-ROM], Information Access, March 1998.

"Vanguard Forecasts." *Business Outlook* [CD-ROM]. Information Access, March 1998.

18. A SOURCE ON A NONPERIODICAL CD-ROM

18. Mary Wollstonecraft Shelley, *Frankenstein*, *Classic Library* [CD-ROM] (Alameda, Calif.: Andromeda, 1993).

Shelley, Mary Wollstonecraft. *Frankenstein*. *Classic Library* [CD-ROM]. Alameda, Calif.: Andromeda, 1993.

19. AN ONLINE BOOK

19. Jane Austen, *Emma* [book online], ed. Ronald Blythe (Harmondsworth, Eng.: Penguin, 1972, accessed 15 December 1998), *Oxford Text Archive;* available from ftp://ota.ox.ac.uk/public/english/Austen/emma.1519; Internet.

Austen, Jane. *Emma* [book online]. Edited by Ronald Blythe. Harmondsworth, Eng.: Penguin, 1972. Accessed 15 December 1998. *Oxford Text Archive*. Available from ftp://ota.ox.ac.uk/public/english/Austen/emma.1519; Internet.

20. AN ARTICLE IN AN ONLINE PERIODICAL

20. Andrew Palfrey, "Choice of Mates in Identical Twins," *Modern Psychology* 4, no. 1 (1996): par. 10 [journal online]; available from http://www.liasu.edu/modpsy/palfrey4(1).htm; Internet; accessed 25 February 1997.

Palfrey, Andrew. "Choice of Mates in Identical Twins." *Modern Psychology* 4, no. 1 (1996): 12 pars. [journal online]. Available from http://www.liasu.edu/modpsy/palfrey4(1).htm; Internet. Accessed 25 February 1997.

40b

Chic

21. An online database

21. *Scots Teaching and Research Network* [database online], ed. John Corbett (Glasgow: University of Glasgow, 2 February 1998, accessed 5 March 1998); available from http://www.arts.gla.ac.uk/www/comet/starn.htm; Internet.

Scots Teaching and Research Network [database online]. Edited by John Corbett. Glasgow: University of Glasgow, 2 February 1998. Accessed 5 March 1998. Available from http://www.arts.gla.ac.uk/www/comet/starn.htm; Internet.

Other sources

22. A government publication

22. House, *Medicare Payment for Outpatient Physical and Occupational Therapy Services*, 102d Cong., 1st sess., 1991, H. Doc. 409, 12-13.

U.S. Congress. House. *Medicare Payment for Outpatient Physical and Occupational Therapy Services*. 102d Cong., 1st sess., 1991. H. Doc. 409.

23. A letter

A published letter:

23. Mrs. Laura E. Buttolph to Rev. and Mrs. C. C. Jones, 20 June 1857, *The Children of Pride: A True Story of Georgia and the Civil War*, ed. Robert Manson Myers (New Haven: Yale University Press, 1972), 334.

Buttolph, Mrs. Laura E. Letter to Rev. and Mrs. C. C. Jones, 20 June 1857. In *The Children of Pride: A True Story of Georgia and the Civil War*, ed. Robert Manson Myers. New Haven: Yale University Press, 1972.

**40b
Chic**

A personal letter:

23. Ann E. Packer, letter to author, 15 June 1998.

Packer, Ann E. Letter to author. 15 June 1998.

24. An interview

24. Warren Christopher, interview by William Lindon, *Frontline*, Public Broadcasting System, 13 February 1998.

Christopher, Warren. Interview by William Lindon. *Frontline*. Public Broadcasting System, 13 February 1998.

25. A work of art

25. John Singer Sargent, *In Switzerland*, watercolor, 1908, Metropolitan Museum of Art, New York.

Sargent, John Singer. *In Switzerland*, watercolor, 1908. Metropolitan Museum of Art, New York.

26. A FILM OR VIDEO RECORDING

> 26. *Serenade*, George Balanchine, San Francisco Ballet, PBS Video, 1985, videocassette.

Serenade. George Balanchine. San Francisco Ballet. PBS Video, 1985. Videocassette.

27. A SOUND RECORDING

> 27. Johannes Brahms, *Concerto no. 2 in B-flat*, Artur Rubinstein, Philadelphia Orchestra, Eugene Ormandy, RCA BRC4-6731, 1992.

Brahms, Johannes. *Concerto no. 2 in B-flat*. Artur Rubinstein. Philadelphia Orchestra. Eugene Ormandy. RCA BRC4-6731, 1992.

Two or more citations of the same source

Reference to the same source cited in the preceding note:

> 8. Janet Lever, "Sex Differences in the Games Children Play," *Social Problems* 23 (1976): 482.

> 9. Ibid., 483.

Reference to a source cited earlier than the preceding note:

> 1. Carol Gilligan, *In a Different Voice: Psychological Theory and Women's Development* (Cambridge: Harvard University Press, 1982), 27.

> 2. Carol Gilligan, "Moral Development in the College Years," *The Modern American College*, ed. A. Chickering (San Francisco: Jossey-Bass, 1981), 286.

> 3. Gilligan, *In a Different Voice*, 47.

Omit the shortened title if you are using only one source by the cited author(s).

41
APA

41
APA DOCUMENTATION STYLE

The documentation style of the American Psychological Association is used in psychology and some other social sciences and is very similar to the styles in sociology, economics, and other disciplines. The following adapts the APA style from the *Publication Manual of the American Psychological Association*, 4th ed. (1994).

NOTE The APA provides occasional updates of its style and answers to frequently asked questions at its Web site at *http://www.apa.org/journals/acorner.html*. For a fee, the

APA site also offers *APA-Style Helper,* a student's companion to the *Publication Manual* that formats papers and source citations in APA style.

41a. APA parenthetical citations

Citation formats

In the APA style, parenthetical citations in the text refer to a list of sources at the end of the text. The basic parenthetical citation contains the author's last name and the date of publication; for direct quotations and other specific borrowings, it also contains the page number.

1. AUTHOR NOT NAMED IN YOUR TEXT

One critic of Milgram's experiments insisted that the subjects "should have been fully informed of the possible effects on them" (Baumrind, 1968, p. 34).

2. AUTHOR NAMED IN YOUR TEXT

Baumrind (1968) insisted that the subjects in Milgram's study "should have been fully informed of the possible effects on them" (p. 34).

3. A WORK WITH TWO AUTHORS

Pepinsky and DeStefano (1987) demonstrate that a teacher's language often reveals hidden biases.

One study (Pepinsky & DeStefano, 1987) demonstrates hidden biases in a teacher's language.

41a
APA

APA Parenthetical Citations

4. A WORK WITH THREE TO FIVE AUTHORS

First reference:

Pepinsky, Dunn, Rentl, and Corson (1993) further demonstrate the biases evident in gestures.

Later references:

In the work of Pepinsky et al. (1993), the loaded gestures include head shakes and eye contact.

5. A WORK WITH SIX OR MORE AUTHORS

One study (Rutter et al., 1996) attempts to explain these geographical differences in adolescent experience.

6. A WORK WITH A CORPORATE AUTHOR

An earlier prediction was even more somber (Lorenz Research, 1997).

7. AN ANONYMOUS WORK

One article ("Right to Die," 1976) noted that a death-row inmate may crave notoriety.

8. ONE OF TWO OR MORE CITED WORKS BY THE SAME AUTHOR(S) PUBLISHED IN THE SAME YEAR

At about age seven, most children begin to use appropriate gestures to reinforce their stories (Gardner, 1973a, pp. 144-145).

(See the reference for this source on p. 172.)

9. TWO OR MORE WORKS BY DIFFERENT AUTHORS

Two studies (Herskowitz, 1994; Marconi & Hamblen, 1990) found that periodic safety instruction can dramatically reduce employees' accidents.

10. A SOURCE REFERRED TO BY ANOTHER SOURCE

Supporting data appear in a study by Wong (cited in Marconi & Hamblen, 1990).

11. AN ELECTRONIC SOURCE

Electronic sources can be cited like printed sources, usually with the author's last name and the publication date. For electronic sources that number paragraphs instead of pages, provide that information in the text citation, substituting "par." (or "pars.") for "p." (or "pp.").

41a
APA

Ferguson and Hawkins (1998) did not anticipate the "evident hostility" of participants (par. 6).

If the source does not have numbering of any kind, provide just the author's name and the date.

Footnotes for supplementary content

When you need to explain something in your text—for instance, commenting on a source or providing data that don't fit into the relevant paragraph—you may place the supplementary information in a footnote. Follow the instructions for footnotes in the Chicago style (p. 158). Be careful not to overuse such notes: they can be more distracting than helpful.

41b. APA reference list

In APA style, the in-text parenthetical citations refer to the list of sources at the end of the text. In this list, titled "References," you include full publication information on every source cited in your paper. The reference list falls at the end of the paper, numbered in sequence with the preceding pages. The sample below shows the elements and their spacing.

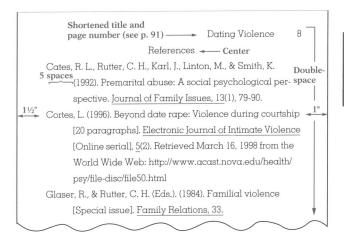

ARRANGEMENT Arrange sources alphabetically by the author's last name or, if there is no author, by the first main word of the title.

SPACING Double-space all entries.

INDENTION Use an appropriate indention for each entry. For papers that will be published, the APA recommends indenting the first line of each entry five to seven spaces, like so:

Rodriguez, R. (1982). <u>A hunger of memory: The education of Richard Rodriguez.</u> Boston: Godine.

When set into type for publication, the initial indentions are then converted into so-called hanging indentions, in which the first line is not indented while the others are. The hanging indention makes it easier for readers to spot authors' names, so the APA recognizes that students who are preparing final copy (not destined for publication) may wish to use the hanging indention for their references, like so:

Rodriguez, R. (1982). <u>A hunger of memory: The education of Richard Rodriguez.</u> Boston: Godine.

Because it is clearer for readers, the hanging indention is used in the sample on the previous page and in the following models for references, with a five-space indention for the second and subsequent lines of each entry.

Ask your instructor which format he or she prefers.

AUTHORS List all authors with last-name first, separating names and parts of names with commas. Use initials for first and middle names. Use an ampersand (&) before the last author's name.

TITLES In titles of books and articles, capitalize only the first word of the title, the first word of the subtitle, and proper nouns;° all other words begin with small letters. In titles of journals, capitalize all significant words. Unless your instructor specifies italics, underline the titles of books and journals, along with any comma or period following. Do not underline or use quotation marks around the titles of articles.

CITY OF PUBLICATION For sources that are not periodicals (such as books or government publications), give the city of publication. The following American cities do not require state names as well: Baltimore, Boston, Chicago, Los Angeles, New York, Philadelphia, and San Francisco. Follow their names with a colon. For all other cities, add a comma after the city name and give the two-letter postal abbreviation of the state. Then put a colon after the state.

PUBLISHER'S NAME Also for nonperiodical sources, give the publisher's name after the place of publication and a colon. Use shortened names for many publishers (such as

APA References

41b
APA

"Morrow" for William Morrow), and omit "Co.," "Inc.," and "Publishers." However, give full names for associations, corporations, and university presses (such as "Harvard University Press"), and do not omit "Books" or "Press" from a publisher's name.

PAGE NUMBERS Use the abbreviation "p." or "pp." before page numbers in books and in newspapers, but *not* in other periodicals. For inclusive page numbers, include all figures: "667–668."

PUNCTUATION Separate the parts of the reference (author, date, title, and publication information) with a period and one space. Do not use a final period in references to electronic sources, which conclude with an electronic address (see pp. 174–75).

Books

1. A BOOK WITH ONE AUTHOR

Rodriguez, R. (1982). A hunger of memory: The education of Richard Rodriguez. Boston: Godine.

2. A BOOK WITH TWO OR MORE AUTHORS

Nesselroade, J. R., & Baltes, P. B. (1979). Longitudinal research in the study of behavioral development. New York: Academic Press.

3. A BOOK WITH AN EDITOR

Dohrenwend, B. S., & Dohrenwend, B. P. (Eds.). (1974). Stressful life events: Their nature and effects. New York: Wiley.

4. A BOOK WITH A TRANSLATOR

Trajan, P. D. (1927). Psychology of animals. (H. Simone, Trans.). Washington, DC: Halperin.

5. A BOOK WITH A CORPORATE AUTHOR

Lorenz Research, Inc. (1997). Research in social studies teaching. Baltimore: Arrow Books.

6. AN ANONYMOUS BOOK

Merriam-Webster's collegiate dictionary (10th ed.). (1997). Springfield, MA: Merriam-Webster.

7. TWO OR MORE WORKS BY THE SAME AUTHOR(S) PUBLISHED IN THE SAME YEAR

Gardner, H. (1973a). The arts and human development. New York: Wiley.

Gardner, H. (1973b). <u>The quest for mind: Piaget, Lévi-Strauss, and the structuralist movement.</u> New York: Knopf.

8. A LATER EDITION

Bollinger, D. L. (1975). <u>Aspects of language</u> (2nd ed.). New York: Harcourt Brace Jovanovich.

9. A WORK IN MORE THAN ONE VOLUME

Reference to a single volume:

Lincoln, A. (1953). <u>The collected works of Abraham Lincoln</u> (R. P. Basler, Ed.). (Vol. 5). New Brunswick, NJ: Rutgers University Press.

Reference to all volumes:

Lincoln, A. (1953). <u>The collected works of Abraham Lincoln</u> (R. P. Basler, Ed.). (Vols. 1-8). New Brunswick, NJ: Rutgers University Press.

10. AN ARTICLE OR CHAPTER IN AN EDITED BOOK

Paykel, E. S. (1974). Life stress and psychiatric disorder: Applications of the clinical approach. In B. S. Dohrenwend & B. P. Dohrenwend (Eds.), <u>Stressful life events: Their nature and effects</u> (pp. 239-264). New York: Wiley.

Periodicals: Journals, magazines, newspapers

41b
APA

11. AN ARTICLE IN A JOURNAL WITH CONTINUOUS PAGINATION THROUGHOUT THE ANNUAL VOLUME

Emery, R. E. (1992). Marital turmoil: Interpersonal conflict and the children of divorce. <u>Psychological Bulletin, 92,</u> 310-330.

12. AN ARTICLE IN A JOURNAL THAT PAGES ISSUES SEPARATELY

Dacey, J. (1998). Management participation in corporate buy-outs. <u>Management Perspectives, 7</u>(4), 20-31.

13. AN ABSTRACT OF A JOURNAL ARTICLE

Emery, R. E. (1992). Marital turmoil: Interpersonal conflict and the children of divorce. <u>Psychological Bulletin, 92,</u> 310-330. (From <u>Psychological Abstracts,</u> 1992, <u>78,</u> Abstract No. 8624A).

14. AN ARTICLE IN A MAGAZINE

Van Gelder, L. (1986, December). Countdown to motherhood:
When should you have a baby? Ms., 37-39.

15. AN ARTICLE IN A NEWSPAPER

Lewis, P. H. (1999, January 21). Many updates cause profitable
confusion. The New York Times, pp. D1, D5.

16. AN UNSIGNED ARTICLE

The right to die. (1976, October 11). Time, 121, 101.

17. A REVIEW

Dinnage, R. (1987, November 29). Against the master and
his men [Review of the book A mind of her own: The
life of Karen Horney]. The New York Times Book Review,
10-11.

Electronic sources

The APA *Publication Manual* includes a few models
for electronic sources. More recently, the APA Web site
(see p. 166) has added new models that extend and in
some ways alter those in the *Publication Manual*. The following examples reflect the more recent guidelines when
appropriate.

Two sources provide more models for electronic sources
based on APA style. Each one also differs from APA style,
however, so ask your instructor which style you should use.

- Columbia online style for the sciences is discussed in
  this book's Chapter 43, page 184. The differences between APA and Columbia are outlined on pages 190–91.
- Xia Li and Nancy B. Crane's *Electronic Style: A Guide
  to Citing Electronic Information* (1993) was a source
  for the APA *Publication Manual*. Li and Crane's formats have since been updated at *http://www.uvm.edu/
  ncrane/estyles/apa.html.*

NOTE Since APA sources do not specify how to break
electronic addresses in references, follow MLA style (p.
152): break only after slashes, and do not hyphenate.

18. A PERIODICAL ARTICLE ON CD-ROM

Emery, R. E. (1992). Marital turmoil: Interpersonal conflict and the
children of divorce [CD-ROM]. Psychological Bulletin, 92, 310-
330. (ERIC Document Reproduction Service No. EJ 426 821)

19. AN ABSTRACT ON **CD-ROM**

Willard, B. L. (1992). <u>Changes in occupational safety standards,</u>
<u>1970-1990</u> [CD-ROM]. Abstract from: UMI-ProQuest File:
Dissertation Abstracts Item: 7770763

20. AN ARTICLE IN AN ONLINE JOURNAL

Palfrey, A. (1996, January). Choice of mates in identical twins.
<u>Modern Psychology</u> [Online serial], <u>4</u>(1). Retrieved Febru-
ary 25, 1997 from the World Wide Web: http://
www.liasu.edu/modpsy/palfrey4(1).htm

21. AN ARTICLE IN AN ONLINE NEWSPAPER

Still, L. (1996, March 3). On the battlefields of business, millions of
casualties. <u>The New York Times on the Web</u> [Online news-
paper]. Retrieved August 17, 1996 from the World Wide
Web: http://www.nytimes.com/specials/downsize/
03down1.htm

22. A RETRIEVABLE ONLINE POSTING

Include postings to listservs and newsgroups in your list
of references only if they are retrievable by others. The
following source is archived and thus retrievable.

Tourville, M. (1998, January 6). European currency reform. <u>Inter-</u>
<u>national Finance Discussion List</u> [Online]. Retrieved Janu-
ary 8, 1999 from the World Wide Web: http://
www.liasu.edu/finance-dl/46732

23. A NONRETRIEVABLE ONLINE POSTING

Personal electronic mail and other online postings that are
not retrievable by others should be cited only in your text.

At least one member of the research team had expressed reser-
vations about the design of the study (L. Kogod, personal communication, February 6, 1999).

24. AN ONLINE DATABASE

Barbour, J. (1998, February 2). The Brus. In J. Corbett (Ed.), <u>Scots</u>
<u>teaching and research network</u> [Online database]. Re-
trieved March 5, 1998 from the World Wide Web:
http://www.arts.gla.ac.uk/www/comet/starn/poetry/brus/
contents.htm

41b
APA

25. SOFTWARE

Project scheduler 8000 [Computer software]. (1999). Orlando, FL:
    Scitor.

Other sources

26. A REPORT

Gerald, K. (1958). Micro-moral problems in obstetric care (Report
    No. NP-71). St. Louis: Catholic Hospital Association.

Jolson, M. K. (1981). Music education for preschoolers (Report No.
    TC-622). New York: Teachers College, Columbia University.
    (ERIC Document Reproduction Service No. ED 264 488)

27. A GOVERNMENT PUBLICATION

U.S. Commission on Civil Rights. (1983). Greater Baltimore com-
    mitment. Washington, DC: Author.

28. AN ABSTRACT OF AN UNPUBLISHED DISSERTATION

Steciw, S. K. (1986). Alterations to the Pessac project of Le Cor-
    busier (Doctoral dissertation, University of Michigan, 1986).
    Dissertation Abstracts International, 46, 565B.

29. AN INTERVIEW

Brisick, W. C. (1988, July 1). [Interview with Ishmael Reed]. Pub-
    lishers Weekly, 41-42.

30. A VIDEOTAPE, RECORDING, OR OTHER AUDIOVISUAL SOURCE

Spielberg, S. (Director). (1993). Schindler's list [Videotape]. Los
    Angeles: Viacom.

Siberry, J. (1995). Caravan. On Maria [CD]. Burbank, CA: Reprise.

**42
CBE**

42
CBE DOCUMENTATION STYLE

Writers in the life sciences, physical sciences, and
mathematics rely for documentation style on *Scientific
Style and Format: The CBE Style Manual for Authors, Editors, and Publishers,* 6th ed. (1994). (CBE is the Council of
Biology Editors.) This book details two styles of in-text ci-

tation: one using author and date (see 42a) and one using numbers (see 42b). Both types of text citation refer to a list of references at the end of the paper (see 42c). Ask your instructor which style you should use.

42a. CBE name-year citations

In the CBE name-year style, parenthetical text citations provide the last name of the author being cited and the source's year of publication. At the end of the paper, a list of references, arranged alphabetically by authors' last names, provides complete information on each source. (See p. 178.)

The CBE name-year style closely resembles the APA name-year style detailed on pages 167–69. You can follow the APA examples for in-text citations, making several notable changes for CBE:

- Do not use a comma to separate the author's name and the date: (Baumrind 1968, p. 34).
- For sources with two authors, separate their names with "and" (not "&"): (Pepinsky and DeStefano 1987).
- For sources with three or more authors, use "and others" (not "et al.") after the first author's name: (Rutter and others 1996).
- For anonymous sources, give the author as "Anonymous" both in the citation and in the list of references: (Anonymous 1976).

42b. CBE number citations

In the CBE number style, raised numbers in the text refer to a numbered list of references at the end of the paper.

Two standard references[1,2] use this term.

These forms of immunity have been extensively researched.[3]

According to one report,[4] research into some forms of viral immunity is almost nonexistent.

Hepburn and Tatin[2] do not discuss this project.

ASSIGNMENT OF NUMBERS The number for each source is based on the order in which you cite the source in the text: the first cited source is 1, the second is 2, and so on.

REUSE OF NUMBERS When you cite a source you have already cited and numbered, use the original number again (see the last example above, which reuses the number 2 from the first example).

42b
CBE

This reuse is the key difference between the CBE numbered citations and numbered references to footnotes or endnotes (pp. 157–59). In the CBE style, each source has only one number, determined by the order in which the source is cited. With notes, in contrast, the numbering proceeds in sequence, so that sources have as many numbers as they have citations in the text.

CITATION OF TWO OR MORE SOURCES When you cite two or more sources at once, arrange their numbers in sequence and separate them with a comma and no space, as in the first example on the previous page.

42c. CBE reference list

For both the name-year and the number styles of in-text citation, provide a list, titled "References," of all sources you have cited. Format the page as shown for APA references on page 169 (but you may omit the shortened title before the page number).

Follow these guidelines for references, noting the important differences in name-year and number styles:

SPACING Single-space each entry, and double-space between entries.

ARRANGEMENT The two styles differ in their arrangement of entries:

NAME-YEAR STYLE

Arrange entries alphabetically by authors' last names.

NUMBER STYLE

Arrange entries in numerical order—that is, in order of their citation in the text.

FORMAT In both styles, begin the first line of each entry at the left margin and indent subsequent lines:

NAME-YEAR STYLE

Hepburn PX, Tatin JM. 1995. Human physiology. New York: Columbia Univ Pr. 1026 p.

NUMBER STYLE

2. Hepburn PX, Tatin JM. Human physiology. New York: Columbia Univ Pr; 1995. 1026 p.

AUTHORS List each author's name with the last name first, followed by initials for first and middle names. (See the examples above.) Do not use a comma after the last name or periods or space with the initials. Do use a comma to separate authors' names.

PLACEMENT OF DATES The two styles differ, as shown in the examples on the facing page.

NAME-YEAR STYLE

The date follows the author's or authors' names.

NUMBER STYLE

The date follows the publication information (for a book) or the title (for a periodical).

JOURNAL TITLES Do not underline or italicize journal titles. For titles of two or more words, abbreviate words of six or more letters (without periods) and omit most prepositions,° articles,° and conjunctions.° Capitalize each word. For example, *Annals of Medicine* becomes Ann Med, and *Journal of Chemical and Biochemical Studies* becomes J Chem Biochem Stud. See the Rowell examples below.

BOOK AND ARTICLE TITLES Do not underline, italicize, or quote a book or an article title. Capitalize only the first word and any proper nouns.° See the Hepburn and Tatin examples opposite and the Rowell examples below.

PUBLICATION INFORMATION FOR JOURNAL ARTICLES Both the name-year and the number styles give the journal's volume number, a colon, and the inclusive page numbers of the article: 28:329-33 in the examples below. (If the journal has an issue number, it follows the volume number in parentheses: 62(2):26-40.) However, the styles differ in the punctuation as well as the placement of the date:

42c
CBE

NAME-YEAR STYLE

The date, after the author's name and a period, is followed by a period:

Rowell LB. 1996. Blood pressure regulation during exercise. Ann Med 28:329-33.

NUMBER STYLE

The date, after the journal title and a space, is followed by a semicolon:

3. Rowell LB. Blood pressure regulation during exercise. Ann Med 1996;28:329-33.

The following examples show both a name-year reference and a number reference for each type of source.

CBE References

42c
CBE

Books

1. A BOOK WITH ONE AUTHOR

Gould SJ. 1987. Time's arrow, time's cycle. Cambridge: Harvard Univ Pr. 222 p.

 1. Gould SJ. Time's arrow, time's cycle. Cambridge: Harvard Univ Pr; 1987. 222 p.

2. A BOOK WITH TWO TO TEN AUTHORS

Hepburn PX, Tatin JM. 1995. Human physiology. New York: Columbia Univ Pr. 1026 p.

 2. Hepburn PX, Tatin JM. Human physiology. New York: Columbia Univ Pr; 1995. 1026 p.

3. A BOOK WITH MORE THAN TEN AUTHORS

Evans RW, Bowditch L, Dana KL, Drummond A, Wildovitch WP, Young SL, Mills P, Mills RR, Livak SR, Lisi OL, and others.

1998. Organ transplants: ethical issues. Ann Arbor: Univ of Michigan Pr. 498 p.

3. Evans RW, Bowditch L, Dana KL, Drummond A, Wildovitch WP, Young SL, Mills P, Mills RR, Livak SR, Lisi OL, and others. Organ transplants: ethical issues. Ann Arbor: Univ of Michigan Pr; 1998. 498 p.

4. A BOOK WITH AN EDITOR

Jonson P, editor. 1997. Anatomy yearbook. Los Angeles: Anatco. 628 p.

4. Jonson P, editor. Anatomy yearbook. Los Angeles: Anatco; 1997. 628 p.

5. A SELECTION FROM A BOOK

Krigel R, Laubenstein L, Muggia F. 1997. Kaposi's sarcoma. In: Ebbeson P, Biggar RS, Melbye M, editors. AIDS: a basic guide for clinicians. 2nd ed. Philadelphia: WB Saunders. p 100-26.

5. Krigel R, Laubenstein L, Muggia F. Kaposi's sarcoma. In: Ebbeson P, Biggar RS, Melbye M, editors. AIDS: a basic guide for clinicians. 2nd ed. Philadelphia: WB Saunders; 1997. p 100-26.

6. AN ANONYMOUS WORK

[Anonymous]. 1992. Health care for multiple sclerosis. New York: US Health Care. 86 p.

6. [Anonymous]. Health care for multiple sclerosis. New York: US Health Care; 1992. 86 p.

7. TWO OR MORE CITED WORKS BY THE SAME AUTHOR PUBLISHED IN THE SAME YEAR

Gardner H. 1973a. The arts and human development. New York: J Wiley. 406 p.

Gardner H. 1973b. The quest for mind: Piaget, Lévi-Strauss, and the structuralist movement. New York: AA Knopf. 492 p.

(The number style does not require such forms.)

Periodicals: Journals, magazines, newspapers

8. AN ARTICLE IN A JOURNAL WITH CONTINUOUS PAGINATION THROUGHOUT THE ANNUAL VOLUME

Ancino R, Carter KV, Elwin DJ. 1983. Factors contributing to viral immunity: a review of the research. Dev Biol 30:156-9.

8. Ancino R, Carter KV, Elwin DJ. Factors contributing to viral immunity: a review of the research. Dev Biol 1983;30:156-9.

42c CBE

9. An article in a journal that pages issues separately

Kim P. 1986 Feb. Medical decision making for the dying. Milbank
    Quar 64(2):26-40.

  9. Kim P. Medical decision making for the dying. Milbank Quar
      1986 Feb;64(2):26-40.

10. An article in a newspaper

Krauthammer C. 1986 June 13. Lifeboat ethics: the case of Baby
    Jesse. Washington Post;Sect A:33(col 1).

  10. Krauthammer C. Lifeboat ethics: the case of Baby Jesse.
       Washington Post 1986 June 13;Sect A:33(col 1).

11. An article in a magazine

Van Gelder L. 1986 Dec. Countdown to motherhood: when
    should you have a baby? Ms.:37-9.

  11. Van Gelder L. Countdown to motherhood: when should you
       have a baby? Ms. 1986 Dec:37-9.

Electronic sources

The CBE's *Scientific Style and Format* includes just a
few models for electronic sources, and they form the basis of the following examples. For additional models and
simpler formats, you can use Columbia online style for
the sciences, discussed in Chapter 43. Pages 191–92 show
how to adapt Columbia style to the CBE styles (both
name-year and number) and details the differences between the styles. Ask your instructor which style you
should use.

Note Since the CBE does not specify how to break
electronic addresses, follow **MLA** style (p. 152): break
only after slashes, and do not hyphenate.

42c
CBE

12. A source on CD-ROM

Reich WT, editor. 1998. Encyclopedia of bioethics [CD-ROM]. New
    York: Co-Health.

  12. Reich WT, editor. Encyclopedia of bioethics [CD-ROM]. New
       York: Co-Health; 1998.

13. An online journal article

Grady GF. 1993 May 2. The here and now of hepatitis B immu-
    nization. Today's Med [serial online]. Available from:
    http://www.fmrt.org/todaysmedicine/Grady050293.html.
    Accessed 1997 Dec 27.

13. Grady GF. The here and now of hepatitis B immunization. Today's Med [serial online] 1993 May 2. Available from: http://www.fmrt.org/todaysmedicine/Grady050293.html. Accessed 1997 Dec 27.

14. AN ONLINE BOOK

Ruch BJ, Ruch DB. 1999. Homeopathy and medicine: resolving the conflict [book online]. New York: Albert Einstein Coll of Medicine. Available from: http://www.einstein.edu/medicine/books/ruch.html. Accessed 1999 Jan 28.

14. Ruch BJ, Ruch DB. Homeopathy and medicine: resolving the conflict [book online]. New York: Albert Einstein Coll of Medicine; 1999. Available from: http://www.einstein.edu/medicine/books/ruch.html. Accessed 1999 Jan 28.

15. COMPUTER SOFTWARE

Project scheduler 8000 [computer program]. 1999. Version 4.1. Orlando (FL): Scitor. 1 computer disk: 3 1/2 in. Accompanied by: 1 manual. System requirements: IBM PC or fully compatible computer; DOS 6.0 or higher; Windows 3.1 or higher; 8 MB RAM; hard disk with a minimum of 2 MB of free space.

15. Project scheduler 8000 [computer program]. Version 4.1. Orlando (FL): Scitor; 1999. 1 computer disk: 3 1/2 in. Accompanied by: 1 manual. System requirements: IBM PC or fully compatible computer; DOS 6.0 or higher; Windows 3.1 or higher; 8 MB RAM; hard disk with a minimum of 2 MB of free space.

**42c
CBE**

Other sources

16. A GOVERNMENT PUBLICATION

Committee on Science and Technology, House (US). 1991. Hearing on procurement and allocation of human organs for transplantation. 102nd Cong., 1st Sess. House Doc. nr 409.

16. Committee on Science and Technology, House (US). Hearing on procurement and allocation of human organs for transplantation. 102nd Cong., 1st Sess. House Doc. nr 409; 1991.

17. A NONGOVERNMENT REPORT

Warnock M. 1992. Report of the Committee on Fertilization and Embryology. Baylor University, Department of Embryology. Waco (TX): Baylor Univ. Report nr BU/DE.4261.

17. Warnock M. Report of the Committee on Fertilization and Embryology. Baylor University, Department of Embryology. Waco (TX): Baylor Univ; 1992. Report nr BU/DE.4261.

18. A SOUND RECORDING, VIDEO RECORDING, OR FILM

Teaching Media. 1993. Cell mitosis [videocassette]. White Plains (NY): Teaching Media. 1 videocassette: 40 min, sound, black and white, 1/2 in.

18. Cell mitosis [videocassette]. White Plains (NY): Teaching Media; 1993. 1 videocassette: 40 min, sound, black and white, 1/2 in.

43

COLUMBIA DOCUMENTATION STYLE FOR ONLINE SOURCES

The style manuals in many disciplines do not yet provide detailed guidelines for citing the many kinds of sources available on the Internet. In response, Janice R. Walker and Todd Taylor wrote *The Columbia Guide to Online Style,* published by Columbia University Press in 1998.

The Columbia Guide offers models for both the humanities and the sciences. The humanities models reflect MLA style (Chapter 39), and the science models reflect APA style (Chapter 41)—although there are differences in both cases. The Columbia models can also be adapted for the other two styles covered in this book: Chicago for the humanities (Chapter 40) and CBE for the sciences (Chapter 42).

NOTE The Web site for *The Columbia Guide* offers an overview of the humanities and science styles and updates. The address *http://www.columbia.edu/cu/cup/cgos/* will take you to the site.

43a
Col

43a. The elements of Columbia online style

Columbia style adapts MLA and APA styles, but it also stresses the likely and important elements that allow readers to trace online sources. These elements may be the same as those in conventional printed sources, but often they are not.

AUTHOR The author may be identified only by a login name (such as *jqsmith*) or a fictitious name (such as *c_major*). List the source by this name if it's all you can find, but take special care in evaluating and using such a source. (See pp. 128–30 on evaluating online sources.) Cite a source with no identifiable author by its title.

TITLE For the title of a complete work, such as a book or periodical, use italics rather than underlining. If your document were posted on the Web, underlining would signal a hypertext link. Also italicize the titles of online sites and the names of information services.

DATE OF ACCESS Online sources may change often, so always provide the date of your access so that readers know just which version you used. The date falls at the end of the citation, in parentheses, and in the format "day mo. year"—for instance, (31 Aug. 1998). If the source's publication or revision date and your access date are identical, use only the access date.

ELECTRONIC ADDRESS Always provide an online source's exact and complete electronic address—the complete path for readers to follow in retrieving the source themselves. The address falls just before the access date with no special introduction or additional punctuation—for instance, finance-dl@weg.isu.edu (31 Aug. 1998). Since Columbia style does not specify how to break long addresses within source citations, follow MLA style (p. 152): break only after slashes, and do not hyphenate.

43b. Online sources in the humanities

Columbia online style adapts most elements of MLA documentation (Chapter 39) to provide a thorough system for documenting online sources in the humanities.

- As in MLA style, a citation in the text provides the author's last name and the page or other number where the borrowed material appears—for instance, One researcher disagrees (Johnson, 143) or Johnson disagrees (143). (See pp. 143–45 for a variety of examples.) However, because many online sources do not use page, paragraph, section, or other numbers, in-text citations of electronic sources may consist only of the author's name.

- Also as in MLA style, a list titled "Works Cited" at the end of your paper arranges your sources alphabetically by the author's last name, or by the first main word of the title if there is no author.

Key differences from MLA style

Columbia online style differs from MLA style (pp. 146–57) in several ways:

COLUMBIA ONLINE STYLE	MLA STYLE
The publication medium is not specially identified.	The publication medium—for instance, "Online posting"—often appears after the title.

COLUMBIA ONLINE STYLE	MLA STYLE
Titles of complete works (books, journals) are italicized.	Titles of complete works are underlined.
The electronic address precedes the date of your access and is not enclosed in angle brackets: finance-dl@weg.isu.edu (23 Feb. 1997).	The electronic address follows the date of your access and is enclosed in angle brackets: 23 Feb. 1997 <finance-dl@weg.isu.edu>.
The date of access is enclosed in parentheses.	The date of access is not enclosed in parentheses.

Ask your instructor which format you should use for online sources.

Chicago style

You can merge Columbia humanities style and Chicago humanities style (Chapter 40) to create citations for online sources that Chicago does not currently cover. The following note and works-cited models show such mergers, drawing on Chicago examples given on page 164.

FOOTNOTE OR ENDNOTE

15. Jane Austen, *Emma*, ed. Ronald Blythe (Harmondsworth, Eng.: Penguin, 1972). *Oxford Text Archive*. ftp://ota.ox.ac.uk/public/english/Austen/emma.1519 (15 Dec. 1998).

43b

Col

Columbia Works-Cited Models for the Humanities

WORKS-CITED ENTRY

Austen, Jane. *Emma*. Edited by Ronald Blythe. Harmondsworth, Eng.: Penguin, 1972. *Oxford Text Archive*.
ftp://ota.ox.ac.uk/public/english/Austen/emma.1519
(15 Dec. 1998).

These Columbia-Chicago mergers differ from the corresponding Chicago models on page 164 in several ways.

COLUMBIA ONLINE STYLE	**CHICAGO STYLE**
The publication medium is not specially identified.	The publication medium—for instance, "book online"—appears after the title in brackets.
The electronic address precedes the date of your access at the end of the entry, and neither is introduced. See the works-cited entry above.	The positions of the electronic address and the access date vary, and both are introduced. In the Chicago works-cited entry for the Austen book, the access date follows the publication date of 1972—Accessed 15 December 1997—and the address falls at the end of the entry—Available from ftp://ota.ox.ac.uk/public/english/Austen/emma.1519; Internet.
The date of access is enclosed in parentheses, and the month is abbreviated.	The date of access is not enclosed in parentheses, and the month is spelled out.

43b
Col

Ask your instructor which format you should use for
online sources.

Models of Columbia humanities style

1. A SITE ON THE WORLD WIDE WEB

Lederman, Leon. *Topics in Modern Physics--Lederman*. 10 Oct.
1997. http://www-ed.fnal.gov/samplers/hsphys/people/
lederman.html (12 Dec. 1997).

2. A REVISED OR MODIFIED SITE

Ruggira, Wendy. "Chiropractic: Past, Present and Future." *Chi-
romen.com*. Mod. 30 Sept. 1998. http://chiromen.com/
chiropractic.htm (4 Feb. 1999).

3. A BOOK

A book previously published in print:

James, Henry. *The Turn of the Screw.* New York: Scribner's,
1908–09. 1998. *American Literary Classics a Chapter a
Day.* http://www.americanliterature.com/TS/TSINDX.HTML
(4 Mar. 1998).

An original book:

Cooper, Phoebe, ed. *Sam and Daphne Maeglin: Selected Correspondence, 1940-1964.* 1999. http://www.alphabetica.org/
maeglin (21 Mar. 1999).

4. AN ARTICLE IN A PERIODICAL

Palfrey, Andrew. "Choice of Mates in Identical Twins." *Modern
Psychology* 4.1 (1996): 12 pars. http://www.liasu.edu/
modpsy/palfrey4(1).htm (25 Feb. 1997).

5. A GROUP OR ORGANIZATION AS AUTHOR

Exxon Corporation. "Managing Risk." *Environment, Health and
Safety Progress Report.* 1998. http://www.exxon.com/
exxoncorp/news/publications/safety_report/index.html
(6 Apr. 1999).

United States. Dept. of State. Bureau of Public Affairs. "History of
the National Security Council, 1947-1997." Aug. 1997.
http://www.whitehouse.gov/WH/EOP/NSC/html/
History.html (6 Feb. 1999).

6. A MAINTAINED OR COMPILED SITE

Scots Teaching and Research Network. Maint. John Corbett.
2 Feb. 1998. U of Glasgow. http://www.arts.gla.ac.uk/
www/comet/starn.htm (5 Mar. 1999).

7. A GRAPHIC, VIDEO, OR AUDIO FILE

Hamilton, Calvin J. "Components of Comets." 1997. *Space Art.*
wysisiwyg://94/http://spaceart.com/solar/eng/comet.htm
(20 Dec. 1998).

8. PERSONAL ELECTRONIC MAIL

Millon, Michele. "Re: Grief Therapy." Personal e-mail (4 May
1999).

9. A POSTING TO A LISTSERV

Tourville, Michael. "European Currency Reform." 6 Jan. 1998.
International Finance Discussion List.
finance-dl@weg.isu.edu (8 Jan. 1998).

10. A POSTING TO A NEWSGROUP OR FORUM

Cramer, Sherry. "Recent Investment Practices." 26 Mar. 1997.
news:biz.investment.current.2700 (3 Apr. 1997).

11. AN ARCHIVED POSTING

Tourville, Michael. "European Currency Reform." 6 Jan. 1998.
International Finance Discussion List. http://
www.weg.isu.edu/finance-dl/46732 (2 Feb. 1998).

12. AN ENCYCLOPEDIA

White, Geoffrey. "Ethnopsychology." *The MIT Encyclopedia of
Cognitive Sciences.* Ed. Rob Wilson and Frank Keil. Cambridge: MIT P, 1997. http://mitpress.mit.edu/MITECS/work/
whiteg_r.html (26 Mar. 1999).

13. A DATABASE

United States. Dept. of Health and Human Services. "Depression
Is a Treatable Illness: A Patient's Guide." Apr. 1993. *Health
Services Technology Assessment Texts.* No. 93-0533.
http://text.nlm.nih.gov/ftrs/
pick?collect=depp&cd=1&t=930533 (26 Sept. 1998).

**43b
Col**

14. A GOPHER OR FTP SITE

Provide directions to a specific source in one of two ways:
give the unique address of the file, as in the example
above; or give the address of the home page, a space, and
the path to the file, as in this example:

Goetsch, Sallie. "And What About Costume?" *Didaskalia:
Ancient Theatre Today* 2.2 (1995). gopher://
gopher.uwarwick.ac.uk Didaskalia/
Didaskalia: Ancient Theatre Today/1995/03Features/
Goetsch (26 May 1999).

15. A TELNET SITE

Johnson, Earl. "My House: Come In." *Houses of Cyberspace.*

7 Aug. 1998. telnet://edwin.ohms.bookso.com.7777 @go #50827, press 10 (11 Aug. 1998).

16. A SYNCHRONOUS COMMUNICATION

Wendy_Librarian_. "Online Integrity (#421)." *Internet Public Library MOO.* telnet://moo.ipl.org.8888 @go #421 (4 Jan. 1999).

17. SOFTWARE

Project Scheduler 8000. Vers. 4.1. Orlando: Scitor, 1999.

43c. Online sources in the sciences

Columbia style adapts most elements of APA style (Chapter 41) to provide a thorough system for documenting online sources in the social, natural, and applied sciences.

- As in APA style, a citation in the text provides the author's last name, the date of publication, and the page or other number where specific borrowings appear— for instance, One researcher called the study "deeply flawed" (Johnson, 1998, p. 143) or Johnson (1998) called the study "deeply flawed" (p. 143). (See pp. 167–69 for a variety of examples.) Because many online sources do not use page, paragraph, or other numbers, citations of specific borrowings from electronic sources often consist only of the author's name and the date.
- Also as in APA style, a list titled "References" at the end of your paper arranges your sources alphabetically by the author's last name, or by the first main word of the title if there is no author.

Key differences from APA style

Though it includes many more kinds of online sources than APA style currently does, Columbia style does differ from APA style (pp. 169–76) in several significant ways.

COLUMBIA ONLINE STYLE	APA STYLE
Titles of complete works (books, journals) are italicized.	Titles of complete works are underlined.
The publication medium is not specially identified.	The publication medium— for instance, "newspaper online"—often appears in brackets after the title.

COLUMBIA ONLINE STYLE	**APA STYLE**
A full publication date after the author's name is in the format "year, month day": 1999, December 12. All other dates are in the format "day mo. year": 12 Dec. 1999.	A full publication date after the author's name is in the format "year, month day": 1999, December 12. All other dates are in the format "month day, year": December 12, 1999.
The electronic address precedes the date of your access, with the date in parentheses—for instance, http://www.thinck.com/insec.html (21 Jan. 1998).	The electronic address follows the date of your access, and the two are linked in a statement—for instance, Retrieved January 21, 1998 from the World Wide Web: http://www.thinck.com/insec.html
A period ends the entry.	A period does not end the entry.

Ask your instructor which format you should use for online sources.

CBE style

CBE style (Chapter 42) currently provides few models for citing online sources. By merging Columbia science style and either the CBE name-year style or the CBE number style, you can create citations for kinds of sources not covered by CBE, such as the Web site below.

43c
Col

NAME-YEAR STYLE

Lederman L. 1997 Oct 10. Topics in modern physics--Lederman. http://www-ed.fnal.gov/samplers/hsphys/people/lederman.html (12 Dec. 1997).

NUMBER STYLE

4. Lederman L. Topics in modern physics--Lederman. 1997 Oct 10. http://www-ed.fnal.gov/samplers/hsphys/people/lederman.html (12 Dec. 1997).

Such a merger of Columbia and CBE styles involves some alterations in the CBE models shown on pages 180–84.

COLUMBIA ONLINE STYLE	**CBE STYLE**
The publication medium is not specially identified.	The publication medium—for instance, "serial online"—appears in brackets after the title.

COLUMBIA ONLINE STYLE	CBE STYLE
The electronic address and the date of your access are not introduced—for instance, finance-dl@weg.isu.edu (23 Feb. 1997).	Both the electronic address and the date of your access are introduced—for instance, Available from: finance-dl@weg.isu.edu. Accessed 1997 Feb 23.
The date of access is enclosed in parentheses and is in the format "day mo. year" (the month abbreviated with a period).	The date of access is not enclosed in parentheses and is in the format "year mo day" (the month abbreviated without a period).

Ask your instructor which format you should use for online sources.

Models of Columbia science style

1. A SITE ON THE WORLD WIDE WEB

Lederman, L. (1997, October 10). *Topics in modern physics--Lederman.* http://www-ed.fnal.gov/samplers/hsphys/people/lederman.html (12 Dec. 1997).

2. A REVISED OR MODIFIED SITE

Ruggira, W. (1998). Chiropractic: Past, present and future (Mod. 30 Sept. 1998). *Chiromen.com.* http://chiromen.com/chiropractic.htm (4 Feb. 1999).

3. A BOOK

A book previously published in print:

James, H. (1998). *The turn of the screw.* New York: Scribner's, 1908-1909. *American literary classics a chapter a day.* http://www.americanliterature.com/TS/TSINDX.HTML (4 Mar. 1998).

An original book:

Cooper, P. (Ed.). (1999). *Sam and Daphne Maeglin: Selected correspondence, 1940-1964.* http://www.alphabetica.org/maeglin (21 Mar. 1999).

4. AN ARTICLE IN A PERIODICAL

Palfrey, A. (1996). Choice of mates in identical twins. *Modern Psychology, 4*(1). http://www.liasu.edu/modpsy/palfrey4(1).htm (25 Feb. 1997).

Columbia Reference Models for the Sciences

5. A GROUP OR ORGANIZATION AS AUTHOR

Exxon Corporation. (1998). Managing risk. *Environment, health and safety progress report.* http://www.exxon.com/ exxoncorp/news/publications/safety_report/index.html (6 Apr. 1999).

U.S. Department of State. Bureau of Public Affairs. (1997, August). History of the National Security Council, 1947-1997. http://www.whitehouse.gov/WH/EOP/NSC/html/ History.html (6 Feb. 1999).

**43c
Col**

6. A MAINTAINED OR COMPILED SITE

Scots teaching and research network. (1998, February 2). (J. Corbett, Maint.). University of Glasgow. http:// www.arts.gla.ac.uk/www/comet/starn.html (5 Mar. 1999).

7. A GRAPHIC, VIDEO, OR AUDIO FILE

Hamilton, C. J. (1997). Components of comets [graphic file]. *Space art.* wysisiwyg://94/http://spaceart.com/solar/eng/comet/htm (20 Dec. 1998).

8. PERSONAL ELECTRONIC MAIL

Millon, M. Re: Grief therapy [personal e-mail]. (4 May 1999).

Note that **APA** style calls for citing nonretrievable sources only in your text (see p. 175).

9. A POSTING TO A LISTSERV

Tourville, M. (1998, January 6). European currency reform. *International finance discussion list.* finance-dl@weg.isu.edu (8 Jan. 1998).

Note that **APA** style calls for citing nonretrievable sources only in your text (see p. 175). Model 11 shows the format for an archived posting, which is retrievable.

10. A POSTING TO A NEWSGROUP OR FORUM

Cramer, S. (1997, March 26). Recent investment practices. news:biz.investment.current.2700 (3 Aug. 1997).

Note that **APA** style calls for citing nonretrievable sources only in your text (see p. 175). Model 11 shows the format for an archived posting, which is retrievable.

11. AN ARCHIVED POSTING

Tourville, M. (1998, January 6). European currency reform. *International finance discussion list.* http://www.weg.isu.edu/ finance-dl/46732 (2 Feb. 1998).

12. AN ENCYCLOPEDIA

White, G. (1997). Ethnopsychology. In R. Wilson & F. Keil (Eds.), *The MIT encyclopedia of cognitive sciences.* Cambridge, MA: MIT Press. http://mitpress.mit.edu/MITECS/work/ whiteg_r.html (26 Mar. 1999).

13. A DATABASE

U.S. Department of Health and Human Services. (1993, April). Depression is a treatable illness: A patient's guide. *Health services technology assessment texts* (No. 93-0533). http:// text.nlm.nih.gov/ftrs/pick?collect=depp&cd=1&t=930533 (26 Sept. 1998).

14. A GOPHER OR FTP SITE

Provide directions to a specific source in one of two ways: give the unique address of the file, as in the example above; or give the address of the home page, a space, and the path to the file, as in this example:

Goetsch, S. (1995). And what about costume? *Didaskalia: Ancient Theatre Today, 2*(2). gopher://gopher.warwicku.ac.uk Didaskalia/Didaskalia: Ancient Theatre Today/1995/ 03Features/Goetsch (26 May 1999).

15. A TELNET SITE

Johnson, E. (1998, August 7). My house: Come in. *Houses of cyberspace*. telnet://edwin.ohms.bookso.com.7777 @go #50827, press 10 (11 Aug. 1998).

16. A SYNCHRONOUS COMMUNICATION

Wendy_Librarian_. Online integrity (#421). *Internet Public Library MOO*. telnet://moo.ipl.org.8888 @go #421 (4 Jan. 1999).

17. SOFTWARE

Project scheduler 8000. (1999). Orlando, FL: Scitor.

43c
Col

WEB SITES FOR WRITING AND RESEARCH

The World Wide Web leads to a huge array of writing resources, both popular and scholarly. The sampling here covers the following topics:

The process of writing
Style, grammar, and punctuation
English as a second language
Document design
Job applications and business writing
Research writing
Citing sources
Online sources in the disciplines

The process of writing

The Online Writery
http://www.missouri.edu/~writery/
Paradigm Online Writing Assistant
http://www.powa.org/
Purdue Online Writing Lab
http://owl.english.purdue.edu/introduction.html
University of Texas Undergraduate Writing Center
http://uwc.fac.utexas.edu/resource/

Style, grammar, and punctuation

The Elements of Style
http://www.cc.columbia.edu:80/acis/bartleby/strunk
Frequently Asked Questions About Writing
http://www2.nu.edu/soas/writing/pages/faq.html
Grammar Girl's Guide to the English Language
http://www.geocities.com/Athens/Parthenon/1489/
Lynch: Guide to Grammar and Style
http://andromeda.rutgers.edu/~jlynch/Writing/
Punctuation Points
http://www.esc.edu/HTMLpages/Writer/pandg/
pmen1.htm
Readability, Clarity, and Style
http://web.calstatela.edu/centers/write_cn/style.htm

See http://www.awlonline.com/littlebrown for more online writing resources and for updates of those given here.

English as a second language

Dave's ESL Café
http://www.eslcafe.com/
English for Internet
http://www.study.com/
ESL Resources
http://www.esl.ohio-state.edu/comp/Resourc.htm
The LinguaCenter Grammar Safari
http://deil.lang.uiuc.edu/web.pages/
grammarsafari.html
The Virtual English Language Center
http://www.comenius.com/

Document design

The Fontsite
http://www.fontsite.com
Ten Common Typesetting Mistakes
http://vera.inforamp.net/~poynton/notes/typesetting/
The 39 Steps Online—A Manhattan College Style Sheet
http://www.manhattan.edu/arts/english/39steps.html
TypoGRAPHIC
http://typographic.rsub.com/index.cgi

Job applications and business writing

Jobweb Résumé Writing Tips
http://www.jobweb.org/catapult/guenov/restips.html
Purdue OWL Business Writing Resources
http://owl.english.purdue.edu/bw/bwresources/
bwresources.html
Résumé Writing Tips by Regina Pontow
http://www.provenresumes.com/

Research writing

PLANNING AND SEARCHING

Doing Research on the Web
http://www.cohums.ohio-state.edu/english/People/
Locker.1/research.htm
Research and Writing Step by Step
http://www.ipl.org/teen/aplus/stepfirst.htm
The Research Paper
http://www.wsu.edu:8080/~brains/general_handouts/
research_guide.html
Research Strategy
http://stauffer.queensu.ca/inforef/strategy.htm
Study Skills Guide
http://www2.csbsju.edu/advising/helplist.html

See also "Online Sources in the Disciplines," opposite.

EVALUATING SOURCES

Evaluating Quality on the Net
  http://www.tiac.net/users/hope/findqual.html
Thinking Critically About World Wide Web Resources
  http://www.library.ucla.edu/libraries/college/instruct/
  web/critical.htm
Using Cyber Sources
  http://www.devry-phx.edu/lrnresrc/dowsc/
  integrty.htm

Citing sources

MLA and APA Styles of Documentation
  http://web.calstatela.edu/centers/write_cn/
  document.htm
Purdue OWL's Documenting Electronic Sources
  http://owl.english.purdue.edu/writers/
  documenting.html
The Writing Center—Documentation Guide
  http://www.wisc.edu/writetest/Handbook/
  Documentation.html

Online sources in the disciplines

VIRTUAL LIBRARIES AND GENERAL REFERENCES

Internet Public Library
  http://www.ipl.org
The Library of Congress
  http://lcweb.loc.gov/
The WWW Virtual Library
  http://www.vlib.org/Home.html

ART

Internet Art Resources
  http://artseek.com/ArtSites/Sites.html
WebMuseum
  http://metalab.unc.edu/wm/paint/

BIOLOGY

Biological, Agricultural, and Medical Sciences
INFOMINE
  http://ranma.ucr.edu/bioag/
The Biology Project
  http://www.biology.arizona.edu/

BUSINESS AND ECONOMICS

Internet Business Library
  http://www.bschool.ukans.edu/IntBusLib/
WWW Resources in Economics
  http://www.helsinki.fi/WebEc/

CHEMISTRY

ChemCenter
  http://www.chemcenter.org/
ChemFinder
  http://www.chemfinder.com/

COMMUNICATION

Communication and Media Studies Database
  http://www.cultsock.ndirect.co.uk/MUHome/cshtml/
Gifts of Speech
  http://gos.sbc.edu/

COMPUTER SCIENCE

Free On-Line Dictionary of Computing
  http://www.nightflight.com/foldoc/
Virtual Computer Library
  http://www.utexas.edu/computer/vcl/

DANCE AND THEATER

McCoy's Guide to Theatre and Performance Studies
  http://www.stetson.edu/departments/csata/
  thr_guid.html
Online Ballet Dictionary
  http://www.abt.org/dictionary/

EDUCATION

Education World
  http://www.education-world.com/
EdWeb: Exploring Technology and School Reform
  http://edweb.gsn.org/

ENGINEERING

ICE: Internet Connections for Engineers
  http://www.englib.cornell.edu/ice/ice-index.html
Thermodynamics Research Library
  http://www.uic.edu/~mansoori/TRL_html

ENVIRONMENTAL SCIENCE

Conservation Databases
  http://www.wcmc.org.uk/cis/
Envirolink Library
  http://www.envirolink.org/library/index.html

ETHNIC OR GENDER STUDIES

Ethnic, Multiracial, and Race Relations on the Internet
  http://www.library.miami.edu/staff/lmc/socrace.html
Voice of the Shuttle Gender Studies Page
  http://humanitas.ucsb.edu/shuttle/gender.html

GEOLOGY

Cornell's Digital Earth
  http://atlas.geo.cornell.edu/

US Geological Survey
   http://info.er.usgs.gov/

HEALTH SCIENCES

Mayo Clinic Health Oasis
   http://www.mayohealth.org/
Medweb Medical Search Engine
   http://WWW.MedWeb.Emory.Edu/MedWeb/
The Sports Medicine Network
   http://www.sportsmedicine.com/

HISTORY

The History Place
   http://www.historyplace.com/
HyperHistory
   http://www.hyperhistory.com/online_n2/History_n2/
   a.html

LANGUAGES AND LITERATURE

Ethnologue Languages of the World
   http://www.sil.org/ethnologue/ethnologue.html
Project Gutenberg: Fine Literature Digitally
Republished
   http://www.promo.net/pg/
Voice of the Shuttle English Literature Page
   http://humanitas.ucsb.edu/shuttle/english.html

MATHEMATICS

Frequently Asked Questions in Mathematics
   http://www.cs.unb.ca/~alopez-o/math-faq/
   math-faq.html

MUSIC

ARCANA: Artists' Research, Composers' Aid, and
Network Access
   http://www.arcananet.org/

PHILOSOPHY AND RELIGION

Philosophy—Electronic Library
   http://www.mnsfld.edu/depts/philosop/aapt.html
Virtual Religion Index
   http://religion.rutgers.edu/links/vrindex.html

PHYSICS AND ASTRONOMY

The Internet Pilot to Physics
   http://physicsweb.org/TIPTOP/
The Astronomy Café
   http://www2.ari.net/home/odenwald/cafe.html

POLITICAL SCIENCE AND GOVERNMENT

American Law Sources Online
   http://www.lawsource.com/also/

The Federal Gateway: US Government Information Clearinghouse
   http://fedgate.org/
Political Science Research Page
   http://www.cudenver.edu/psrp/psrp.html

PSYCHOLOGY

Internet Mental Health
   http://www.mentalhealth.com/p.html
Psychcrawler
   http://www.psychcrawler.com/index1.html

SOCIOLOGY AND ANTHROPOLOGY

Anthropology Resources on the Internet
   http://www.ameranthassn.org/resinet.htm
The SocioWeb
   http://www.socioweb.com/~markbl/socioweb/

GLOSSARY OF USAGE

This glossary provides notes on words or phrases that often cause problems for writers. The recommendations for standard written English are based on current dictionaries and usage guides. Items labeled NONSTANDARD should be avoided in final drafts of academic and business writing. Those labeled COLLOQUIAL and SLANG appear in some informal writing and may occasionally be used for effect in more formal academic and career writing. (Words and phrases labeled *colloquial* include those labeled *informal* by many dictionaries.) See Chapter 5 for more on levels of language.

a, an   Use *a* before words beginning with consonant sounds: *a historian, a one-o'clock class, a university.* Use *an* before words that begin with vowel sounds, including silent *h*'s: *an orgy, an L, an honor.*

The article before an abbreviation depends on how the abbreviation is read: *She was once an AEC aide* (*AEC* is read as three separate letters); *Many Americans opposed a SALT treaty* (*SALT* is read as one word, *salt*).

See also pp. 52–54 on the uses of *a/an* versus *the.*

accept, except   *Accept* is a verb° meaning "receive." *Except* is usually a preposition° or conjunction° meaning "but for" or "other than"; when it is used as a verb, it means "leave out." *I can accept all your suggestions except the last one. I'm sorry you excepted my last suggestion from your list.*

advice, advise   *Advice* is a noun,° and *advise* is a verb.° *Take my advice; do as I advise you.*

affect, effect   Usually *affect* is a verb,° meaning "to influence," and *effect* is a noun, meaning "result": *The drug did not affect his driving; in fact, it seemed to have no effect at all.* (Note that *effect* occasionally is used as a verb meaning "to bring about": *Her efforts effected a change.* And *affect* is used in psychology as a noun meaning "feeling or emotion": *One can infer much about affect from behavior.*)

all ready, already   *All ready* means "completely prepared," and *already* means "by now" or "before now": *We were all ready to go to the movie, but it had already started.*

all right   *All right* is always two words. *Alright* is a common misspelling.

all together, altogether   *All together* means "in unison," or "gathered in one place." *Altogether* means "entirely." *It's not altogether true that our family never spends vacations all together.*

allusion, illusion   An *allusion* is an indirect reference, and an *illusion* is a deceptive appearance: *Paul's constant <u>allusions</u> to Shakespeare created the <u>illusion</u> that he was an intellectual.*

a lot   *A lot* is always two words, used informally to mean "many." *Alot* is a common misspelling.

among, between   In general, use *between* only for relationships of two and *among* for more than two.

amount, number   Use *amount* with a singular noun that names something not countable (a noncount noun°): *The <u>amount</u> of <u>food</u> varies.* Use *number* with a plural noun that names more than one of something countable (a count noun°): *The <u>number</u> of <u>calories</u> must stay the same.*

and/or   *And/or* indicates three options: one or the other or both (*The decision is made by the mayor <u>and/or</u> the council*). If you mean all three options, *and/or* is appropriate. Otherwise, use *and* if you mean both, *or* if you mean either.

anxious, eager   *Anxious* means "nervous" or "worried" and is usually followed by *about*. *Eager* means "looking forward" and is usually followed by *to*. *I've been <u>anxious about</u> getting blisters. I'm <u>eager</u> [not <u>anxious</u>] <u>to</u> get new cross-training shoes.*

anybody, any body; anyone, any one   *Anybody* and *anyone* are indefinite pronouns;° *any body* is a noun° modified by *any; any one* is a pronoun° or adjective° modified by *any. How can <u>anybody</u> communicate with <u>any body</u> of government? Can <u>anyone</u> help Amy? She has more work than <u>any one</u> person can handle.*

any more, anymore   *Any more* means "no more"; *anymore* means "now." Both are used in negative constructions: *He doesn't want <u>any more</u>. She doesn't live here <u>anymore</u>.*

anyways, anywheres   Nonstandard for *anyway* and *anywhere*.

are, is   Use *are* with a plural subject° (*books <u>are</u>*), *is* with a singular subject (*book <u>is</u>*). See pp. 40–42.

as   Substituting for *because, since,* or *while, as* may be vague or ambiguous: *<u>As</u> we were stopping to rest, we decided to eat lunch.* (Does *as* mean "while" or "because"?) *As* never should be used as a substitute for *whether* or *who. I'm not sure <u>whether</u> [not <u>as</u>] we can make it. That's the man <u>who</u> [not <u>as</u>] gave me directions.*

as, like   See *like, as*.

at this point in time   Wordy for *now, at this point,* or *at this time.*

awful, awfully Strictly speaking, *awful* means "awe-inspiring." As intensifiers meaning "very" or "extremely" (*He tried awfully hard*), *awful* and *awfully* should be avoided in formal speech or writing.

a while, awhile *Awhile* is an adverb;° *a while* is an article° and a noun.° *I will be gone awhile* [not *a while*]. *I will be gone for a while* [not *awhile*].

bad, badly In formal speech and writing, *bad* should be used only as an adjective;° the adverb° is *badly*. *He felt bad because his tooth ached badly*. In *He felt bad*, the verb *felt* is a linking verb° and the adjective *bad* modifies the subject° *he*, not the verb *felt*. See also p. 50.

being as, being that Colloquial for *because,* the preferable word in formal speech or writing: *Because* [not *Being as*] *the world is round, Columbus never did fall off the edge.*

beside, besides *Beside* is a preposition° meaning "next to." *Besides* is a preposition meaning "except" or "in addition to" as well as an adverb° meaning "in addition." *Besides, several other people besides you want to sit beside Dr. Christensen.*

between, among See *among, between.*

bring, take Use *bring* only for movement from a farther place to a nearer one and *take* for any other movement. *First, take these books to the library for renewal, then take them to Mr. Daniels. Bring them back to me when he's finished.*

can, may Strictly, *can* indicates capacity or ability, and *may* indicates permission: *If I may talk with you a moment, I believe I can solve your problem.*

climatic, climactic *Climatic* comes from *climate* and refers to weather: *Last winter's temperatures may indicate a climatic change. Climactic* comes from *climax* and refers to a dramatic high point: *During the climactic duel between Hamlet and Laertes, Gertrude drinks poisoned wine.*

complement, compliment To *complement* something is to add to, complete, or reinforce it: *Her yellow blouse complemented her black hair.* To *compliment* something is to make a flattering remark about it: *He complimented her on her hair. Complimentary* can also mean "free": *complimentary tickets.*

conscience, conscious *Conscience* is a noun° meaning "a sense of right and wrong"; *conscious* is an adjective° meaning "aware" or "awake." *Though I was barely conscious, my conscience nagged me.*

continual, continuous *Continual* means "constantly recurring": *Most movies on television are continually interrupted by commercials. Continuous* means "unceasing": *Some cable channels present movies continuously without commercials.*

could of   See *have, of.*

criteria   The plural of *criterion* (meaning "standard for judgment"): *Our criteria are strict. The most important criterion is a sense of humor.*

data   The plural of *datum* (meaning "fact"). Though *data* is often used as a singular noun, most careful writers still treat it as plural: *The data fail [not fails] to support the hypothesis.*

device, devise   *Device* is the noun,° and *devise* is the verb:° *Can you devise some device for getting his attention?*

different from, different than   *Different from* is preferred: *His purpose is different from mine.* But *different than* is widely accepted when a construction using *from* would be wordy: *I'm a different person now than I used to be* is preferable to *I'm a different person now from the person I used to be.*

disinterested, uninterested   *Disinterested* means "impartial": *We chose Pete, as a disinterested third party, to decide who was right. Uninterested* means "bored" or "lacking interest": *Unfortunately, Pete was completely uninterested in the question.*

don't   *Don't* is the contraction for *do not,* not for *does not: I don't care, you don't care,* and *he doesn't [not don't] care.*

due to   *Due* is an adjective° or noun;° thus *due to* is always acceptable as a subject complement:° *His gray hairs were due to age.* Many object to *due to* as a preposition° meaning "because of" (*Due to the holiday, class was canceled*). A rule of thumb is that *due to* is always correct after a form of the verb *be* but questionable otherwise.

eager, anxious   See *anxious, eager.*

effect   See *affect, effect.*

elicit, illicit   *Elicit* is a verb° meaning "bring out" or "call forth." *Illicit* is an adjective° meaning "unlawful." *The crime elicited an outcry against illicit drugs.*

emigrate, immigrate   *Emigrate* means "to leave one place and move to another": *The Chus emigrated from Korea. Immigrate* means "to move into a place where one was not born": *They immigrated to the United States.*

enthused   Sometimes used colloquially as an adjective° meaning "showing enthusiasm." The preferred adjective is *enthusiastic: The coach was enthusiastic [not enthused] about the team's victory.*

etc.   *Etc.,* the Latin abbreviation for "and other things," should be avoided in formal writing and should not be used to refer to people. When used, it should not substitute for precision, as in *The government provides health care, etc.,* and it should not end a list beginning *such as* or *for example.*

everybody, every body; everyone, every one *Everybody* and *everyone* are indefinite pronouns:° *Everybody* [or *every-one*] *knows Tom steals. Every one* is a pronoun° modified by *every,* and *every body* a noun° modified by *every.* Both refer to each thing or person of a specific group and are typically followed by *of: The game commissioner has stocked every body of fresh water in the state with fish, and now every one of our rivers is a potential trout stream.*

everyday, every day *Everyday* is an adjective° meaning "used daily" or "common"; *every day* is a noun° modified by *every: Everyday problems tend to arise every day.*

everywheres Nonstandard for *everywhere.*

except See *accept, except.*

explicit, implicit *Explicit* means "stated outright": *I left explicit instructions. Implicit* means "implied, unstated": *We had an implicit understanding.*

farther, further *Farther* refers to additional distance (*How much farther is it to the beach?*), and *further* refers to additional time, amount, or other abstract matters (*I don't want to discuss this any further*).

feel Avoid this word in place of *think* or *believe: She thinks* [not *feels*] *that the law should be changed.*

fewer, less *Fewer* refers to individual countable items (a plural count noun°), *less* to general amounts (a noncount noun,° always singular): *Skim milk has fewer calories than whole milk. We have less milk left than I thought.*

further See *farther, further.*

get *Get* is easy to overuse; watch out for it in expressions such as *it's getting better* (substitute *improving*), *we got done* (substitute *finished*), and *the mayor has got to* (substitute *must*).

good, well *Good* is an adjective,° and *well* is nearly always an adverb:° *Larry's a good dancer. He and Linda dance well together. Well* is properly used as an adjective only to refer to health: *You look well.* (*You look good,* in contrast, means "Your appearance is pleasing.") See also p. 50.

hanged, hung Though both are past-tense forms° of *hang, hanged* is used to refer to executions and *hung* is used for all other meanings: *Tom Dooley was hanged* [not *hung*] *from a white oak tree. I hung* [not *hanged*] *the picture you gave me.*

have, of Use *have,* not *of,* after helping verbs° such as *could, should, would, may,* and *might: You should have* [not *should of*] *told me.*

he, she; he/she Convention has allowed the use of *he* to mean "he or she," but most writers today consider this usage inaccurate and unfair because it excludes females. The construction *he/she*, one substitute for *he*, is awkward and objectionable to many readers. The better choice is to use *he or she*, to recast the sentence in the plural, or to rephrase. For instance: *After the infant learns to creep, he or she progresses to crawling. After infants learn to creep, they progress to crawling. After learning to creep, the infant progresses to crawling.* See also pp. 20–21 and 46–47.

herself, himself   See *myself, herself, himself, yourself.*

hisself   Nonstandard for *himself.*

hopefully   *Hopefully* means "with hope": *Freddy waited hopefully.* The use of *hopefully* to mean "it is to be hoped," "I hope," or "let's hope" is now very common; but since many readers continue to object strongly to the usage, you should avoid it. *I hope* [not *Hopefully*] *Eliza will be here soon.*

idea, ideal   An *idea* is a thought or conception. An *ideal* (noun°) is a model of perfection or a goal. *Ideal* should not be used in place of *idea: The idea* [not *ideal*] *of the play is that our ideals often sustain us.*

if, whether   For clarity, use *whether* rather than *if* when you are expressing an alternative: *If I laugh hard, people can't tell whether I'm crying.*

illicit   See *elicit, illicit.*

illusion   See *allusion, illusion.*

immigrate   See *emigrate, immigrate.*

implicit   See *explicit, implicit.*

imply, infer   Writers or speakers *imply,* meaning "suggest": *Jim's letter implies he's having a good time.* Readers or listeners *infer,* meaning "conclude": *From Jim's letter I infer he's having a good time.*

irregardless   Nonstandard for *regardless.*

is, are   See *are, is.*

is when, is where   These are faulty constructions in sentences that define: *Adolescence is a stage* [not *is when a person is*] *between childhood and adulthood. Socialism is a system in which* [not *is where*] *government owns the means of production.*

its, it's   *Its* is the pronoun° *it* in the possessive case:° *That plant is losing its leaves. It's* is a contraction for *it is: It's likely to die if you don't water it.* See also p. 72.

kind of, sort of, type of   In formal speech and writing, avoid using *kind of* or *sort of* to mean "somewhat": *He was rather* [not *kind of*] *tall.*
　　Kind, sort, and *type* are singular: *This kind of dog is easily trained.* Errors often occur when these singular nouns are

combined with the plural adjectives° *these* and *those: These kinds* [not *kind*] *of dogs are easily trained. Kind, sort,* and *type* should be followed by *of* but not by *a: I don't know what type of* [not *type* or *type of a*] *dog that is.*

Use *kind of, sort of,* or *type of* only when the word *kind, sort,* or *type* is important: *That was a strange* [not *strange sort of*] *statement.*

lay, lie   *Lay* means "put" or "place" and takes a direct object:° *We could lay the tablecloth in the sun.* Its main forms are *lay, laid, laid. Lie* means "recline" or "be situated" and does not take an object: *I lie awake at night. The town lies east of the river.* Its main forms are *lie, lay, lain.*

less   See *fewer, less.*

lie, lay   See *lay, lie.*

like, as   In formal speech and writing, *like* should not introduce a full clause.° The preferred choice is *as* or *as if: The plan succeeded as* [not *like*] *we hoped.* Use *like* only before a word or phrase: *Other plans like it have failed.*

literally   This word means "actually" or "just as the words say," and it should not be used to intensify expressions whose words are not to be taken at face value. The sentence *He was literally climbing the walls* describes a person behaving like an insect, not a person who is restless or anxious. For the latter meaning, *literally* should be omitted.

lose, loose   *Lose* means "mislay": *Did you lose a brown glove? Loose* usually means "unrestrained" or "not tight": *Ann's canary got loose.*

may, can   See *can, may.*

may be, maybe   *May be* is a verb,° and *maybe* is an adverb° meaning "perhaps": *Tuesday may be a legal holiday. Maybe we won't have classes.*

may of   See *have, of.*

media   *Media* is the plural of *medium* and takes a plural verb.° *All the news media are increasingly visual.* The singular verb is common, even in the media, but most careful writers still use the plural verb.

might of   See *have, of.*

must of   See *have, of.*

myself, herself, himself, yourself   The *-self* pronouns° refer to or intensify another word or words: *Paul did it himself; Jill herself said so.* In formal speech or writing, avoid using the *-self* pronouns in place of personal pronouns:° *No one except me* [not *myself*] *saw the accident. Michiko and I* [not *myself*] *planned the ceremony.*

nowheres   Nonstandard for *nowhere*.

number   See *amount, number*.

of, have   See *have, of*.

OK, O.K., okay   All three spellings are acceptable, but avoid this colloquial term in formal speech and writing.

people, persons   Except when emphasizing individuals, prefer *people* to *persons: We the* *people* *of the United States . . . ; Will the person or* *persons* *who saw the accident please notify. . . .*

percent (per cent), percentage   Both these terms refer to fractions of one hundred. *Percent* always follows a numeral (*40 percent* *of the voters*), and the word should be used instead of the symbol (*%*) in nontechnical writing. *Percentage* usually follows an adjective (*a* *high percentage*).

persons   See *people, persons*.

phenomena   The plural of *phenomenon* (meaning "perceivable fact" or "unusual occurrence"): *Many* *phenomena are* *not recorded. One* *phenomenon is* *attracting attention.*

plus   *Plus* is standard as a preposition° meaning "in addition to": *His income* *plus* *mine is sufficient.* But *plus* is colloquial as a conjunctive adverb:° *Our organization is larger than theirs;* *moreover* [not *plus*], *we have more money.*

precede, proceed   *Precede* means "come before": *My name* *precedes* *yours in the alphabet. Proceed* means "move on": *We were told to* *proceed* *to the waiting room.*

prejudice, prejudiced   *Prejudice* is a noun;° *prejudiced* is an adjective.° Do not drop the *-d* from *prejudiced: I knew that my parents were* *prejudiced* [not *prejudice*].

principal, principle   *Principal* is an adjective° meaning "foremost" or "major," a noun° meaning "chief official," or, in finance, a noun meaning "capital sum." *Principle* is a noun only, meaning "rule" or "axiom." *Her* *principal* *reasons for confessing were her* *principles* *of right and wrong.*

proceed, precede   See *precede, proceed*.

raise, rise   *Raise* means "lift" or "bring up" and takes a direct object:° *The Kirks* *raise* *cattle.* Its main forms are *raise, raised, raised. Rise* means "get up" and does not take an object: *They must* *rise* *at dawn.* Its main forms are *rise, rose, risen.*

real, really   In formal speech and writing, *real* should not be used as an adverb;° *really* is the adverb and *real* an adjective.° *Popular reaction to the announcement was* *really* [not *real*] *enthusiastic.*

reason is because Although colloquially common, this construction should be avoided in formal speech and writing. Use a *that* clause after *reason is: The reason he is absent is that* [not *is because*] *he is sick.* Or: *He is absent because he is sick.*

respectful, respective *Respectful* means "full of (or showing) respect": *Be respectful of other people. Respective* means "separate": *The French and the Germans occupied their respective trenches.*

rise, raise See *raise, rise.*

sensual, sensuous *Sensual* suggests sexuality; *sensuous* means "pleasing to the senses." *Stirred by the sensuous scent of meadow grass and flowers, Cheryl and Paul found their thoughts turning sensual.*

set, sit *Set* means "put" or "place" and takes a direct object:° *He sets the pitcher down.* Its main forms are *set, set, set. Sit* means "be seated" and does not take an object: *She sits on the sofa.* Its main forms are *sit, sat, sat.*

should of See *have, of.*

since *Since* mainly relates to time: *I've been waiting since noon.* But *since* is also often used to mean "because": *Since you ask, I'll tell you.* Revise sentences in which the word could have either meaning, such as *Since you left, my life is empty.*

sit, set See *set, sit.*

somebody, some body; someone, some one *Somebody* and *someone* are indefinite pronouns;° *some body* is a noun° modified by *some;* and *some one* is a pronoun° or an adjective° modified by *some. Somebody ought to invent a shampoo that will give hair some body. Someone told James he should choose some one plan and stick with it.*

sometime, sometimes, some time *Sometime* means "at an indefinite time in the future": *Why don't you come up and see me sometime? Sometimes* means "now and then": *I still see my old friend Joe sometimes. Some time* means "span of time": *I need some time to make the payments.*

somewheres Nonstandard for *somewhere.*

sort of, sort of a See *kind of, sort of, type of.*

supposed to, used to In both these expressions, the *-d* is essential: *I used to* [not *use to*] *think so. He's supposed to* [not *suppose to*] *meet us.*

sure and, sure to; try and, try to *Sure to* and *try to* are the correct forms: *Be sure to* [not *sure and*] *buy milk. Try to* [not *Try and*] *find some decent tomatoes.*

take, bring See *bring, take.*

than, then   *Than* is a conjunction° used in comparisons, *then* an adverb° indicating time: *Holmes knew then that Moriarty was wilier than he had thought.*

that, which   *That* always introduces restrictive clauses:° *We should use the lettuce that Susan bought* (*that Susan bought* limits *lettuce* to a particular lettuce). *Which* can introduce both restrictive and nonrestrictive clauses,° but many writers reserve *which* only for nonrestrictive clauses: *The leftover lettuce, which is in the refrigerator, would make a good salad* (*which is in the refrigerator* simply provides more information about the lettuce we already know of). Restrictive clauses (with *that* or *which*) are not set off by commas; nonrestrictive clauses (with *which*) are. See also pp. 65–66.

that, who, which   Use *that* to refer to most animals and to things: *The animals that escaped included a zebra. The rocket that failed cost millions.* Use *who* to refer to people and to animals with names: *Dorothy is the girl who visits Oz. Her dog, Toto, who accompanies her, gives her courage.* Use *which* only to refer to animals and things: *The river, which runs a thousand miles, empties into the Indian Ocean.*

their, there, they're   *Their* is the possessive° form of *they: Give them their money.* *There* indicates place (*I saw her standing there*) or functions as an expletive° (*There is a hole behind you*). *They're* is a contraction° for *they are: They're going fast.*

theirselves   Nonstandard for *themselves.*

then, than   See *than, then.*

these, this   *These* is plural; *this* is singular. *This pear is ripe, but these pears are not.*

these kind, these sort, these type, those kind   See *kind of, sort of, type of.*

thru   A colloquial spelling of *through* that should be avoided in all academic and business writing.

to, too, two   *To* is a preposition;° *too* is an adverb° meaning "also" or "excessively"; and *two* is a number. *I too have been to Europe two times.*

toward, towards   Both are acceptable, though *toward* is preferred. Use one or the other consistently.

try and, try to   See *sure and, sure to; try and, try to.*

type of   Don't use *type* without *of: It was a family type of* [not *type*] *restaurant.* Or, better: *It was a family restaurant.* See also *kind of, sort of, type of.*

uninterested   See *disinterested, uninterested.*

unique   *Unique* means "the only one of its kind" and so cannot sensibly be modified with words such as *very* or *most:*

That was a <u>unique</u> [not *a very unique* or *the most unique*] *movie.*

used to   See *supposed to, used to.*

wait for, wait on   In formal speech and writing, *wait for* means "await" (*I'm <u>waiting for</u> Paul*), and *wait on* means "serve" (*The owner of the store herself <u>waited on</u> us*).

weather, whether   The *weather* is the state of the atmosphere. *Whether* introduces alternatives. *The <u>weather</u> will determine <u>whether</u> we go or not.*

well   See *good, well.*

whether, if   See *if, whether.*

which, that   See *that, which.*

who, which, that   See *that, who, which.*

who's, whose   *Who's* is the contraction° of *who is: <u>Who's</u> at the door? Whose* is the possessive° form of *who: <u>Whose</u> book is that?*

would have   Avoid this construction in place of *had* in clauses that begin *if* and state a condition contrary to fact: *If the tree <u>had</u>* [not *<u>would have</u>*] *withstood the fire, it would have been the oldest in town.*

would of   See *have, of.*

you   In all but very formal writing, *you* is generally appropriate as long as it means "you, the reader." In all writing, avoid indefinite uses of *you,* such as *In one ancient tribe <u>your</u> first loyalty was to <u>your</u> parents.*

your, you're   *Your* is the possessive° form of *you: <u>Your</u> dinner is ready. You're* is the contraction° of *you are: <u>You're</u> bound to be late.*

yourself   See *myself, herself, himself, yourself.*

GLOSSARY OF TERMS

This glossary defines the terms and concepts of basic English grammar, including every term marked ° in the text.

absolute phrase   A phrase that consists of a noun° or pronoun° plus the *-ing* or *-ed* form of a verb° (a participle°): *Our accommodations arranged, we set out on our trip. They will hire a local person, other things being equal.*

active voice   The verb form° used when the sentence subject° names the performer of the verb's action: *The drillers used a rotary blade.* For more, see *voice.*

adjective   A word used to modify a noun° or pronoun:° *beautiful morning, ordinary one, good spelling.* Contrast *adverb.* Nouns, word groups, and some verb° forms may also serve as adjectives: *book sale; sale of old books; the sale, which occurs annually; increasing profits.*

adverb   A word used to modify a verb,° an adjective,° another adverb, or a whole sentence: *warmly greet* (verb), *only three people* (adjective), *quite seriously* (adverb), *Fortunately, she is employed* (sentence). Word groups may also serve as adverbs: *drove by a farm, plowed the fields when the earth thawed.*

agreement   The correspondence of one word to another in person,° number,° or gender.° Mainly, a verb° must agree with its subject° (*The chef orders eggs*), and a pronoun° must agree with its antecedent° (*The chef surveys her breakfast*). See also pp. 40–42 and 45–47.

antecedent   The word a pronoun° refers to: *Jonah, who is not yet ten, has already chosen the college he will attend* (*Jonah* is the antecedent of the pronouns *who* and *he*).

appositive   A word or word group appearing next to a noun° or pronoun° that renames or identifies it and is equivalent to it: *My brother Michael, the best horn player in town, won the state competition* (*Michael* identifies which brother is being referred to; *the best horn player in town* renames *My brother Michael*).

article   The words *a, an,* and *the.* Articles always signal that a noun follows. See p. 203 for how to choose between *a* and *an.* See pp. 52–54 for the rules governing *a/an* and *the.*

auxiliary verb   See *helping verb.*

case   The form of a pronoun° or noun° that indicates its function in the sentence. Most pronouns have three cases. The SUBJECTIVE CASE is for subjects° and subject comple-

ments:° *I, you, he, she, it, we, they, who, whoever.* The OBJEC-
TIVE CASE is for objects:° *me, you, him, her, it, us, them,
whom, whomever.* The POSSESSIVE CASE is for ownership:
*my/mine, your/yours, his, her/hers, its, our/ours, their/theirs,
whose.* Nouns use the subjective form (*dog, America*) for all
cases except the possessive (*dog's, America's*).

clause A group of words containing a subject° and a predicate.° A MAIN CLAUSE can stand alone as a sentence: <u>*We can go
to the movies.*</u> A SUBORDINATE CLAUSE cannot stand alone as a
sentence: *We can go <u>if Julie gets back on time.</u>* For more, see
subordinate clause.

collective noun A word with singular form that names a
group of individuals or things: for instance, *team, army, family, flock, group.* A collective noun generally takes a singular
verb and a singular pronoun: *The <u>army is</u> prepared for <u>its</u> role.*
See also pp. 41 and 47.

comma splice A sentence error in which two sentences
(main clauses°) are separated by a comma without *and,
but, or, nor,* or another coordinating conjunction.° Splice:
The book was long, it contained useful information. Revised:
*The book was long**;** it contained useful information.* Or: *The
book was long, <u>and</u> it contained useful information.* See pp.
59–60.

comparison The form of an adverb° or adjective° that
shows its degree of quality or amount. The POSITIVE is the
simple, uncompared form: *gross, clumsily.* The COMPARATIVE
compares the thing modified to at least one other thing:
grosser, more clumsily. The SUPERLATIVE indicates that the
thing modified exceeds all other things to which it is being
compared: *grossest, most clumsily.* The comparative and superlative are formed either with the endings *-er* and *-est* or
with the words *more* and *most* or *less* and *least.*

complement See *subject complement.*

complex sentence See *sentence.*

compound-complex sentence See *sentence.*

compound construction Two or more words or word
groups serving the same function, such as a compound sub-
ject° (<u>*Harriet and Peter* </u>*poled their barge down the river*), a
compound predicate° (*The scout <u>watched and waited</u>*), or a
compound sentence (*<u>He smiled, and I laughed</u>*).

compound sentence See *sentence.*

conditional statement A statement expressing a condition
contrary to fact and using the subjunctive mood° of the verb:
If she <u>were</u> mayor, the unions would cooperate.

TERMS

conjunction　A word that links and relates parts of a sentence. See *coordinating conjunction* (*and, but,* etc.), *correlative conjunction* (*either . . . or, both . . . and,* etc.), and *subordinating conjunction* (*because, if,* etc.).

conjunctive adverb　An adverb° that can relate two complete sentences (main clauses°) in a single sentence: *We had hoped to own a house by now; <u>however</u>, prices are still too high.* The main clauses are separated by a semicolon or a period. Some common conjunctive adverbs: *accordingly, also, anyway, besides, certainly, consequently, finally, further, furthermore, hence, however, incidentally, indeed, instead, likewise, meanwhile, moreover, namely, nevertheless, next, nonetheless, now, otherwise, similarly, still, then, thereafter, therefore, thus, undoubtedly.*

contraction　A condensed expression, with an apostrophe replacing the missing letters: for example, *doesn't* (*does not*), *we'll* (*we will*).

coordinating conjunction　A word linking words or word groups serving the same function: *The dog <u>and</u> cat sometimes fight, <u>but</u> they usually get along.* The coordinating conjunctions are *and, but, or, nor, for, so, yet.*

coordination　The linking of words or word groups that are of equal importance, usually with a coordinating conjunction.° *He <u>and</u> I laughed, <u>but</u> she was not amused.* Contrast *subordination.*

correlative conjunction　Two or more connecting words that work together to link words or word groups serving the same function: *<u>Both</u> Michiko <u>and</u> June signed up, but <u>neither</u> Stan <u>nor</u> Carlos did.* The correlatives include *both . . . and, just as . . . so, not only . . . but also, not . . . but, either . . . or, neither . . . nor, whether . . . or, as . . . as.*

count noun　A word that names a person, place, or thing that can be counted (and so may appear in plural form): *camera/cameras, river/rivers, child/children.*

dangling modifier　A modifier that does not sensibly describe anything in its sentence. Dangling: *<u>Having arrived late</u>, the concert had already begun.* Revised: *Having arrived late, <u>we found that</u> the concert had already begun.* See p. 56.

determiner　A word such as *a, an, the, my,* and *your* that indicates that a noun follows. See also *article.*

direct address　A construction in which a word or phrase indicates the person or group spoken to: *Have you finished, <u>John</u>? <u>Farmers</u>, unite.*

direct object　A noun° or pronoun° that identifies who or what receives the action of a verb:° *Education opens <u>doors</u>.* For more, see *object* and *predicate.*

direct question A sentence asking a question and concluding with a question mark: *Do they know we are watching?* Contrast *indirect question.*

direct quotation Repetition of what someone has written or said, using the exact words of the original and enclosing them in quotation marks: *Feinberg writes, "The reasons are both obvious and sorry."*

double negative A nonstandard form consisting of two negative words used in the same construction so that they effectively cancel each other: *I don't have no money.* Rephrase as *I have no money* or *I don't have any money.* See also pp. 51–52.

ellipsis The omission of a word or words from a quotation, indicated by the three spaced periods of an ELLIPSIS MARK: *"that all . . . are created equal."* See also pp. 78–80.

expletive construction A sentence that postpones the subject° by beginning with *there* or *it* and a form of *be: It is impossible to get a ticket. There are no more seats available.*

first person See *person.*

fused sentence (run-on sentence) A sentence error in which two complete sentences (main clauses°) are joined with no punctuation or connecting word between them. Fused: *I heard his lecture it was dull.* Revised: *I heard his lecture; it was dull.* See pp. 59–60.

future perfect tense The verb tense expressing an action that will be completed before another future action: *They will have heard by then.* For more, see *tense.*

future tense The verb tense expressing action that will occur in the future: *They will hear soon.* For more, see *tense.*

gender The classification of nouns° or pronouns° as masculine (*he, boy*), feminine (*she, woman*), or neuter (*it, computer*).

generic *he* *He* used to mean *he or she.* For ways to avoid *he* when you intend either or both genders, see pp. 21 and 46–47.

generic noun A noun° that does not refer to a specific person or thing: *Any person may come. A student needs good work habits. A school with financial problems may shortchange its students.* A singular generic noun takes a singular pronoun° (*he, she,* or *it*). See also *indefinite pronoun* and pp. 46–47.

gerund A verb form that ends in *-ing* and functions as a noun:° *Working is all right for killing time.* For more, see *verbals and verbal phrases.*

gerund phrase See *verbals and verbal phrases.*

helping verb (auxiliary verb) A verb° used with another verb to convey time, possibility, obligation, and other mean-

TERMS

ings: *You should write a letter. You have written other letters.* The MODALS are the following: *be able to, be supposed to, can, could, had better, had to, may, might, must, ought to, shall, should, used to, will, would.* The other helping verbs are forms of *be, have,* and *do.* See also pp. 30–32.

idiom   An expression that is peculiar to a language and that may not make sense if taken literally: for example, *dark horse, bide your time,* and *by and large.*

imperative   See *mood.*

indefinite pronoun   A word that stands for a noun° and does not refer to a specific person or thing. A few indefinite pronouns are plural: *both, few, many, several.* A few more may be either singular or plural depending on the context: *all, any, more, most, some.* But most are only singular: *anybody, anyone, anything, each, either, everybody, everyone, everything, neither, nobody, none, no one, nothing, one, somebody, someone, something.* The singular indefinite pronouns take singular verbs and are referred to by singular pronouns: *Something makes its presence felt.* See also *generic noun* and pp. 41 and 46–47.

indicative   See *mood.*

indirect object   A noun° or pronoun° that identifies to whom or what something is done: *Give them the award.* For more, see *object* and *predicate.*

indirect question   A sentence reporting a question and ending with a period: *Writers wonder if their work must always be lonely.* Contrast *direct question.*

indirect quotation   A report of what someone has written or said, but not using the exact words of the original and not enclosing the words in quotation marks. Quotation: *"Events have controlled me."* Indirect quotation: *Lincoln said that events had controlled him.*

infinitive   A verb form° consisting of the verb's dictionary form plus *to: to swim, to write.* For more, see *verbals and verbal phrases.*

infinitive phrase   See *verbals and verbal phrases.*

intensive pronoun   See *pronoun.*

interjection   A word standing by itself or inserted in a construction to exclaim or command attention: *Hey! Ouch! What the heck did you do that for?*

interrogative pronoun   A word that begins a question and serves as the subject° or object° of the sentence. The interrogative pronouns are *who, whom, whose, which,* and *what. Who received the flowers? Whom are they for?*

intransitive verb   A verb° that does not require a following word (direct object°) to complete its meaning: *Mosquitoes buzz. The hospital may close.* For more, see *predicate.*

irregular verb   See *verb forms.*

linking verb   A verb that links, or connects, a subject° and a word that renames or describes the subject (a subject complement°): *They are golfers. You seem lucky.* The linking verbs are the forms of *be,* the verbs of the senses (*look, sound, smell, feel, taste*), and a few others (*appear, become, grow, prove, remain, seem, turn*). For more, see *predicate.*

main clause   A word group that contains a subject° and a predicate,° does not begin with a subordinating word, and may stand alone as a sentence: *The president was not overbearing.* For more, see *clause.*

main verb   The part of a verb phrase° that carries the principal meaning: *had been walking, could happen, was chilled.* Contrast *helping verb.*

misplaced modifier   A modifier so far from the term it modifies or so close to another term it could modify that its relation to the rest of the sentence is unclear. Misplaced: *The children played with firecrackers that they bought illegally in the field.* Revised: *The children played in the field with firecrackers that they bought illegally.*

modal   See *helping verb.*

modifier   Any word or word group that limits or qualifies the meaning of another word or word group. Modifiers include adjectives° and adverbs° as well as words and word groups that act as adjectives and adverbs.

mood   The form of a verb° that shows how the speaker views the action. The INDICATIVE MOOD, the most common, is used to make statements or ask questions: *The play will be performed Saturday. Did you get tickets?* The IMPERATIVE MOOD gives a command: *Please get good seats. Avoid the top balcony.* The SUBJUNCTIVE MOOD expresses a wish, a condition contrary to fact, a recommendation, or a request: *I wish George were coming with us. If he were here, he'd come. I suggested that he come. The host asked that he be here.*

noncount noun   A word that names a person, place, or thing and that is not considered countable in English (and so does not appear in plural form): *confidence, information, silver, work.* See p. 53 for a longer list.

nonrestrictive clause   See *nonrestrictive element.*

nonrestrictive element   A word or word group that does not limit the word it refers to and that is not essential to the meaning of the sentence. Nonrestrictive elements are usually set off by commas: *Sleep,* <u>*which we all need,*</u> *occupies a third of our lives.* *His wife,* <u>*Patricia,*</u> *is a chemist.* Contrast *restrictive element.* See also pp. 65–66.

noun A word that names a person, place, thing, quality, or idea: *Maggie, Alabama, clarinet, satisfaction, socialism.* See also *collective noun, count noun, generic noun, noncount noun,* and *proper noun.*

noun clause See *subordinate clause.*

number The form of a word that indicates whether it is singular or plural. Singular: *I, he, this, child, runs, hides.* Plural: *we, they, these, children, run, hide.*

object A noun° or pronoun° that receives the action of or is influenced by another word. A DIRECT OBJECT receives the action of a verb° or verbal° and usually follows it in a sentence: *We watched the* <u>*stars.*</u> An INDIRECT OBJECT tells for or to whom something is done: *Reiner bought* <u>*us*</u> *tapes.* An OBJECT OF A PREPOSITION usually follows a preposition° and is linked by it to the rest of the sentence: *They are going to* <u>*New Orleans.*</u>

objective case The form of a pronoun° when it is the object° of a verb° (*call* <u>*him*</u>) or the object of a preposition° (*for* <u>*us*</u>). For more, see *case.*

object of preposition See *object.*

parallelism Similarity of grammatical form between two or more coordinated elements: <u>*Rising prices*</u> *and* <u>*declining incomes*</u> *left many people in* <u>*bad debt*</u> *and* <u>*worse despair.*</u> See also pp. 13–15.

parenthetical expression A word or construction that interrupts a sentence and is not part of its main structure, called *parenthetical* because it could (or does) appear in parentheses: *Mary Cassatt (*<u>*1845–1926*</u>*) was an American painter. Her work,* <u>*incidentally,*</u> *is in the museum.*

participial phrase See *verbals and verbal phrases.*

participle See *verbals and verbal phrases.*

particle A preposition° or adverb° in a two-word verb: *catch* <u>*on*</u>*, look* <u>*up*</u>*.*

parts of speech The classes into which words are commonly grouped according to their form, function, and meaning: nouns, pronouns, verbs, adjectives, adverbs, conjunctions, prepositions, and interjections. See separate entries for each part of speech.

passive voice The verb form° used when the sentence subject° names the receiver of the verb's action: *The mixture* <u>*was stirred*</u>*.* For more, see *voice.*

past participle The *-ed* form of most verbs:° *fished, hopped.* Some verbs form their past participles in irregular ways: *be-*

gun, written. For more, see *verbals and verbal phrases* and *verb forms*.

past perfect tense The verb tense expressing an action that was completed before another past action: *No one <u>had heard</u> that before*. For more, see *tense*.

past tense The verb tense expressing action that occurred in the past: *Everyone <u>laughed</u>*. For more, see *tense*.

past-tense form The verb form used to indicate action that occurred in the past, usually created by adding -*d* or -*ed* to the verb's dictionary form (*smiled*) but created differently for most irregular verbs (*began, threw*). For more, see *verb forms*.

perfect tenses The verb tenses indicating action completed before another specific time or action: *have walked, had walked, will have walked*. For more, see *tense*.

person The form of a verb° or pronoun° that indicates whether the subject is speaking, spoken to, or spoken about. In the FIRST PERSON the subject is speaking: *I am, we are*. In the SECOND PERSON the subject is spoken to: *you are*. In the THIRD PERSON the subject is spoken about: *he/she/it is, they are*.

personal pronoun *I, you, he, she, it, we*, or *they*: a word that substitutes for a specific noun° or other pronoun. For more, see *case*.

phrase A group of related words that lacks a subject° or a predicate° or both: *She ran <u>into the field</u>*. *She tried <u>to jump the fence</u>*. See also *absolute phrase, prepositional phrase, verbals and verbal phrases*.

plain form The dictionary form of a verb: *buy, make, run, swivel*. For more, see *verb forms*.

plural More than one. See *number*.

positive form See *comparison*.

possessive case The form of a noun° or pronoun° that indicates its ownership of something else: *<u>men's</u> attire, <u>your</u> briefcase*. For more, see *case*.

predicate The part of a sentence that makes an assertion about the subject.° The predicate may consist of an intransitive verb° (*The earth <u>trembled</u>*), a transitive verb° plus direct object° (*The earthquake <u>shook</u> buildings*), a linking verb° plus subject complement° (*The result <u>was chaos</u>*), a transitive verb plus indirect object° and direct object (*The government <u>sent</u> the <u>city aid</u>*), or a transitive verb plus direct object and object complement (*The citizens <u>considered</u> the <u>earthquake</u> a <u>disaster</u>*).

preposition A word that forms a noun° or pronoun° (plus any modifiers) into a PREPOSITIONAL PHRASE: *<u>about</u> love, <u>down</u> the steep stairs*. The common prepositions: *about, above, according to, across, after, against, along, along with, among*,

around, as, at, because of, before, behind, below, beneath, be-
side, between, beyond, by, concerning, despite, down, during,
except, except for, excepting, for, from, in, in addition to, in-
side, in spite of, instead of, into, like, near, next to, of, off, on,
onto, out, out of, outside, over, past, regarding, since, through,
throughout, till, to, toward, under, underneath, unlike, until,
up, upon, with, within, without.

prepositional phrase   A word group consisting of a prepo-
sition° and its object.° Prepositional phrases usually serve as
adjectives° (*We saw a movie about sorrow*) and as adverbs°
(*We went back for the second show*).

present participle   The *-ing* form of a verb:° *swimming, fly-*
ing. For more, see *verbals and verbal phrases.*

present perfect tense   The verb tense expressing action
that began in the past and is linked to the present: *Dogs have*
buried bones here before. For more, see *tense.*

present tense   The verb tense expressing action that is occurring now, occurs habitually, or is generally true: *Dogs*
bury bones here often. For more, see *tense.*

principal parts   The three forms of a verb from which its
various tenses are created: the PLAIN FORM (*stop, go*), the PAST-
TENSE FORM (*stopped, went*), and the PAST PARTICIPLE (*stopped,*
gone). For more, see *tense* and *verb forms.*

progressive tenses   The verb tenses that indicate continuing (progressive) action and use the *-ing* form of the verb: *A*
dog was burying a bone here this morning. For more, see *tense.*

pronoun   A word used in place of a noun,° such as *I, he,*
everyone, who, and *herself.* See also *indefinite pronoun, inter-*
rogative pronoun, personal pronoun, relative pronoun.

proper noun   A word naming a specific person, place, or
thing and beginning with a capital letter: *David Letterman,*
Mt. Rainier, Washington, US Congress.

regular verb   See *verb forms.*

relative pronoun   A word that relates a group of words to a
noun° or another pronoun.° The relative pronouns are *who,*
whom, whoever, whomever, which, and *that. Ask the woman*
who knows all. This may be the question that stumps her. For
more, see *case.*

restrictive clause   See *restrictive element.*

restrictive element   A word or word group that is essential
to the meaning of the sentence because it limits the word it
refers to: removing it would leave the meaning unclear or too
general. Restrictive elements are *not* set off by commas:
Dorothy's companion the Scarecrow lacks a brain. The man

who called about the apartment said he'd try again. Contrast *nonrestrictive element*. See also pp. 65–66.

run-on sentence   See *fused sentence*.

-s form   See *verb forms*.

second person   See *person*.

sentence   A complete unit of thought, consisting of at least a subject° and a predicate° that are not introduced by a subordinating word. Sentences can be classed on the basis of their structure: A SIMPLE SENTENCE contains one main clause:° *I'm leaving*. A COMPOUND SENTENCE contains at least two main clauses: *I'd like to stay, but I'm leaving*. A COMPLEX SENTENCE contains one main clause and at least one subordinate clause:° *If you let me go now, you'll be sorry*. A COMPOUND-COMPLEX SENTENCE contains at least two main clauses and at least one subordinate clause: *I'm leaving because you want me to, but I'd rather stay*.

sentence fragment   A sentence error in which a group of words is set off as a sentence even though it begins with a subordinating word or lacks a subject° or a predicate° or both. Fragment: *She was not in shape for the race. Which she had hoped to win*. Revised: *She was not in shape for the race, which she had hoped to win*. See pp. 57–58.

series   Three or more items with the same function: *We gorged on ham, eggs, and potatoes*.

simple sentence   See *sentence*.

simple tenses   See *tense*.

singular   One. See *number*.

split infinitive   The usually awkward interruption of an infinitive° and its marker *to* by a modifier: *Management decided to not introduce the new product*. See p. 55.

squinting modifier   A modifier that could modify the words on either side of it: *The plan we considered seriously worries me*.

subject   In grammar, the part of a sentence that names something and about which an assertion is made in the predicate:° *The quick, brown fox jumped lazily* (simple subject); *The quick, brown fox jumped lazily* (complete subject).

subject complement   A word that renames or describes the subject° of a sentence, after a linking verb.° *The stranger was a man* (noun°). *He seemed gigantic* (adjective°).

subjective case   The form of a pronoun° when it is the subject° of a sentence (*I called*) or a subject complement° (*It was I*). For more, see *case*.

subjunctive   See *mood*.

TERMS

subordinate clause   A word group that consists of a subject° and a predicate,° begins with a subordinating word such as *because* or *who,* and is not a question: *They voted for whoever seemed to care the least because they mistrusted politicians.* Subordinate clauses may serve as adjectives° (*The car that hit Fred was running a red light*), as adverbs° (*The car hit Fred when it ran a red light*), or as nouns° (*Whoever was driving should be arrested*). Subordinate clauses may *not* serve as complete sentences.

subordinating conjunction   A word that forms a complete sentence into a word group (a subordinate clause°) that can serve as an adverb° or a noun.° *Everyone was relieved when the meeting ended.* Some common subordinating conjunctions: *after, although, as, as if, as long as, as though, because, before, even if, even though, if, if only, in order that, now that, once, rather than, since, so that, than, that, though, till, unless, until, when, whenever, where, whereas, wherever, while.*

subordination   The use of grammatical structures to de-emphasize one element in a sentence by making it dependent on rather than equal to another element. Through subordination, *I left six messages; the doctor failed to call* becomes *Although I left six messages, the doctor failed to call* or *After six messages, the doctor failed to call.*

tag question   A question attached to the end of a statement and composed of a pronoun,° a helping verb,° and sometimes the word *not: It isn't raining, is it? It is sunny, isn't it?*

tense   The form of a verb° that expresses the time of its action, usually indicated by the verb's endings and by helping verbs. See also *verb forms.*

PRESENT   Action that is occurring now, occurs habitually, or is generally true

SIMPLE PRESENT Plain form or -s form	PRESENT PROGRESSIVE *Am, is,* or *are* plus -*ing* form
I *walk.*	I *am walking.*
You/we/they *walk.*	You/we/they *are walking.*
He/she/it *walks.*	He/she/it *is walking.*

PAST   Action that occurred before now

SIMPLE PAST Past-tense form (-*d* or -*ed*)	PAST PROGRESSIVE *Was* or *were* plus -*ing* form
I/he/she/it *walked.*	I/he/she/it *was walking.*
You/we/they *walked.*	You/we/they *were walking.*

FUTURE   Action that will occur in the future

SIMPLE FUTURE *Will* plus plain form	FUTURE PROGRESSIVE *Will be* plus -*ing* form
I/you/he/she/it/we/they will walk.	I/you/he/she/it/we/they will be walking.

PRESENT PERFECT Action that began in the past and is linked to the present

PRESENT PERFECT *Have* or *has* plus past participle (*-d* or *-ed*)	**PRESENT PERFECT PROGRESSIVE** *Have been* or *has been* plus *-ing* form
I/you/we/they *have walked.*	I/you/we/they *have been walking.*
He/she/it *has walked.*	He/she/it *has been walking.*

PAST PERFECT Action that was completed before another past action

PAST PERFECT *Had* plus past participle (*-d* or *-ed*)	**PAST PERFECT PROGRESSIVE** *Had been* plus *-ing* form
I/you/he/she/it/we/they *had walked.*	I/you/he/she/it/we/they *had been walking.*

FUTURE PERFECT Action that will be completed before another future action

FUTURE PERFECT *Will have* plus past participle (*-d* or *-ed*)	**FUTURE PERFECT PROGRESSIVE** *Will have been* plus *-ing* form
I/you/he/she/it/we/they *will have walked.*	I/you/he/she/it/we/they *will have been walking.*

transitional expression A word or phrase that links sentences and shows the relations between them. Transitional expressions can signal various relationships (examples in parentheses): addition or sequence (*also, besides, finally, first, furthermore, in addition, last*); comparison (*also, likewise, similarly*); contrast (*even so, however, in contrast, nevertheless, still*); examples (*for example, for instance, specifically, that is*); intensification (*indeed, in fact, of course, truly*); place (*below, elsewhere, here, nearby, to the east*); time (*afterward, at last, earlier, immediately, meanwhile, shortly, simultaneously*); repetition or summary (*all in all, in brief, in other words, in short, in summary, that is*); and cause and effect (*as a result, consequently, hence, otherwise, therefore, thus*).

transitive verb A verb° that requires a following word (a direct object°) to complete its meaning: *We raised the roof.* For more, see *predicate.*

verb A word that expresses an action (*bring, change*), an occurrence (*happen, become*), or a state of being (*be, seem*). A verb is the essential word in a predicate,° the part of a sentence that makes an assertion about the subject.° With endings and helping verbs,° verbs can indicate tense,° mood,° voice,° number,° and person.° For more, see separate entries for each of these aspects as well as *verb forms.*

verbals and verbal phrases VERBALS are verb forms used as adjectives,° adverbs,° or nouns.° They form VERBAL PHRASES with objects° and modifiers. A PRESENT PARTICIPLE adds -*ing* to the dictionary form of a verb (*living*). A PAST PARTICIPLE usually adds -*d* or -*ed* to the dictionary form (*lived*), although irregular verbs form the past participle in other ways (*begun, swept*). A participle or PARTICIPIAL PHRASE usually serves as an adjective: *Strolling shoppers fill the malls.* A GERUND is the -*ing* form of a verb used as a noun. Gerunds and GERUND PHRASES can do whatever nouns can do: *Shopping satisfies personal needs.* An INFINITIVE is the verb's dictionary form plus *to*: *to live.* Infinitives and INFINITIVE PHRASES may serve as nouns (*To design a mall is to create an artificial environment*), as adverbs (*Malls are designed to make shoppers feel safe*), or as adjectives (*The environment supports the impulse to shop*).

Note that a verbal *cannot* serve as the only verb in the predicate° of a sentence. For that, it requires a helping verb:° *Shoppers were strolling.*

verb forms   Verbs have five distinctive forms. The PLAIN FORM is the dictionary form: *A few artists live in town today.* The -*s* FORM adds -*s* or -*es* to the plain form: *The artist lives in town today.* The PAST-TENSE FORM usually adds -*d* or -*ed* to the plain form: *Many artists lived in town before this year.* Some verbs' past-tense forms are irregular, such as *began, fell, swam, threw, wrote.* The PAST PARTICIPLE is usually the same as the past-tense form, although, again, some verbs' past participles are irregular (*begun, fallen, swum, thrown, written*). The PRESENT PARTICIPLE adds -*ing* to the plain form: *A few artists are living in town today.*

REGULAR VERBS are those that add -*d* or -*ed* to the plain form for the past-tense form and past participle. IRREGULAR VERBS create these forms in irregular ways (see above).

verb phrase   See *phrase.* A verb° of more than one word that serves as the predicate° of a sentence: *The movie has started.*

voice   The form of a verb° that tells whether the sentence subject° performs the action or is acted upon. In the ACTIVE VOICE the subject acts: *The city controls rents.* In the PASSIVE VOICE the subject is acted upon: *Rents are controlled by the city.* The actor in a passive sentence may be stated (*the city*) or not stated: *Rents are controlled.* See also pp. 39–40.

INDEX

242 · Index

INDEX

244 • Index

DETAILED CONTENTS